URBANIZATION IN AUSTRALIA:
THE POST-WAR EXPERIENCE

Urbanization in Australia
THE POST-WAR EXPERIENCE

EDITED BY
I. H. BURNLEY

CAMBRIDGE
AT THE UNIVERSITY PRESS
1974

Published by the Syndics of the Cambridge University Press
Bentley House, 200 Euston Road, London NW1 2DB
American Branch: 32 East 57th Street, New York, N.Y. 10022

© Cambridge University Press 1974

Library of Congress Catalogue Card Number: 73-77261

ISBNS: 0 521 20250 7 hard covers
        0 521 09827 0 paperback (Australia only)

Printed and bound in Great Britain
at The Pitman Press, Bath

cc

Contents

FIGURES

Contributors

Dr I. H. Burnley, Lecturer in Population and Cultural Geography, University of New South Wales; formerly Research Fellow in Demography, Australian National University.

Dr C. Y. Choi, Lecturer in Sociology, The Chinese University of Hong Kong; formerly Post Doctoral Fellow, Population Enquiry Unit, Australian National University.

Mr P. Harrison, Senior Research Fellow, Urban Research Unit, Australian National University.

Mr G. J. Hugo, Scholar in Demography, Research School of Social Sciences, Australian National University.

Mr D. T. Rowland, Scholar in Demography, Research School of Social Sciences, Australian National University.

Dr F. J. B. Stilwell, Lecturer in Economics, University of Sydney.

Mr R. J. Stimson, Lecturer in Urban Geography, Flinders University of South Australia.

Mr E. Vandermark, National Capital Development Commission, Canberra; formerly of the Urban Research Unit, Australian National University.

Dr H. Ware, Research Fellow in Demography, Australian National University.

Preface

The purpose of this book has been to bring together in an integrated form new research being undertaken on urbanization in contemporary Australia. This topic has not been treated in a unitary volume before and until now had to be perused through consultation of various papers and monographs on specialized aspects of urban development, more especially those dealing with economics and city planning. Secondly, areas particularly neglected have been those connected with the *demographic* and ecological aspects of the urbanization *process* in post-war Australia.[1] In particular, the time dimension and intercensal change have not been reviewed; even specialized papers in the geographic and sociological literature take cities or towns at particular points in time rather than follow approaches in which time series analyses are important.[2] The particular emphases of the book will not suit everybody's taste; no book on such a multi-disciplinary field possibly could – but attention has been given to economic and city planning elements in the urbanization process. The politics of cities has not been covered, partly due to space limitations, but also because monographs and papers already exist on particular aspects of the politics of cities, some of which consist of volumes of papers at various conferences dealing broadly with the politics of urban growth in Australia. The emphasis is on *metropolitan growth* and change which has absorbed so much of population increase in post-war Australia.

The book is divided into three sections: (i) the growth of cities; (ii) the impact and consequences of urbanization – urban residential and social structure and differentiation; and (iii) the regularity and developmental role of planning of various types in handling the impact of urbanization on Australian society. Although the authors' intentions are an analysis of the basic (but neglected) elements of urban growth, form and character of the recent Australian urbanization experience, they have in places criticized or made suggestions as to the changing or improvement of government and public policy towards cities.

The first, and largest section of the work treats the economic demographic and social aspects of the evolution of Australia's cities in the post-war period. Dr Stilwell puts forward interesting and original ideas on the reasons for the evolution of the striking pattern of metropolitan primacy as do Messrs Rowland and Hugo in their discussions of internal migration in the States of Victoria and South Australia respectively, ideas which complement those of Stilwell and also earlier writers such as A. J. Rose and K. Robinson. Drs Burnley and Choi analyse the demographic components – natural increase, internal and international migration in metropolitan growth – and stress in particular the importance of migration. Burnley also discusses the general urbanization trend post-war of the Australian population, stressing population centralization and the impact of immigration, not only on city growth, but also on population changes within the large metropolitan areas. Finally Burnley and Choi undertake a simple set of population projections of the metropolitan centres based on post-war trends and assuming little or no decentralization.

In Part II, dealing in particular with social and residential differentiation in the large metropolitan centres which have become World Cities in the post-war period, Mr Stimson discusses rapidly growing Adelaide, in particular using the social area analysis schemata, while Burnley discusses the implications of social segregation in the large metropolises of Sydney and Melbourne and the role of the heavy, heterogeneous post-war immigration in social differentiation and segregation of areas. Dr Helen Ware reviews some of the findings of the survey of fertility and family formation in Melbourne, discussing the extent of family limitation in an industrialized metropolitan setting and socio-economic and cultural differences in fertility, some of which are connected with the rural–urban transition with international migration.

In Part III, also dealing with the impact and consequences of urbanization, the role of planning is studied, particularly its impact on city morphology and land use structure by Peter Harrison, and on urban renewal and the urban environment by Elzo Vandermark.

A few points about sources. In most of the demographic analyses, metropolitan statistical divisions have been used rather than metropolitan area boundaries because of the relative ease in standardization of boundaries backwards through time. For certain tabulations, however, data are only available at the *metropolitan area* level rather than the larger metropolitan division, particularly with immigrant group and economic characteristics of populations, and these in some instances have had to be used interchangeably. Whenever this has been done, acknowledgement is made. Wherever possible, 1971 population data have been used but as only simple numbers by sex by L.G.A. were available in October 1972, much of the analysis is based on 1947–66 trends and on the 1966 census in particular. In some instances, 1961 boundaries have had to be used as in part of Elzo Vandermark's study, and in accompanying illustrations. In the illustrations accompanying the immigrant contribution to metropolitan growth chapter, metropolitan *area* boundaries are utilized as at 1966. These differences may account for some variation between figures quoted by various authors although the differences are mostly relatively small.

Perhaps the ultimate justification of the study along with the paucity of research on the urbanization theme in Australia is that with 85 per cent of its population in urban centres, and with a rapid rate of growth post-war, Australia ranks as one of the three most urbanized countries on earth. With the rapid growth of population between 1947 and 1971 from 7.56 to 12.71 million, Australia, gaining population at 2.2 per cent per annum, started on an unprecedented expansion of mineral exploitation, manufacturing and tertiary industry with associated metropolitan expansion. It is the social parameters and aspects of this growth and some of the implications for Australian society that are the main theme of this volume.

1973   I. H. Burnley

NOTES

1 With the notable exception of F. Lancaster Jones's study of the social areas of Melbourne (*Dimensions of Urban Social Structure*, A. N. U. Press, 1969).
2 Once again, the important exception here is Bernard Barrett's study of the inner suburbs of Melbourne (*The Inner Suburbs, the Evolution of an Industrial Area*, Melbourne University Press, 1971).

Acknowledgements

I would like to thank the following persons without whose aid, advice and counsel this work would not have been possible: Mr Ken Crawford of the Bureau of Census and Statistics, Canberra; Professors W. D. Borrie and J. C. Caldwell of the Department of Demography, Australian National University, Canberra; Mrs Patricia Pyne and Mr W. Naughton, also of the Australian National University, and Dr C. A. Price for his stimulation and encouragement.

PART I

The growth of cities

I

The urbanization of the Australian population 1947–1971

I. H. BURNLEY

A high degree of urbanization has for long been characteristic of Australia as it is of most industrialized countries. However, there is a certain uniqueness in the Australian situation since as with New Zealand, a large proportion of its G.N.P. has been derived from the export of pastoral products. This uniqueness is further enhanced in that along with industrialized Japan and the United Kingdom, Australia is among the first three countries in degree of urbanization. The high incidence of urbanization post-war, however, has been mainly the result of industrial growth, and associated tertiary industries became a very important factor influencing the growth of State capitals and of some large towns. In 1947, according to current boundary definitions, 50.7 per cent of the total population in Australia was found in State capital cities (i.e. metropolitan areas) and 18.1 per cent in 'other urban' areas. In total, the proportion of Australia's population enumerated in urban areas was 68.8 per cent in 1947, while by 1971 this figure had increased to 85.6 per cent. In 1971 the proportion of the population in metropolitan areas (State capitals) was 60.1 per cent, an increase of 10 per cent over the 1947 figure.

There is a clear trend of continuing urbanization, as Table 1.1 indicates.

For Australia as a whole, the proportion of the population resident in rural areas fell from 31.1 per cent in 1947 to only 14.7 per cent in 1971, the greatest drop occurring between 1947 and 1954. In view of the continuous increase in the proportion of the population in urban areas, it can be expected that rural proportions would have declined and this was consistently the case throughout all States.[1] The absolute numbers in most rural areas also fell throughout the period, due to increased mechanization on farms, lack of an adequate living for all farm family members, declining rural incomes throughout the whole period in many dairy farming areas, and in the 1968–71 period the severe rural recession for wool producers which led to out-migration not only of the young between ages 16 and 25 but whole family movement in many districts. Thus in some districts, particularly north-western and south-eastern New South Wales and in western Victoria, rural population declines of 5–10 per cent were recorded between the 1966 and 1971 censuses.

In South Australia, there were significant rural population losses in the

1947–66 period, there being a decline after boundary readjustments of 11,500 (6 per cent) between 1961 and 1966 alone.[2] Hugo found in South Australia a lack of a sufficient range and number of jobs and educational opportunities open to school leavers, particularly females, in rural areas. Furthermore, the substitution of capital investment for labour inputs in primary industry has markedly increased production per unit of manpower throughout most pastoral rural areas of Australia in the 1947–71 era.

TABLE 1.1. *Percentage distribution of population in urban and rural divisions of Australia 1947–1971*

| | Year | | | | |
	1947 %	1954 %	1961 %	1966 %	1971 %
Metropolitan	50.72	54.06	56.26	58.23	60.13
Other urban	18.14	24.88	25.88	25.13	25.53
Rural	31.14	21.06	17.86	16.64	14.34
Per cent	100.00	100.00	100.00	100.00	100.00
Total no.	7,560,755	8,963,161	10,482,900	11,530,775	12,711,574

Notes
(1) Based on current boundary definitions.
(2) Metropolitan areas are all capital cities plus Canberra.
(3) 1971 figures include the Aboriginal population.
Source: Censuses of the Commonwealth of Australia, 1947, 1954, 1961, 1966 and 1971.

But because markets for most primary products have become relatively inelastic, established members of the primary industry workforce have in fact become redundant, a process which began of course much earlier, and its results in Australia were already evident in the 1933 census. Not all rural areas lost population however; in areas of closer settlement for soldier settlers and richer irrigation areas there were rural population gains. Post-war immigration of divers ethnic groups contributed to the latter.

Throughout the 1947–71 period there were increases in proportions of the population resident in cities of 100,000 or more persons, as Table 1.2 indicates. Centres of 100,000 or more persons have commonly been taken as a reliable index of urbanization,[3] provided anomalous city states like Singapore, Hong Kong, Kuwait and the like are not included. Even in 1947 at the beginning of the period under discussion, Australia had a higher proportion of the population in cities of 100,000 or more people than Canada, France and the Netherlands, and the same proportion as the United States (56 per cent), but a significantly lesser percentage than in

England and Wales. By 1971, the proportion of the Australian population resident in centres of 100,000 or more persons had increased to 64.5 per cent, still significantly below England and Wales but higher than most other industrialized nations. The most significant increase in Australia was that in the proportion of the population in cities of 500,000 or more, as the rapidly growing State capitals of Brisbane, Adelaide and Perth passed the half million mark and the absolute number of persons in cities of more than 500,000 increased from 2,976,000 to 7,372,000. Meanwhile, the proportion of the population in cities of one million or more increased slightly from 39 to 40 per cent. In actual fact, of course, by 1971, as Sydney and Melbourne had reached populations well over 2 million, 40 per cent of the population were in centres of over 2.5 million, a much greater proportion than in highly urbanized Britain and a percentage not exceeded elsewhere (excepting the city states mentioned). However, if the highly urbanized north-east of the United States and the Tokyo–Osaka and adjacent cities in Japan are considered as integrated connurbations,[4] then these two countries may compare with Australia in the proportion of the population in cities of 2.5 million or more.

There has been considerable debate on indices of urbanization as Arriaga and Kingsley Davis have testified,[4] and there are difficulties in the

TABLE 1.2. *Cumulative proportions of the population in various size classes of cities in Australia 1947, 1966 and 1971*

	Year					
	1947		1966		1971	
	Number	%	Number	%	Number	%
Above 1 million	2,975,914	39.31	4,556,370	39.28	5,106,010	40.11
Above 500,000	2,975,914	39.31	6,553,843	56.50	7,372,085	57.91
Above 100,000	4,256,273	56.15	7,283,715[a]	62.79	8,209,126	64.49
Total population	7,579,358	100.00	11,599,498	100.00	12,728,461	100.00

[a] Includes Canberra-Queanbeyan as one urban area.

Source: Censuses of the Commonwealth of Australia, 1947, 1966 and 1971.

usage of relative figures which do not take into account the size of the cities in a given country. Where this is done, as in a study by Arriaga, in which the mean city size of residence of the urban population and the proportion of the population which is urban are considered together, Australia still ranks among the five most urbanized countries in the world. Again, the social and economic characteristics of urbanism are very difficult to measure in a standard way but it is probable that with the diffusion of urban values to rural areas, and to the non-peasant, highly capitalistic graziers and pastoralists through the mass media, the press and frequent city visiting, Australia has one of the two or three most urban societies in the world.

Factors in urban growth in non-metropolitan urban areas 1947–1971

Between 1947 and 1971, the officially designated non-metropolitan 'other urban' areas increased their share in the total population from 18.4 per cent in 1947 to 25.9 per cent in 1961 with a slight decline to 25.5 per cent in 1971. Some of this change reflected variations in definition of 'other urban' areas and the physical spread of towns into areas formerly classified as rural, but the growing importance of 'other urban' areas, especially the industrial cities of Wollongong and Geelong, but also the larger country towns, has been evident.

For urban areas other than the metropolitan State capitals (and Canberra), the rate of growth was in general higher than that of the metropolitan cities until 1961, and became lower for the periods 1961–6 and 1966–71. The number of relatively large towns over 10,000 in population size (excluding capital cities) increased from 34 in 1947 to 66 in 1971. In population, these towns contained just over 10 per cent of the total Australian population in 1947 but increased to 15.1 per cent in 1961 and 15.7 per cent in 1971. Whereas in 1947 there was only one non-metropolitan city over 50,000 and containing only 1.68 per cent of the Australian population, by 1971 there were eight such centres containing 6.97 per cent of the population. Thus major growth occurred among the largest non-metropolitan cities. In 1947, only Newcastle (N.S.W.) had a population of over 50,000 persons, whereas by 1961, cities of 50,000 population and over included also Geelong (Victoria) and Wollongong (N.S.W.), as well as Launceston and suburbs (Tasmania), Ballarat (Victoria), Townsville (Queensland) and Toowoomba (Queensland), while the Latrobe Valley urban area (Victoria) was just under 50,000. By 1966, to the list of seven in 1961 was added Goldcoast, adjacent to Brisbane and straddling the New South Wales–Queensland boundaries, which grew continuously to become the second largest urban area in Queensland. It had a population of approximately 53,200 in 1966 and 69,700 in 1971.

Geelong, Wollongong and Newcastle grew as relatively specialized industrial cities, Wollongong and Newcastle in particular becoming Australia's major steel-producing towns, being located close to coal supplies. Wollongong had the fastest rate of growth of these industrial cities, gaining heavily through both internal and international migration. The Latrobe Valley urban area was also an industrial complex, being Victoria's basic source of power and fuel, and an important supplier of town gas; thus it became attractive to industries requiring large quantities of fuel. It was not a steel producer, but has tended to concentrate on paper pulp manufacture and chemicals.[5] Ballarat, formerly a mining centre, developed light manufacturing as well as growing as a market town and regional centre, while the Queensland cities of Toowoomba and Townsville developed as market towns and ports serving large rural hinterlands and also as light manufacturing centres. Goldcoast specialized as a tourist and resort centre.

Not only did the number of non-metropolitan large cities increase in the 1947–71 period, but each of them has also grown. Newcastle, for example, had a population of 127,000 in 1947 but in 1971 the population had almost doubled to 249,960. Wollongong grew even more rapidly: from only 62,960 people on 1954 it grew to 185,890 in 1971, three times the 1954 population in only seventeen years.

The number of towns with populations more than 10,000 but smaller than 50,000 also increased, from 33 (1947) to 57 (1971), but the proportion of total Australian population which they contained increased only slightly, from 8.58 per cent in 1947 to 8.73 per cent in 1971. The rates of growth of these small to medium sized cities and towns were lower than that of the total country and it appears that some towns in this size class might have experienced population loss through out-migration. Country urban centres tended to retain their aggregate natural increase in population but were able to absorb only 10 per cent of the out-migration from rural areas between 1954 and 1966.[6]

Growth of the metropolitan State capitals 1947–1971

Australia has not had one dominant primate city but rather two competing rivals, Sydney and Melbourne, throughout the twentieth century. However, because of the separate origin of the States as sovereign colonies in the late eighteenth and nineteenth centuries, each State had its capital geographically distant from those of other States and centrally located (with the exception of Brisbane) within it. In fact, as Rose has pointed out, the four State capitals of Brisbane, Sydney, Melbourne and Adelaide are spaced at regular intervals between 400 and 480 air miles from each other around the coast of south-east Australia.[7] Rose, Bunker, Robinson, Clarke[8] and others have commented, however, on the extent of metropolitan primacy *within each State*. Thus in Victoria, metropolitan Melbourne was over twenty times the size of the next largest centre, Geelong, in 1971, and in South Australia, Adelaide was also more than twenty times the size of the next largest centre. In New South Wales, Sydney was over eight times larger than the second largest centre, Newcastle. But if Newcastle, Sydney and Wollongong are seen as one urbanizing region (as Clarke argues because of their functional interdependence)[9] the next largest urban centre in New South Wales was over sixty times smaller in 1971. Only in

Queensland and Tasmania has metropolitan primacy been more moderate and the population relatively decentralized.[10]

In all the mainland States, population centralization increased significantly in the 1947–71 period, i.e. an increasing proportion of the population of each State became resident in its primate or capital city. Whereas in 1947, 49 per cent of New South Wales' population resided in Sydney, by 1971 over 60 per cent were located in Sydney. Melbourne's proportion of Victoria's population also increased markedly from 53 per cent to over 70 per cent and Adelaide's from 52 to over 71 per cent of South Australia's population. In Western Australia, Perth's share of the State population increased from 47 to 67 per cent in the 1947–71 period.

In the metropolitan areas, although all capital cities substantially increased their share of population in their States, percentage intercensal increases differed very much between capital cities. This was the case after standardization of statistical boundaries as at the 1966 census statistical division, a procedure followed throughout this work. For the 1947–54 period, the population of Perth increased by almost 28 per cent and Adelaide's increased by 26.5 per cent. Sydney's and Melbourne's increases were considerably less, being only 17.9 and 13.2 per cent respectively, compared with the national increase of 18.5 per cent. In the next intercensal period, 1954–61, Sydney remained the slowest growing metropolis, but Melbourne grew by 24.8 per cent. Brisbane grew much more slowly – 19.5 per cent in 1954–61 as contrasted with almost 25 per cent in 1947–54, and other State capitals also grew much more slowly. During 1961–6, which is a five year intercensal period, Brisbane and Adelaide grew very fast, by 22.3 and 25.4 per cent respectively, or at an annual rate of 4.7 per cent for Brisbane and 5 per cent for Adelaide. Sydney and Melbourne grew by 2.25 per cent a year during this period. Hobart had the lowest growth rate from 1954 – 1.2 per cent a year for 1954–61, and 1.7 per cent a year for 1961–6.

Between 1966 and 1971, Perth grew very rapidly with the expansion of mineral exploitation and associated tertiary activities in Western Australia, increasing its population from 500,340 to 639,600, or an increase of 27.8 per cent. Growth rates for other State capitals during 1966–71 declined slightly, although they were still significantly higher than the State averages. The more rapid growth of Brisbane, Adelaide and Perth was in part the result of a much greater net gain through internal migration than in Sydney and Melbourne,[11] a movement which was not merely rural–urban but was almost certainly inter-metropolitan. Though largely compensated by receiving the bulk of overseas immigrants, Sydney and Melbourne grew during the post-war period at much slower rates than other State capital cities except Hobart.

Immigration and population composition of cities

A vitally important element in the growth of Australia's larger cities has been immigration in the 1947–71 period. The major urban areas became attractive to migrants, especially those from eastern and southern Europe. Occupational opportunities were limited in smaller towns or rural areas where unemployment levels, whole low by international standards, were higher than in larger centres. The attraction in the large cities was the availability of employment in rapidly expanding heavy industry – car assembly in Geelong, South Melbourne, Adelaide and Sydney, steel production with the establishment of new plant in Wollongong, building and construction and allied service trades in Melbourne in particular, but also in Sydney and Adelaide. In these industries and in manufacturing, in particular, semi-skilled and unskilled migrants could find openings and ambitious persons establish themselves as independent craftsmen–businessmen and the like.

When various size classes of cities are examined, as in Table 1.3, it can be seen that the largest cities on the whole had a much higher proportion of their population born overseas at the 1966 census than the lesser cities and smaller urban centres.

TABLE 1.3. *Urban centre size and proportion (per cent) of the population born overseas 1966*

Size of centre (persons)		Per cent born overseas							
		0–4	5–9	10–14	15–19	20–24	25–29	30+	Total
Above 500,000	No.	—	—	—	1	1	3	—	5
	Per cent of centres				20.0	20.0	60.0		100.0
90,000–300,000	No.	—	—	2	—	1	2	—	5
	Per cent of centres			40.0		20.0	40.0		100.0
40,000–65,000	No.	1	3	3	—	—	—	—	7
	Per cent of centres	14.3	42.9	42.9					100.1
20,000–40,000	No.	—	10	1	1	1	—	1	14
	Per cent of centres		71.4	7.1	7.1	7.1		7.1	99.8
10,000–20,000	No.	2	15	12	2	2	1	—	34
	Per cent of centres	5.9	44.1	35.3	5.9	5.9	2.9		100.0
5,000–10,000	No.	16	29	11	2	3	—	—	61
	Per cent of centres	24.4	47.5	18.0	3.3	4.9			100.1
Below 5,000	No.	128	114	98	4	7	—	7	358
	Per cent of centres	35.7	31.8	27.4	1.1	1.9		1.9	99.8

Note. Includes all 'urban centres' designated as such at the 1966 census.

Source: Unpublished census data by collectors' districts and local government areas, 1966. Birthplace data for the 1971 census by sub areas was unavailable.

In only one State capital larger than half a million in population size, Brisbane, did the overseas-born constitute less than 20 per cent of the population, while in three – Perth, Melbourne and Adelaide – immigrants comprised 25–29 per cent of the population compared with 18 per cent of the total population of Australia. Of the five centres with populations between 90,000 and 300,000, two (Newcastle and Hobart) had migrant proportions below the national average and three proportions over 20 per cent (two over 25 per cent). All of the seven centres between 40,000 and 65,000 had migrant proportions under 15 per cent (two under 10 per cent). At the bottom end of the scale, of the 358 urban centres below 5,000, 340 (94.9 per cent) had foreign-born proportions below 10 per cent and 128 (35.7 per cent) foreign-born proportions under 5 per cent, compared with 18 per cent of the total population of Australia. The very small percentage of minor urban centres with relatively high proportions of their population born overseas were mainly special function towns associated with mining activities or small industrial centres close to the major metropolitan areas, or towns which have become dormitory suburbs.

The favouring of the large capital cities, more especially Sydney, Melbourne and Adelaide, by immigrants has had an effect on the masculinity ratio of the population in these cities as well as the age composition. The masculinity ratios of almost all the immigrant groups in Australia were consistently higher than those of the Australian-born in rural, non-metropolitan urban, and metropolitan areas in 1966. Thus in rural areas, masculinity ratios of the eight largest immigrant groups ranged from 128 to 235 compared with the rural rate for the total population of 116. In the metropolitan areas, masculinity ratios ranged from 100 (German-born) to 149 (Yugoslav-born) with a mean of 112 for the overseas-born compared with 97.4 for the total population and 92 for the Australian-born. The relatively low metropolitan masculinity of the Australian-born, while reflecting higher male mortality of upper ages and the result of a male-selective net migration loss of the Australian-born overseas probably reflected also a female-selective (in the 15–30 age group) rural and small town to metropolitan internal migration.

The effect of the male-dominant immigration to the large cities was to lessen the imbalance of the sexes, although because of cultural and linguistic difficulties, particularly with groups from eastern and southern Europe, this did not facilitate intermarriage with the host society population. Among east European former Displaced Persons (especially Poles), there was a surplus of single men in the original drafts between the ages of 16 and 25, many of whom never married and have resided in rooming houses or in flats or cottages on their own. This was also the case with the Italians and Yugoslav-born, so much so with the latter that the Federal government recently acted to modify immigrant selection and negotiate new migration agreements with Yugoslavia to encourage more female migration. On the whole, however, sex ratios have been more balanced among north-west European settlers in the metropolitan areas except for the Netherlands-born, and *family* migration has been the dominant role with north-west European settlers in the process of residential adjustment and suburban expansion. For southern and central Europeans, more especially in inner and middle distance suburbs, family settlement was the prevalent residential form in the urbanization process although single men immigrant concentrations in inner suburban rooming house districts with declining total populations also developed.

Workforce changes in the urbanization process

Other demographic trends of significance in the post-war metropolitanization process were changes in workforce characteristics. With the relatively rapid growth of the largest cities, more especially Sydney, Melbourne and Adelaide, there was an expansion of the labour force within which manufacturing was very important. It was only in the post-war era that the heavy industry base of the Australian economy was established: hitherto, with the exception of the iron and steel industry in Newcastle, and the embryonic steel industry at Port Kembla (Wollongong), much of Australian manufacturing consisted of assembling, processing and manufacturing from imported raw materials or from Australian rural-produced raw materials; light engineering and service industries were also important. Post-war, iron and steel manufacture from native raw materials was extended in Australia, with associated heavy engineering, and large-scale vehicle and other assembly works and petro-chemical manufacture were developed in the three southern State capitals of Sydney, Melbourne and Adelaide. In 1966, 34.4, 37.7 and 32.3 per cent of the workforce in Sydney, Melbourne and Adelaide respectively were employed in manufacturing (industry group), compared with 25.2, 22.7 and 22.9 per cent of the Brisbane, Perth and Hobart metropolitan area workforces. Immigration played a major part in the growth of the manufacturing labour force in the southern cities, and in all State capitals the labour force grew at a faster rate than the total population. This was substantially because the age composition of migrants was concentrated in the working age groups (16–65 and in particular 20–45).[12] Another important reason however was increased female participation in the workforce: in 1966, 33 per cent of Sydney's workforce consisted of women, while 33 per cent of Melbourne's and 31 per cent of the Brisbane, Adelaide, Perth, Canberra and Hobart labour forces was female. Between 1966 and 1970, female labour force participation increased significantly, particularly that of married women. In May 1969, 39 per cent of married women (in the nation as a whole) aged 30–44 years were employed. It is estimated that over two-thirds of the inflow of women into the labour force between 1966 and 1970 consisted of immigrants.

Despite the growth of manufacturing and heavy industry in Australia's large cities between 1947 and 1966, the manufacturing proportion of the labour force actually declined in this period: in Sydney from 37.1 per cent to 34.4 per cent, in Melbourne from 40.7 to 37.7 per cent, in Adelaide from 35.6 to 32.3, and in Hobart from 26.4 to 22.9 per cent. Meanwhile, those employed in the finance, property, public authority (not elsewhere included), defence and community and business service components of tertiary industry actually increased their proportion in the workforce: from 17.2 per cent in 1947 to 21.4 per cent in Sydney in 1966, from 16.4 to 20.2 per cent in Melbourne, 19.4 to 25.3 per cent in Perth and 22.1 to 28.4 per cent in Hobart. The 'whire collar' sector of tertiary industry in fact increased to become almost as large numerically as the 'blue collar' sector in manufacturing, and the building and construction part of the tertiary group. The 1947–71 period in the urban history of Australia has been one of the growth of an industrial structure and at the same time a transition towards a post-industrial society.

Conclusion

Australia has clearly emerged in the post-war world as one of the most urbanized countries in the world, whatever indices of urbanization are used as measurement. The basic pattern has been the further increase in primacy of the metropolitan capital cities within their respective States; the rapid growth of two industrial non-metropolitan cities (Wollongong and Geelong) and the very rapid growth of the national capital, Canberra; with a notable absence of any intermediate sized centres in the urban hierarchy of the respective States with the exception of Queensland and Tasmania in which Toowoomba, Townsville and Launceston respectively have had healthy growth rates; and with the exception of a few market towns servicing rural areas, slow growth of a plethora of small country towns and population decline in some. Of the total Australian population increase of 5,149,100 between 1947 and 1971, 78 per cent occurred in the metropolitan centres (capital cities) along with Wollongong, Newcastle and Geelong, and over 70 per cent took place in the capital cities alone. Because of an absolute population decline in rural areas, all the population increase was in fact absorbed in urban centres, although of course there were a few rural areas in which population increased and a number of small country towns and mining towns in which population declined.

Following the early establishment in Sydney and Melbourne of government and economic centralization of trade, wool and gold exporting, and through industrialization, these two primate cities have multiplied their economic and demographic dominance within their own State regions. In the nineteenth century and early twentieth century, they tended to dominate the other capital cities and their regions as well, but in the post-war period their demographic dominance of the other capital cities (except Hobart) decreased. In fact the other State capitals grew faster than either Sydney or Melbourne in the 1947–71 period. The populations of Adelaide, Perth and Brisbane increased by 104, 130 and 94 per cent respectively in this twenty-four year period, whereas those of Sydney and Melbourne increased by only 65 and 92 per cent respectively, despite heavy overseas immigration to them. The rate of growth of Sydney was actually slightly lower than that of the total population of Australia.

As far as the host society (Australian-born) population is concerned, Sydney and Melbourne experienced almost no net gain through internal migration and for much of the period suffered Australian-born losses (see subsequent chapters), both overseas and to other Australian cities and States. This tendency of the Australian-born to move from the larger cities has been paralleled in part in post-war Japan, as Kuroda has shown,[13] although this has not meant mere suburbanization but movement to other distinct urban places as well; it has followed recent trends in the connurbations of Great Britain. Of course, in Great Britain and Japan, two highly urbanized countries, there has not been the massive immigration from overseas which has dominated Sydney's and Melbourne's growth.

Because of heavy overseas immigration and natural increase, however, Sydney's population increased by 1,100,790 between 1947 and 1971, and at the latter date there were 2.8 million persons in Sydney, which ranked 27th in size among world city-regions. Sydney in fact had a population in 1971 equal to the West Midlands conurbation, Britain's second largest urban agglomeration after London, and was larger than Canada's metropolitan centres. Only seven metropolitan areas in North America were larger than Sydney. Melbourne too in the period of post-war urbanization become a World City, ranking (by estimation) 36th or 37th among the urbanizing regions of the world. If Newcastle and Wollongong are considered along with Sydney as part of one urbanizing region, that of the New South Wales Central Coast – a terminology coined by George Clarke[14] – with a population of 3.3 million, Sydney would rank higher on the world scale of metropolitan area size.

The urbanization process typified by metropolitan expansion in Australia has differed considerably from that of large cities elsewhere, in that population densities have been much lower in Sydney, Melbourne and the other capital cities than in British, European and North American cities of comparable function and size. Thus in 1966, the average densities of persons per square mile in Sydney and Melbourne respectively were 4,908 and 4,794, compared with 9,810 persons per square mile in the New York–north-eastern New Jersey urbanized area in 1950,[15] although this latter figure had dropped a little by 1960. Density averages were significantly lower in all the other State capitals ranging from 2,940 per square mile in Brisbane to 3,580 in Adelaide in 1966.

However, the post-war trend in Australia has been one of increasing density, from 2,678 per square mile in metropolitan Sydney in 1954 to 4,908 in 1966, and a similar increase took place in Melbourne. This has been partly the result of increasing construction of multi-storey apartment blocks and owner-occupier three to four storey home unit (apartment) dwellings, and while home ownership is likely to remain high in urban Australia, the *type* of homes constructed in the future may change more towards the European pattern of semi-detached (duplex) or owner-occupier medium density apartment blocks, rather than the traditional detached bungalow on its suburban one-sixth to one-eighth acre lot. This will be necessary in Sydney because of environmental limitations to low density urban sprawl. It is only in central and some eastern suburbs of Sydney and in Carlton and harbour-side St Kilda, Melbourne, that population densities begin to approach those regarded as medium densities in the large cities of the north-east United States (densities over 11,000 per square mile), and the pockets of densities over 20,000 per square mile are found only in a few limited modern apartment block areas, or three-storey nineteenth century terraces in inner Sydney.

As Kingsley Davis aptly states with reference to the urbanized north-eastern seaboard of the United States, population cannot long expand, especially in Sydney and in Adelaide, without a rise in density. Persistent metropolitan population growth promises to frustrate the ceaseless search for space – for ample residential blocks, wide-open suburban school grounds, sprawling shopping centres, one-floor factories, broad motorways. How the host society population feels about large agglomerations may be best indicated by the data on net migration loss of the Australian-born from Sydney and Melbourne presented in a later chapter: there may be a headlong effort to escape them. The bigger the city, the higher the cost of space on the whole; yet the more the level of living rises, the more that more people are willing to pay (or have to pay) for low-density living. It seems probable in Australia's largest cities that life in low-density surroundings will become too dear for the great majority. It seems plain that the only way to stop urban crowding and to solve most of the urban problems (housing, schools, renewal) besetting Sydney and Melbourne is to reduce the overall rate of population growth, and for Australia's largest cities this means reducing immigration.

NOTES

1 C. Y. Choi, 'Components of population changes in non-metropolitan urban areas, 1947–1971', in national population enquiry: *Australia's Population and the Future*, Working Paper no. 9.
2 Graeme J. Hugo, 'Some spatial aspects of the pattern of internal migration within South Australia 1961–1966', 43rd A.N.Z.A.A.S. Congress, Geographical Sciences Section, Brisbane, May 1971.
3 Edvardo E. Arriaga, 'A new approach to the measurements of urbanization, Economic Development and Cultural Change, *18*, no. 2, January 1970, pp. 208–9.
4 Arriaga, 'New approach'; Ana Casis and Kingsley Davis, 'Urbanization in Latin America', *Milbank Memorial Fund Quarterly*, *24*, no. 3, July 1946, pp. 292–314.
5 J. Zubrzycki, *Settlers of the Latrobe Valley*, A.N.U. Press, 1964, p. 10.
6 John C. Steinke, *Regional Trends in Australian Population Distribution, 1947–1966*, Department of Decentralization and Development, Sydney, 1971, p. 7.
7 A. J. Rose, *Patterns of Cities*, Nelson, 1967, p. 195.
8 A. J. Rose, 'Dilemma down under: metropolitan primacy as the normal state', *Pacific Viewpoint*, 7, 1966, pp. 1–27; R. Bunker, 'The metropolis in Australia', in *Readings in Urban Growth*, Department of Geography, University of Sydney, 1963; K. W. Robinson, 'The distinctive character of Australian urban growth', in *Readings in Urban Growth*.
9 George Clarke, 'Urban Australia', in A. F. Davies and S. Encel (eds.), *Australian Society, a Sociological Introduction*, second ed., Cheshire, 1970, p. 54.
10 J. H. Holmes, 'Macrogeographic analysis of population distributions of Australian States', Institute of Australian Geographers Conference, Canberra, February 1972.
11 I. H. Burnley and C. Y. Choi, 'Internal migration in Australia 1947–1966, with special reference to interstate movements and the growth of capital cities', Institute of Australian Geographers Conference, Canberra, February 1972.
12 R. T. Appleyard, 'The population', in A. F. Davies and S. Encel (eds.), *Australian Society, a Sociological Introduction*, second ed., Cheshire, 1970, p. 8.
13 T. Kuroda, 'Demographic aspects of urbanization in Japan: the new dimension of internal migration and urbanization', *Proceedings of the International Population Conference*, London, 1969, vol. IV, pp. 2916–20.
14 Clarke, 'Urban Australia', p. 56.
15 Kingsley Davis, 'The urbanization of the human population', in *Cities*, A 'Scientific American' Book, Penguin, 1967.

2

Economic factors and the growth of cities

F. J. B. STILWELL*

Economic analysis of urban growth

The high degree of urbanization in Australia determines the environmental fabric of economic and social life. On the one hand, it can be regarded partly as the *outcome* of certain economic forces, such as the need for proximity between different industries and the desire to obtain the benefits of scale economies in the provision of infra-structure. On the other hand, the highly urbanized structure is a *cause* of important economic and social effects, such as the pattern of land prices, the extent of congestion and pollution, and the degree of inequality in the income distribution. In these ways, economic considerations are interwoven in all aspects of urbanization.

However, economists have been very little concerned to date with questions relating to urbanization and the environmental fabric. Various reasons for this can be identified. Most generally, the neglect would appear to reflect economists' preoccupation with readily quantifiable variables such as gross national product, unemployment and inflation levels, rather than less easily measurable variables relating to the living conditions of sub-groups within the population.

Secondly, urban environmental studies have been accorded a low status within the economic profession because of their necessarily interdisciplinary nature. As Richardson notes, 'urban economists frequently have to endure the condescension of their purist colleagues because they are not concerned with the great traditional themes and because they fraternise with sociologists, planners and similar types'.[1]

Finally a special reason for the neglect of urban environmental studies in Australia. To my mind, this reflects a continuing attachment to the 'developing country' ideology. What this means is that politicians, public administrators and businessmen imply that Australia must accept whatever urban–rural pattern is necessary for rapid national economic development. Fundamentally, there are two implicit value judgements here, that faster national economic growth is necessarily a good thing, and that such growth is best achieved by minimizing the constraints on private enterprise. Both these propositions are highly questionable, and recent books by Mishan[2] and others have helped to expose the fallacies underlying 'growthmania' and the laissez-faire outlook. Nevertheless, their persistence in Australia accounts for the lack of concern to date with the 'side-issues of urban environment relative to the "main issue" of stimulating national economic growth'.

The prevalence of this particular ideology has had important repercussions on the intra-urban distribution of economic activities and on the balance between metropolitan and non-metropolitan growth. This chapter concentrates on the latter aspect. The former is important but is more appropriately dealt with in Part II of this book where emphasis is placed on the internal structure of urban areas. Here we are concerned with city growth in a more aggregate sense. An initial distinction can be drawn between the following two questions:

a. What *descriptive* role can economic analysis play in explaining Australia's particular pattern of urban growth?
b. What *prescriptive* role can economic analysis play in the formulation of public policies towards urban growth?

This chapter concentrates largely on the former. The general theme adopted is that economic analysis does have a potentially useful function in the analysis of urbanization, but that its proper role is as part of a more generalized institutional-historical approach. The greatest potential contribution of economics to urban studies is not through the construction of elegant space-subscripted general equilibrium models, so much as in terms of a more directly political view of socio-economic systems. Frank argues that 'social science must be political science'[3] and in the Australian case it is very clear that the political structure has set the framework within which economic forces have been allowed to operate. One such effect has already been noted: the predominantly laissez-faire outlook of political leadership has allowed the centralizing economic forces full reign in the urbanization process.

More fundamentally, the colonial-capitalist heritage has largely determined the pattern of population growth. The prominence of a few coastal centres is a legacy from the British imperial era which resources were taken out through ports which also served as colonial administrative centres. This dominance has been accentuated by the capitalist means of domestic economic organization. Under such a system, where location decisions are primarily in the hands of private enterprise, it is natural to develop further the already partially developed. As Rose puts it, 'growth begets growth'.[4] Once cities are established and pass a certain size, vested interests of business (and those of local government) lead to a process of cumulative causation. The dual economy outcome is familiar to students of under-development: the pursuit of private profit through 'building on the best' often leads to impressive growth rates but at the expense of balanced development. Capitalist development, even when most successful, is always a 'trickle-down' development.

In Australia, there have been special forces causing this 'trickle-down' from the early-established centres to be even slower than is normal in capitalist economies. Some of these are considered in detail later in this chapter, including the Federal organization, interstate variations in railway gauges, the relatively recent start to the process of *national* development, the concentration of manufacturing industry close to the ports and the special situation of the agricultural sector. An analytical framework for studying Australian urbanization must be capable of handling such influences. This suggests that conventional models (e.g. of the central place or urban-base type) are likely to be too constraining. These are briefly discussed later in this chapter but the main emphasis is on the effect of economic forces in building on the colonial-capitalist heritage. In part, this can be illustrated through an analysis of urban industrial structure (as in the third section of this chapter): in part, it requires a more general analysis of the process of cumulative causation in consolidating the imbalance within the economy (as in the fourth section of this chapter, pp. 37–43).

Economic trends

First we need to build a general picture of post-war trends in urban growth. This requires an initial decision regarding the most appropriate measure of economic activity. Richardson notes this difficulty that 'a special problem facing the urban economist is that he usually lacks a satisfactory measure of urban growth'.[5] However, his further assertion that demographic data are 'a very poor proxy for an index of growth' is questionable. Admittedly, economists usually prefer to measure growth in income terms because of the implied link between income and welfare. However, in studying urbanization, there are a number of reasons why demographic data (including information on employment as well as population) are normally more useful.

Firstly, the link between income and welfare is of dubious validity in a situation where individuals' assessment of their own well-being depends on the relative well-being of other persons. This is what is known to economists as the problem of interdependent utility functions, and it is a particularly intense problem in urban areas where the proximity of persons to each other makes interdependence the rule rather than the exception. Secondly, the link between income and welfare becomes even more dubious where the attempts of any one individual to improve his welfare have direct effects on the ability of others to improve their welfare. This is the problem of 'externalities' or 'spillover' effects and, once again, it is a particularly recurrent problem in urban areas because of the close proximity of different economic activities. Thirdly, there is a more direct link between many social problems of urbanization (congestion, provision of adequate public services etc.) and population growth, than between those social problems and growth measured in income terms.

For these reasons, no apology is necessary for examining economic trends mainly in terms of demographic data. Even if adequate regional income data were available, it would still be desirable to give primary attention to population and employment statistics. The main practical problem in presenting such information relates to the extent of disaggregation. It would be possible to tabulate data on a very localized basis but the resulting statistics would be highly indigestible. Moreover, it is the essence of the social scientist that he be able to selectively condense vast masses of information. As Boulding says, 'knowledge is always gained by the orderly loss of information, that is, by condensing and abstracting and indexing the great buzzing confusion of information that comes from the world around us into a form we can appreciate and comprehend'.[6] Bearing this in mind, and recognizing the primacy of the State capitals, the most appropriate initial classification is according to the three-fold breakdown: metropolitan, other urban and rural. This gives a conveniently small set of information and, although there have been some boundary changes in the post-war period, it remains the most useful starting point for demographic analysis, particularly since our concern is more with total urban growth than with the growth of population in areas which were classified as urban at some historical date. Moreover, it places useful emphasis on an essential qualitative difference between the seven major metropolitan areas and other urban places.

The information presented in Table 2.1 summarizes the post-war trends in population shares. Clearly, the various States and Territories vary considerably in the relative importance of metropolitan, urban and rural habitation. The dominance of the State capitals is greatest in Victoria and South Australia, where over two persons in every three live in the metropolitan areas, but only in Tasmania and Queensland do the State capitals contain less than half of the population. However, all the States exhibit the same tendency towards increased metropolitan dominance. The share of population in the rural areas has fallen in all States and, while the areas in the 'other urban' category have generally maintained a fairly stable share, the metropolitan areas have continued to forge ahead.

The outcome is that Australia has become one of the world's most urbanized nations. Its urban emphasis has always been well above average, despite the myth of the 'outback' nation. However, according to a recent survey cited by Van Dugteren,[7] it now tops this particular league-table with 88 per cent of the population in urban areas, ahead of Japan with 84 per cent, Germany 82 per cent, Denmark and the U.K. with 80 per cent and the United States in sixth place with 75 per cent. This classification would appear to be based on a slightly different definition of urban areas from that

TABLE 2.1. *Post-war population trends by States and Territories*

		Total population[a] (000s)	Proportion of total in		
			Metropolitan	Other urban	Rural
New South Wales	1947[b]	2,977	55.3	27.2	17.5
	1954	3,417	54.5	28.3	17.2
	1961	3,906	55.9	29.5	14.6
	1966	4,225	57.9	28.7	13.4
	1971[c]	4,584	59.3	29.4	11.3
Victoria	1947[b]	2.051	63.0	18.2	18.8
	1954	2,444	62.4	19.2	18.4
	1961	2,926	65.4	19.6	15.0
	1966	3,217	65.6	20.0	14.4
	1971[c]	3,494	68.4	19.4	12.2
Queensland	1947[b]	1,105	36.4	34.4	29.2
	1954	1,315	38.2	35.0	26.8
	1961	1,517	41.0	35.4	23.6
	1966	1,662	43.2	33.6	23.2
	1971[c]	1,820	44.9	34.6	20.5
Western Australia	1947[b]	499	54.6	16.7	28.7
	1954	638	54.7	16.5	28.8
	1961	734	57.3	17.1	25.6
	1966	834	60.0	16.8	23.2
	1971[c]	1,025	62.4	19.2	18.4
South Australia	1947[b]	644	59.4	13.7	26.9
	1954	795	60.8	13.9	25.3
	1961	965	60.9	18.3	20.8
	1966	1,090	66.8	15.9	17.3
	1971[c]	1,171	69.1	15.6	15.3
Tasmania	1947[b]	257	30.3	33.5	36.2
	1954	308	30.9	35.1	34.0
	1961	349	33.2	37.4	29.4
	1966	371	32.2	38.2	29.6
	1971[c]	389	33.3	40.2	26.5
A.C.T.	1947[b]	17	89.7	—	10.3
	1954	30	93.3	—	6.7
	1961	59	95.9	—	4.1
	1966	96	96.1	—	3.9
	1971[c]	144	98.0	—	2.0
Northern Territory	1947[b]	11	—	66.0	34.0
	1954	16	—	66.8	33.2
	1961	27	—	63.2	36.8
	1966	37	—	77.4	22.6
	1971[c]	85	—	64.7	35.3

[a] Excludes migratory population.
[b] Vernon Report, vol. II, p. 537: 'At the 1954 Census urban areas previously confined to cities and towns outside the metropolitan area which were separately incorporated, were redefined to include non-municipal towns with populations of 1,000 and over (750 in Tasmania). Without adjustment, this would have had the statistical effect of increasing the proportion of the population in urban, relative to rural areas. Because of this, the 1947 figures have been adjusted to 1954 boundaries and definitions by the Commonwealth Statistician.'
[c] 1971 figures include full-blood Aboriginals (not included in other census figures).

Sources: Report of the Committee of Economic Enquiry (Vernon Report), vol. II; Commonwealth Bureau of Census and Statistics: Censuses of the Commonwealth of Australia, 1954, 1961, 1966 and 1971.

used in Table 2.1. However, the general point is clear: Australia is a remarkably urbanized nation and any analysis of its distribution of economic activities must concentrate on explaining this high degree of urbanization and, more particularly, the dominance of the metropolitan areas.

The importance of this overall analysis of the reasons for metropolitan dominance is accentuated by the implied normative aspect. Some commentators have argued that such concentration reflects people's 'revealed preference' for metropolitan living. While a general appraisal of normative aspects of urbanization must await further research, some comments on this particular fallacy must be made right away.

Metropolitan living can be deduced to be a revealed preference by analysis of population movements, but only if the following two conditions hold: (*a*) that the urbanization is due to population movements where a real choice between different types of settlement exists, and (*b*) that there are no adverse spillovers or external diseconomies of individual location decisions on the rest of the community.

On the former point, there is much evidence that no real choice exists. Most of the metropolitan growth stems from four sources:

(1) natural increase of births over deaths;
(2) migration of persons from overseas (whose choice is determined more by the location of personal contacts and the policies of the Department of Immigration than by any more general informed evaluation of the desirability of alternative locations);
(3) the inclusion of persons living in areas adjacent to metropolitan areas who have been swamped by metropolitan expansion; and
(4) persons whose choice of location is constrained by job availability (particularly persons in professional and scientific occupations for whom even those few medium-sized centres that do exist in Australia do not provide suitable job opportunities).

Moreover, it should be clear that the decision of any person or business to locate in an urban area will normally have effects on the welfare of persons already living in that area. In such circumstances, it is improper to draw conclusions about the welfare of the community as a whole from the revealed preferences of some members of it. Bearing this cautionary statement in mind, more detailed comments on the individual States and Territories can be made as follows:

New South Wales

In one sense, Sydney's dominance of the State is understated in Table 2.1 because the two major secondary centres, Newcastle and Wollongong, also lie in the central coast region. Both are primarily coal-based developments and with current populations of 300,000 and 186,000 persons respectively, form the largest secondary centres in the nation as well as the State. Elsewhere, the major feature of population distribution in the State is a number of country centres with population numbers in the range of 15,000 to 30,000 (Wagga Wagga, Albury-Wodonga, Tamworth, Maitland, Orange, Goulbourn, Lismore, Armidale, Dubbo, Bathurst and Grafton). Most of these have been fairly slow growing, although Wagga Wagga and Albury-Wodonga seem to be becoming natural growth centres, while Armidale has expanded faster than average because of the establishment of a university and a teachers' college there. The far-west mining town of Broken Hill is slowly declining in population as ores are gradually depleted. So too is the coal mining town of Lithgow in the Blue Mountains. Indeed, the only really fast growing areas in the 'other urban' category are Gosford, Woy Woy and The Entrance, all of which are popular retirement areas and can be considered northern extensions of the Sydney area. Disaggregation of the statistics thus reveals the magnetism of Sydney regarding post-war growth in the State: the central area is capturing the lion's share of growth, while the mineral-based and country towns play no major role in capturing population as the decline of the rural areas continues.

Victoria

Melbourne's domination of growth within its State is even stronger than that of Sydney. Indeed, in the five years to 1971, it actually captured more than 100 per cent of Victoria's population growth, indicating a net decline in non-metropolitan areas. The largest secondary centre, Geelong (population 115,000), is close by on Port Phillip Bay, and one of the fastest growing areas in the 'other urban' category, Werribee, is contiguous to the metropolis. To the east lie the coal-based towns of the Latrobe Valley, but population numbers there have stabilized and even begun to decline in recent years. That leaves the only counter-magnets as Ballarat and Bendigo (both initially founded as the result of gold discoveries) and, to a lesser degree, the towns of Shepparton, Warmambool, Wangaratta and Mildura. They have grown slowly, certainly less rapidly in percentage terms than the Albury-Wodonga area on the border with New South Wales. Overall, it is very clear that Melbourne's absolute and relative dominance of the State is relentlessly increasing.

Queensland

Here the picture is rather different because there are a number of major secondary centres. Townsville, Toowoomba and Rockhampton are the largest, but Cairns, Mackay, Bundaberg, Maryborough and Gladstone are also of importance because of their domination of particular regions within the State. Most have been growing steadily in the post-war period, and both Townsville and Gladstone have accelerated their growth in the sixties. There are two other special cases in the 'other urban' category, the Gold Coast and Mt Isa. Both are based on resource exploitation of different types, it being 'sun and sand' in the former case and mining of minerals in the latter, and both have had very rapid growth performances. Nevertheless, even in the light of all these developments, the 'other urban' areas have failed to increase their share of the State's population. The rural sector has declined here as elsewhere, but the long-term trend is for this to be associated with increasing dominance of Brisbane. So, even here, where secondary centres have some importance, increased metropolitan dominance is the order of the day.

Western Australia

This has been the State with the fastest rate of growth, some of which has been associated with the great mineral discoveries of the sixties. New settlements have developed, such as Port Hedland, Kambalda, Mt Newman and Tom Price, but the major growth has been in the existing urban areas, particularly Perth. Indeed, there is very little alternative to a Perth location in Western Australia: the only distinctive centres with a population above 10,000 are Bunbury, Geraldton, Albany and the old established mining town of Kalgoorlie. Physical conditions severely restrict possibilities of settlement. The result is that, despite the mineral developments elsewhere in the State, Perth and its associated urban areas absorbed nearly four out of every five additional persons in the five years to 1971.

South Australia

In terms of secondary centres this State is not dissimilar to Western Australia. The only urban places with a population over 10,000 are Whyalla, Mount Gambier, Port Pirie and Port Augusta. The first of these continues to grow rapidly because of the expansion of its steel manufacturing base and the last, another industrial town which supplies about a third of the State's electricity, has shown significant growth, especially during the fifties. However, Adelaide's dominance continues unrivalled: its proportion of the State's population is now the highest of all the States.

Tasmania

Apart from being geographically detached, this State is the 'odd man out' in a number of ways. Firstly, the proportion of the population in rural areas remains outstandingly high. Secondly, metropolitan dominance is the least of all the States: only one in three persons lives in Hobart, and again unlike the other States, this proportion is relatively stable. Thirdly, there is some shift of focus in the State away from the southern metropolis towards the northern parts of the island. Although Launceston, the second largest town, has expanded only fairly slowly in the last decade, the six towns that stretch 40 miles along the north coast from Wynyard to Latrobe have formed an important growth centre, capturing nearly 30 per cent of the State's population increase in the five years to 1971. The result is that only in this State has the population share of the 'other urban' areas shown a significant and sustained expansion.

A. C. T.

The Capital Territory is Australia's showpiece of urban planning. Its population can be regarded as almost wholly metropolitan, although the integration of bushland areas between suburbs gives it quite a different character from other metropolitan areas. Also its socio-economic base is quite distinct because of its reliance on government activities. According to Linge, 'persons employed under the Public Service Act form 38 per cent of the workforce, those in public authorities and organisations supported by funds from the Government (such as ANU and CSIRO) make up another 25 per cent and the remaining 37 per cent are in private employment'.[8]

Since much of this private sector employment is in the provision of services, Canberra's rapid rate of build-up can be best understood in terms of decisions on public service expansion, rather than in terms of any more general model of the dynamics of the urban growth process.

Northern Territory

The population has expanded rapidly over the post-war period as this relatively uninhabited region has begun to be opened up. Its main centre, Darwin, now has a population of 35,000, and Alice Springs at 11,000 must be the best known of its size in Australia. Other expanding settlements are Katherine, Tennant Creek and the newly established bauxite-producing town of Nhulunbuy. One complication in the interpretation of population statistics is the inclusion of Aborigines in the published census tabulations for the first time in 1971. Since Aborigines predominate in rural rather than urban areas, the figures in Table 2.1 cannot be taken as indicating a genuine decline in the population share of the urban areas. Indeed, a recalculation of the 1966 figures including Aborigines indicates an urban share of only 53 per cent. The overall pattern, then, is that of rapid development with the major population growth centred on existing urban areas: indeed, Darwin alone captured nearly half of total population growth in the five years to 1971.

The foregoing analysis has been couched exclusively in terms of population numbers. This is a necessary but not sufficient element in the study of urbanization. One problem raised by Bate[9] is that differences in the age or sex composition of different towns may have a significant effect on their relative economic potential. Subsequent chapters of this book have much to say on such topics. The more fundamental issue to which we now turn attention is the relationship between economic and social factors in the urbanization process. The central issue is that of *industrialization*, and Appendixes 2.1 and 2.2 lay the groundwork for a detailed study of the importance of industrial structure in urban growth. These tables show, for 1954 and 1966 respectively, the industrial composition of the workforce in each of the metropolitan, other urban and rural regions within each State. The following section poses the question, 'to what extent can the pattern of industrialization which each region developed up to 1954 explain subsequent trends in urbanization?'. Trends in workforce numbers in the different metropolitan, other urban and rural areas closely mirror the population trends. Hence, any explanation of workforce trends by reference to the effects of industrialization provides a valuable explanation of the sort of population trends outlined earlier.

Growth and industrial structure

One of the most obvious characteristics of a town or region's growth potential is its industrial structure. If it specializes in industries for which demand is growing rapidly nationally (and internationally), its rate of growth is likely to be faster than if it specializes in stagnant or declining industries. The issue here is whether this hypothesis provides an adequate explanation of growth patterns in Australia.

The analytical procedure for distinguishing the effects of industrial structure is a standardization technique usually known as shift and share analysis. This is now a well-established tool of regional analysis: see for example, Perloff, Dunn, Lampard and Muth, Fuchs, Thirlwall, or Stilwell.[10] There is no reason to prevent its application at the urban area level being equally fruitful. A previous application to Australian regional statistics by Bunker led the author to conclude that it 'appears to be a good tool to dissect the way in which Australian states have grown since the war'.[11]

More rapturously, Dunn describes it as achieving 'a delightful wedding of the horizontal and vertical dimensions of regional analysis'.[12] In fact, the technique is subject to certain conceptual and empirical limitations, as catalogued by Stilwell,[13] but it provides a useful means of distinguishing between:

(a) employment growth in an area which would have occurred if the area had just maintained its share of national employment (the 'regional share' component);

(b) employment growth in an area above or below this regional share which can be attributed to the particular industrial composition of the area (the 'proportionality shift' or 'industrial mix' component);

(c) employment growth in an area above or below the regional share which cannot be explained by these industrial mix considerations (the 'differential shift' component).

The last of these elements is a residual which is not explained within the model itself. To that extent the model is incomplete, but it is still of value in helping to identify the relative magnitude of the proportionality and differential shifts. Subsequent attention can then be turned more directly to the latter item, to see if it reflects some natural locational advantage or disadvantage, interregional growth spillovers or even the effects of regional policy instruments used by governments.

The results of the shift and share analysis applied to the data shown in Appendixes 2.1 and 2.2 are presented in Table 2.2. However, care in interpretation is necessary in the light of the following four points.

(1) The analysis relates to the time period 1954 to 1966. Ideally a longer period should be studied in order to assess the effects of industrialization trends over the whole post-war period. However, the only sufficiently comprehensive and reliable data source is the census, and results of the 1971 enumeration are not yet available at the time of writing. Also, the 1947 census data are not strictly comparable with later years, partly because of changes in industrial classification and also because of the high proportion of persons classified in the 'other industries' category as a result of inadequate information. Hence, we are necessarily restricted to a twelve year study period. However, because industrial structure changes relatively slowly over time, proportionality shifts are fairly stable, so the effects of industrial structure on growth can be fairly confidently generalized.

(2) The analysis is based on a classification of the workforce into 23 industries, of which 3 are in primary, 7 are in manufacturing and 13 are in service sectors. As a rule, the finer the industrial classification, the greater the proportionality shifts relative to the differential shifts. As noted elsewhere, there is no absolute ideal degree of disaggregation, but this analysis uses a finer classification than most previous Australian studies. Indeed, the finest possible classification is used, so that the analysis is quite sensitive to small differences in industrial structure between regions.

(3) There are some technical problems associated with the interpretation of proportionality effects. Shift and share analysis is a very mechanical process (the mathematics of which is summarized in Appendix 2.3). As Mackay notes,[14] the analysis does not isolate the multiplier or inter-industry linkage effects of industrial structure on growth. The result is that the proportionality shift is best regarded as a minimum estimate of the structural effects. This is particularly important in the case of Sydney and Melbourne because of the additional consideration of relative size. Because these two areas account for about 40 per cent of the total workforce, they heavily weight the national average with which they are compared in the calculation of proportionality shifts. As such, one would not expect the calculated shifts into and out of these areas to appear as

TABLE 2.2. *Shift and share analysis of employment growth 1954–1966*

		Actual (ooo persons)	Growth %	Regional (ooo persons)	Share %	Proportionality shift (ooo persons)	%	Differential shift (ooo persons)	%
N.S.W.	Metropolitan	+ 308.3	+ 38.3	+ 253.1	+ 31.4	+ 52.0	+ 6.5	+ 3.2	+ 0.4
	Other urban	+ 93.9	+ 25.3	+ 116.9	+ 31.4	+ 8.8	+ 2.4	− 31.8	− 8.6
	Rural	+ 37.7	+ 1.7	+ 70.3	+ 31.4	− 43.7	− 19.6	− 22.8	− 10.2
VIC	Metropolitan	+ 268.5	+ 39.6	+ 213.3	+ 31.4	+ 36.3	+ 5.4	+ 18.9	+ 2.8
	Other urban	+ 62.4	+ 34.3	+ 57.3	+ 31.4	+ 5.0	+ 2.7	+ 0.2	+ 0.1
	Rural	+ 5.4	+ 3.0	+ 56.0	+ 31.4	− 31.2	− 17.5	− 19.4	− 10.9
QLD	Metropolitan	+ 88.3	+ 43.5	+ 63.9	+ 31.4	+ 13.7	+ 6.7	+ 10.8	+ 5.3
	Other urban	+ 36.9	+ 20.9	+ 55.4	+ 31.4	+ 1.1	+ 0.6	− 19.6	− 11.1
	Rural	+ 10.8	+ 7.3	+ 46.4	+ 31.4	− 34.2	− 23.2	− 1.4	− 1.0
TAS	Metropolitan	+ 10.4	+ 27.1	+ 12.0	+ 31.4	+ 3.5	+ 9.2	− 5.2	− 13.6
	Other urban	+ 14.8	+ 35.5	+ 13.1	+ 31.4	+ 0.7	+ 1.6	+ 1.0	+ 2.4
	Rural	+ 3.9	+ 10.5	+ 11.9	+ 31.4	− 6.7	− 17.6	− 1.3	− 3.3
S.A.	Metropolitan	+ 103.8	+ 52.4	+ 62.3	+ 31.4	+ 12.2	+ 6.2	+ 29.3	+ 14.8
	Other urban	+ 26.1	+ 61.5	+ 13.3	+ 31.4	+ 0.6	+ 1.4	+ 12.1	+ 28.7
	Rural	− 0.4	+ 0.5	+ 24.9	+ 31.4	− 14.3	− 18.1	− 11.0	− 13.8
W.A.	Metropolitan	+ 58.6	+ 41.4	+ 44.5	+ 31.4	+ 8.9	+ 6.3	+ 5.1	+ 3.6
	Other urban	+ 14.7	+ 37.0	+ 12.5	+ 31.4	+ 2.0	+ 4.9	+ 4.2	+ 10.4
	Rural	+ 7.5	+ 10.1	+ 23.6	+ 31.4	− 13.4	− 17.9	− 2.6	− 3.5
N.T.	Metropolitan	+ 8.1	+ 144.5	+ 1.8	+ 31.4	+ 0.6	+ 11.2	+ 5.7	+ 101.8
	Other urban	+ 1.9	+ 56.6	+ 1.1	+ 31.4	+ 0.5	− 14.0	+ 1.3	+ 39.1
A.C.T.	Metropolitan	+ 29.8	+ 232.9	+ 4.0	+ 31.4	+ 2.7	+ 20.8	+ 23.1	+ 180.6
	Rural	+ 0.5	+ 51.5	+ 0.3	+ 31.4	+ 0.04	− 4.5	+ 0.2	+ 24.6
Total	Metropolitan	+ 867.7	+ 41.8	+ 653.2	+ 31.4	+ 129.4	+ 6.2	+ 85.1	+ 4.1
	Other urban	+ 256.8	+ 29.9	+ 270.3	+ 31.4	+ 14.8	+ 1.7	− 28.2	+ 2.8
	Rural	+ 33.4	+ 4.5	+ 234.5	+ 31.4	− 144.1	− 19.3	− 56.9	+ 8.0
Grand Total		+ 1157.9	+ 31.4	+ 1157.9	+ 31.4	0	0	0	0

Source: Commonwealth Bureau of Census and Statistics: Censuses of the Commonwealth of Australia, 1954 and 1966.

large as those of areas of smaller workforce size, such as the Territories, where the weighting in the national total is so much smaller.

(4) Finally, there is the problem of changes in the boundaries of areas for which workforce statistics are compiled. Many have been subject to definitional changes as the metropolitan area boundaries have been adjusted in the light of peripheral urbanization, and 'other urban' area boundaries have been widened to take account of new built-up areas. However, one important point to note in this regard is that the effect of these changes would show up wholly in the differential shift. Thus, the analysis of the impact of industrial structure on growth, shown in the proportionality shifts, is not distorted. Moreover, it could be argued that if boundary enlargements are the result of urban areas spreading outwards, we would actually want to include these additional persons in our differential shift calculations, which purport to illustrate the strength of urban growth pressures over and above industry mix effects. In practice, it appears that the effect of metropolitan boundary changes is not one of sufficient magnitude to change the direction of differential shifts except in the case of Adelaide, and special comments are made on that particular case at a later stage.

Bearing these practical problems in mind we can now go on with the detailed interpretation of Table 2.2. The first two columns show the absolute and relative growth of workforce by area and these mirror the earlier population data in that the most striking feature is the contrast between the rapid growth in all metropolitan areas and the stagnation of the rural areas. The 'other urban' category has generally featured steady growth, although much less in absolute terms than the metropolitan areas in all cases except Tasmania. The high percentage growth figures for the A.C.T. and Northern Territory reflect the small size of the base year workforce. The next two columns of Table 2.2 show the growth each area would have experienced if it had just maintained its 1954 share of the nation's workforce. Thus, the regional share of Sydney, which contained 22 per cent of Australia's workforce in 1954, is 253.1 thousand, which is 22 per cent of the extra workforce in Australia over the following twelve years. The difference between the regional share and the actual workforce growth is known as the total shift. In Sydney, for example, there was an inward total shift of 55.2 thousand persons while in rural N.S.W. there was an outward total shift of 66.5 thousand persons. The important step is the separation of this total shift in the final columns of the table into proportionality and differential shifts.

First we look at the proportionality shifts. Positive values indicate an economic specialization conducive to rapid growth. All the metropolitan areas come in this category, as do the 'other urban' areas in New South Wales, Victoria, Queensland, South Australia, Tasmania and the Northern

Territory. Negative proportionality shifts are found in all rural areas and also the 'other urban' areas of Western Australia. This is explicable because of the relative dependence of these towns on industries such as mining and quarrying which, partly as a result of productivity gains, were nationally among the slowest growing industries in terms of numbers employed. The performance of the rural areas can be attributed to similar structural factors. Primary industries were the slowest growing over the whole period: hence, on grounds of industrial composition alone, the rural areas could have expected to feature a relative decline.

Overall, the general picture is clearly one of centralization accentuated by the effects of industrialization. The metropolitan areas and, to a lesser extent, the other urban areas, had economic specializations conducive to rapid growth, featuring activities such as engineering, printing, finance and property management, public authorities and community and business services. The rural areas, on the other hand, faced relative stagnation because they had largely missed out on the industrialization process and continued to be dependent on primary industries.

Turning to the differential shifts, it is clear that these have reinforced such tendencies. By and large, the metropolitan areas feature positive shifts while the rural areas feature negative shifts, with most of the areas in the 'other urban' category in an intermediate position. What this means is that the metropolitan areas captured an even larger share of national employment growth than their favourable industrial structure suggested. The rural areas, which would have suffered a declining share in national workforce because of their industrial structure alone, suffered an even sharper decline.

More detailed comments are as follows, beginning with the metropolitan areas. First, it is clear that Hobart is an exceptional case. Not only is it the only State capital to feature negative differential shifts but such effects more than outweigh the positive proportionality shifts. Thus, the relatively slow growth of Hobart is revealed as only partly a reflection of its economic specialization. It must also be interpreted in the light of a change in focus to the more northern parts of the island which lie closer to the mainland. This in turn can be seen as part of a more general problem for the Tasmanian economy, that the island as a whole is peripheral to the main national markets.

Adelaide is something of a problem as far as this analysis is concerned. The difficulty is one of boundary changes associated with the rapid build-up of the satellite town of Elizabeth (in retrospect more of a suburb than a satellite). This development was recognized as part of the Adelaide metropolitan area for the purposes of the 1966 census. Subtracting the estimated numbers of persons involved, it would appear that Adelaide (as defined in 1954 and 1961) has actually featured negative differential growth over the

1954–66 period. This reflects how successfully growth was diverted to Elizabeth, and bodes well for the suggested new development at Murray Bridge. On the other hand, if Elizabeth is regarded as part of Adelaide, then the whole area has had differential growth of a similar intensity to the other metropolitan centres, or even slightly stronger. Certainly, employment growth within the State has been markedly concentrated on the capital city and its surrounding areas.

Canberra's differential growth has also been very large, especially when considered in relative terms. (It appears somewhat smaller than Adelaide's in absolute terms.) Thus, as well as having the most growth-oriented economic specialization, its experience of differential growth is also outstanding. Of course, one of the elements in the differential shift is the effects of government policy and, to this extent, the figures show the success of planning in the build-up of the national capital.

As for Sydney, the most striking feature is how small is the differential growth effect relative to that in the other State capitals. This may reflect many different considerations but one possible interpretation is in terms of the diseconomies of urban scale. However, even if such diseconomies are starting to predominate, this does not necessarily imply that the rate of expansion in the Sydney area will decline. Its very favourable industrial structure continues to secure it an increasing share of the nation's economic growth. Thus, even diseconomies of urban scale are not a sufficient condition to reduce the trend towards metropolitan primacy. The cumulative expansionary pressures deriving from industrial structure can, and do, outweigh any such equilibrating tendencies.

Among the 'other urban' groupings, positive differential shifts are found in Victoria, Tasmania, South Australia, Western Australia and the Northern Territory. The first two are quite small in absolute terms. The figures for South Australia should be interpreted in the light of the boundary changes discussed earlier. However, to the extent that Elizabeth can be regarded as an urban centre distinct from the Adelaide metropolis, then differential growth has been outstanding. The situation in Western Australia can be attributed mainly to the mineral boom which gives a great boost to the development of towns particularly in the Pilbara region. The Northern Territory's differential growth, which is quite startling in percentage terms, reflects the rapid development of the Territory and urbanization in Darwin in particular.

The exceptional cases in the 'other urban' category are New South Wales and Queensland. This is very interesting because these are the two States which have the best-developed secondary centres (Newcastle and Wollongong in New South Wales and the string of medium-sized coastal centres in Queensland). Yet differential growth has been negative, indicating less growth of employment than their industrial structure would have led one to expect. This is bad news for the decentralists: even in the two States with major alternatives in metropolitan location to the metropolitan areas, there is no evidence of the trend towards metropolitan dominance being reversed. On the contrary, the growth of these secondary centres has been much less than their industrial composition would normally suggest.

Turning to the rural areas, the differential effects are all negative with the exception of the two Territories.

Rural growth in the A.C.T. is best regarded as a Canberra spillover effect: there was actually a decline in the numbers engaged in primary industries, while the main growth sectors were construction and public authority employment. Similarly, in the Northern Territory the differential growth was not due directly to employment expansion in the rural sector so much as growth in the tertiary sector. In the other rural areas the decline in primary production was only partially offset by growth in other sectors. Not surprisingly, manufacturing and service growth were slower than in the urban areas: on average over half the employment is in farming and declining activity in that sector has had downward multiplier effects on all other sources of employment. Such effects hit particularly hard at the service industries. As for manufacturing, with some relatively minor exceptions, there just has not been significant decentralization to country areas.

In summary, the analysis presented here provides a partial, but far from complete, explanation of post-war growth trends. The most general classification of areas is as shown in Table 2.3. Those in the left-hand column can be regarded as having inherited an industrial base which is favourable to further growth. Of these the ten areas in the top two boxes have grown faster than the initial advantage would have suggested, while those in the bottom two boxes have grown more slowly. 'Other urban' Queensland still managed to grow faster in terms of employment than the national average, but metropolitan Tasmania and the 'other urban' areas of N.S.W. actually grew more slowly than the national average as a result. Looking at the right-hand column of Table 2.3 we see the areas which inherited a relatively unfavourable economic specialization. These are all the rural areas, plus the 'other urban' areas of Western Australia. Only the rural areas in the two Territories had growth of sufficient magnitude to offset this initial disadvantage. In all other cases, growth was even slower than the industrial composition would have suggested.

Economic models

We now have the framework for analysing the interaction between economic and institutional factors in the determination of urban growth patterns. The form of economic specialization is revealed as a partial but incomplete explanation of post-war trends. The two questions which remain unanswered are:

(a) What is the historical explanation of the economic specialization which the various metropolitan and other urban areas inherited in the post-war period?
(b) What determined the pattern of differential growth as revealed by the preceding shift and share analysis?

TABLE 2.3. *General classification of areas according to values of proportionality and differential shifts in employment growth 1954–1966*

			Proportionality effect (P)	
			Positive	Negative
Differential effect (D)	Positive	D > P	South Australia (Metropolitan) South Australia (Other urban) Tasmania (Other urban) Northern Territory (Other urban)	A.C.T. (Rural) Northern Territory (Rural)
		P > D	New South Wales (Metropolitan) Victoria (Metropolitan) Queensland (Metropolitan) Western Australia (Metropolitan) A.C.T. (Metropolitan) Victoria (Other urban)	Western Australia (Other urban)
	Negative	P > D	Queensland (Other urban)	New South Wales (Rural) Victoria (Rural) Queensland (Rural) Tasmania (Rural) South Australia (Rural) Western Australia (Rural)
		D > P	New South Wales (Other urban) Tasmania (Metropolitan)	

What is particularly required in the latter case is a systematic explanation of why the main metropolitan areas are growing even faster than their industrial structure would lead us to expect, and why the rural areas are faring even worse than theirs would lead us to expect. It is to models potentially capable of providing answers to such questions that we now turn.

Various authors have sought to classify the theories of urban and regional growth. The particular classification adopted here derives partly from that of Richardson,[15] who emphasizes the application of theories to urban areas, and partly from my own classification[16] which concentrates on more general regional growth models.

(1) The first model derives from the well-established *theory of central places*. According to this theory, the rate of growth of an urban area is determined by the demand for goods and services in its hinterland. Summaries are to be found in the works of Ullman and Berry.[17] Much of the theory relates to the spatial relationships between population centres at different levels in the urban hierarchy, but as a model of urban growth, it can be summarized in the postulate that growth of an urban centre is a function of its hinterland size and income levels within that hinterland. There is certain evidence that these factors provide a partial explanation of urban growth trends in the U.S.A. and intuitively one would expect the model to have certain explanatory power in Australia. Right from the days of earliest settlement, each major urban place has had a fairly clearly defined hinterland and has been responsible for serving that hinterland in a number of ways (supplying domestic manufactures, acting as a focal point for import and export activities, providing administrative, financial, legal and other professional services, and so on).

Moreover, the central place theory offers some insights into the differences in growth rates between the various State capitals. McCarty[18] argues along such lines in attributing the rapid growth of Melbourne and Sydney to their large productive hinterlands and the absence of important urban rivals. Brisbane also has had a large hinterland but it is sparser and it has been shared with other regional centres such as Rockhampton, Mackay and Townsville. Hobart's slow growth can be likewise attributed to its small and relatively stagnant hinterland, which it has had to share with Launceston. Bringing the argument up to date, Perth's rapid growth performance in the 1960s can be at least partly attributed to the remarkable mineral discoveries in its Western Australian hinterland.

However, as a general theory of urban growth, this central place theory suffers from two problems of particular importance in the Australian context:

(a) It ignores the internal growth-generating forces within cities. National economies can grow economically by other means than by becoming colonial powers: so it is with cities. Hinterland expansion is not a prerequisite for urban growth, although it may provide one possible means to that end.

(*b*) It does not clearly distinguish between causes and effects or urbanization. The growth of hinterlands may be restricted by the size and facilities of their central places, just as the growth of central places depends in part on their hinterland size. To adopt an analytical procedure capable of handling such interaction is particularly important in Australia, because the establishment of urban centres actually preceded hinterland development.

(2) *Urban base theory* differs from central place theory in that it does not rely on the delineation of a geographically bounded hinterland: rather, it sees the rate of urban growth as determined by the amount of exports of goods and services from the urban area, whatever their destination. Secondly, it recognizes that some economic activities in any urban area are locally oriented. Thus, while the export-oriented activities are seen as the propulsive influences on urban growth, explanation of overall urban trends requires specific consideration of the relationship between the growth of the export and local service sectors. In these ways, urban base theory is rather more general than central place theory.

Testing this model in the Australian context is made impossible by the lack of data on urban exports and in interregional trade in general. Qualitatively, there is no doubt of the association between the metropolitan centres and exporting activities. However, much of the trade through the ports has concerned produce originating outside the urban areas, so that much of the stimulus to metropolitan growth is better interpreted as reflecting a service function rather than a genuine export-generating function. More fundamentally, there is some objection to urban base theory on theoretical grounds. Two objections are particularly important:

(*a*) Its central tenet, as articulated by Pfouts, 'that exporting activity is the source and wellspring of urban economic growth'[19] is too naive. National economies can grow by other means than promoting exports. Similarly, cities can grow through other expenditure injections into the local economy, such as autonomous public authority or private enterprise investment.

(*b*) Like the central place theory, urban base theory also ignores some aspects of interdependence between different cities and regions. An increase in one area's prosperity will normally lead to an increase in its import expenditure (given that there is no immediate reduction in the marginal propensity to import). This increases exports of other areas, causing rises in income which in turn feedback to the first area via interregional trade. Such cumulative interactions are not adequately encompassed within the urban base theory.

These considerations suggest that the urban base model should be widened to take account of the importance of exogenous forces other than exports and of the importance of interregional interaction. This means we need to develop fully fledged 'macro' models, of the type outlined by Tiebout.[20] A necessary requirement is information for each area on total income and its components, consumption, private investment, public investment, exports and imports. However, no such data are collected in Australia.

(3) *Supply-oriented models* of urban growth attempt to rectify the usual over-emphasis on demand considerations. Richardson's argument that 'in the long run a city's capacity for growth is determined less by export sales than by the in-migration of labour and inflows of capital'[21] suggests the need for a theory which relates growth of cities to their ability to attract resources from outside.

The neo-classical economic approach is to regard such resource flow as a response to resource price differentials. Thus, the fastest growing areas would be those in which the monetary return to capital and labour is highest. Testing this hypothesis in the Australian context is hampered by the lack of suitable data on the returns to capital. Nevertheless, there is piecemeal evidence to suggest that it is broadly consistent with the intra-national labour migration experience of the post-war period. The migratory flows have been largely from low wage country areas to high wage urban areas, although the picture is obscured by the attempts at wage and salary standardization embodied in the workings of the Australian arbitration system.

However, there is little evidence of the equilibrating tendencies which neo-classical theory would predict. More fundamentally, the problem with this conventional view of migration is its neglect of non-economic elements. On the one hand, there is clear evidence that some location decisions are not directly financially motivated (e.g. the desire of immigrants to cluster together with members of their own nationality). On the other hand, there are decisions taken with a view to financial gain but not explicable within a neo-classical framework because of imperfect or distorted information. An example here would be the choice of a metropolitan business location, not because of higher realized profits, but because of what Friedmann calls the 'failure to perceive peripheral investment opportunities'.[22] For these various reasons, it is clear that conventional economic models will fail to provide an adequate explanation of migratory flows.

Thus, while the central place and urban base models are deficient because of their neglect of supply variables, the ideal analytical orientation requires more flexibility than is offered by neo-classical models of resource supply. What is required is a model capable of handling demand–supply interaction. For example, it is imperative to recognize that migration of labour changes the distribution of demand in the economy as well as the supply. The host regions experience a rise in income, exaggerated by investment as well as multiplier effects, while donor regions suffer a fall in income because of emigration. Thus, migratory flows can have cumulatively disequilibrating effects. In the Australian case, the effect is to reinforce metropolitan primacy because the rural–urban migration adds to expansionary effects in the cities, where aggregate demand is already most buoyant. Moreover, the effects are reinforced by the selective nature of migration. It is generally the younger and more enterprising sectors of any community who move out and, since these constitute the 'enterpreneurs of tomorrow', the long-run effect on the distribution of demand is to further reinforce the primacy of the metropolitan centres. Such influences are recognized only in the centre–periphery model, the most general of all urban growth theories.

(4) *The centre–periphery model*, as developed from the work of Myrdal and Friedmann,[23] provides a synthesis of demand and supply oriented models, incorporating them within a historical-institutional framework. Supply-side considerations are seen as interacting with demand-side considerations to compound tendencies for metropolitan growth. The central hypothesis is that growth centres, having developed for an assortment of historical/geographical reasons, develop cumulative advantages so that the gap between their prosperity and the rest of the nation tends to widen. Some of the reasons for these cumulative effects have already been noted, e.g. localization and urbanization economies, failure of businessmen to perceive non-metropolitan investment opportunities and the selective nature of migration. The beauty of the centre–periphery approach is that it integrates these primarily economic factors with more general social and political considerations, e.g. the power of vested interests in securing concentration and the inability of local government in peripheral areas to reverse the centralizing process because of their lack of resources and the less egalitarian bias in their political systems.

Conventional attempts to correlate urbanization pressures with the existing size of urban centres tend to be excessively mechanistic. The usual hypothesis is that factors such as indivisibilities, industrial diversification, local market size and the supply of entrepreneurship enable large cities to grow faster than small ones. Some investigators have modified this theory to take account of some minimum 'threshold' level that must be reached before these propulsive effects set in. Others have sought to impose upper limits as constraints on the general size–growth correlations. However, a fundamental problem remains, that any attempt to construct a theory of urban growth on such correlations is incapable of distinguishing between the various potential causal links. Richardson cites some of these as:

(*a*) large-scale economies in the use of social overhead capital, urban government and private business services;

(*b*) the size of the local market;

(*c*) the advantage of access to a metropolitan labour pool and to developed capital markets;

(*d*) the saving in transport costs in a relatively self-contained local economy;

(*e*) localization economies due to the agglomeration of several firms within an industry.

The conceptual separation between some of these influences is blurred enough: empirical separation is almost impossible. What this means is that we must recognize the interdependence of these various cumulating influences in explaining how the major Australian cities have capitalized on their initial advantage and the general inertia in location patterns. Relating this back to the earlier shift and share analysis, the differential shift component can be interpreted as reflecting the strength of these interacting forces. It is not only a measure of growth due to external economies, but also incorporates multiplier and inter-industry linkage effects as well as the cumulative supply-side advantages of urban scale.

Applied to Australia and its particular historical experience, the main elements of a centre–periphery view of urbanization are as follows:

(*a*) The dominance of a few cities began in the colonial period when the first settlements were convict settlements. Sydney was first settled in 1788, and an important element in the subsequent development of Hobart, Perth, Brisbane and Adelaide was spatial separation. In part, it was necessary for reasons of internal security to isolate the individual prison settlements and in part it was a defensive strategy designed to maximize security against external aggressors such as the French. Thus, Hobart was established in southern Tasmania partly in an attempt to consolidate the claim to the intervening land. In Adelaide's case there was the special reason for isolation that, not being a prison settlement, it needed clear separation from 'contaminated' areas. A further explanation of early settlement patterns noted by Bird[24] is the desire for centrality in potential agricultural areas. Thus, relatively few factors were responsible for the original settlement of the capital city areas. Desirable physical conditions such as fresh water and flat land were important in the selection of sites. but general situations are more explicable in terms of internal security, national defence and centrality in potential agricultural areas.

(*b*) Metropolitan dominance became further entrenched as a result of the imperialist relationship with Britain. Imports of a whole range of commodities from Britain and exports of gold, wool and other resources gave the port settlements a strongly commercial role. In addition, they served as centres from which the British administered the colonies. The joint incidence of these commercial and administrative functions led to further reinforcement of the extreme centrality in the pattern of urbanization.

Thus, the resource development phase did not lead to the growth of new population centres, as it has done in other countries. In part, this was because one of the major export industries, wool, favoured a thinly spread population distribution. Moreover, central control favoured settlement rather than the growth of more independent self-contained communities. In this sense, Australia was in the unusual position, noted by Glynn,[25] that urbanization developed in advance of rural settlement. The country towns that were developed adopted the role of marketing and service centres but failed to develop the industrial and commercial functions necessary for the development of autonomous regions. Even the gold discoveries in the middle of the nineteenth century failed to lead to the establishment of new urban centres. The miners involved were naturally mobile. Moreover, Ryan[26] suggests that the tendency to extensive population distribution was reinforced in this period as disappointed miners who had invested in the diggings turned eventually to rural activities.

(*c*) Transportation technology can be regarded as another force leading to metropolitan primacy. As noted by Robinson[27] countries which developed before the advent of railways faced a technology more conducive to the development of multiple urban centres. Australia, on the other hand, being relatively recently developed, had not the need for a population distribution of this sort. True, railways did serve as new foci for marketing and processing farm products, and some hamlets did develop along railway routes. However, no major centres developed: the railways (and roads too) became focussed on the existing metropolitan centres. Thus, due to modern technology, these centres were able to serve larger hinterlands than would have been previously possible, with the result that metropolitan primacy was unchallenged by new urban areas. (Note the link between the centre–periphery approach and central place theory here.)

(*d*) The particular form of political organization adopted in the twentieth century added further pressure for centralization. While the Federal system prevented any one metropolitan area from becoming dominant, it certainly reinforced the dominance of each metropolitan area within its own State. The capital city of each State naturally became the focal point for administrative functions, with depressing effects on initiative in non-metropolitan areas. Also, the Federal organization provides a historical explanation of interstate variation in railway gauges. Given that each State regulated its own railways and that these focussed on the capital cities, such variation formed an effective barrier to interstate trade and the decentralization of manufacturing industries. Overall, it now seems clear that the spatial separation of the major colonial centres favoured a Federal organization of the nation, and that this political change provided further impetus to metropolitan dominance within each State.

(*e*) Throughout this century, the industrial specialization of the metropolitan centres has given them cumulative advantages in securing a rising share of the nation's economic growth. On the other hand, the rural areas have been facing a declining demand for their products. Coupled with the trends towards mechanization in agriculture this had led to a steady flow of migrants from country to urban areas. Industrialization and the development of tertiary sectors have been mainly concentrated in the metropolitan areas. This is not to say that such activities could not occur elsewhere because of locational unsuitability: only that because of interdependence in location decisions new secondary and tertiary centres are not normally established.

The importance of interdependence is revealed by the fact that the only major successes in the development of new urban areas have involved massive investment in resource exploitation by particular companies (Newcastle, Wollongong, Broken Hill, Mt Isa, and, to a lesser extent, Gladstone). Where such initiatives have occurred they have been followed by an inflow of secondary industries, usually with commercial success. But such instances are the exception rather than the rule. Cumulative causation has been the order of the day. The metropolitan areas have grown, not because of the inherent unsuitability of other areas, but because of the general inability of the private enterprise system to change the direction of industrial growth.

In relation to the earlier shift and share analysis, what this means is that the economic heritage of the metropolitan areas was most conducive to growth in the post-war period. This is what is revealed by the positive proportionality shifts in the metropolitan areas and the negative shifts in all rural areas: the former have a heritage conducive to capitalist development, while the latter (and to some extent the 'other urban' areas too) have not.

(*f*) The trends towards centralization are further reinforced by the internationalism of the capitalist system. This is largely because international flows of both labour and capital resources are biased towards the major cities. On the demographic side, there is a natural tendency for immigrants to congregate in the largest cities, because the larger the city the greater the likelihood of having personal contacts there. On the investment side, dependence on overseas capital involves a restriction of the possibility of domestic economic management. The international corporation, because of its interest in major markets for its products, naturally seeks to establish its overseas subsidiaries in or near the largest cities. As such, international capitalism tends to be a centralizing force within the domestic economy.

(*g*) Finally, the imbalance between the metropolitan areas and the periphery is accentuated by current government policies. Max Neutze has written on some of the problems of co-ordination between the various levels of government,[28] and this certainly does provide an obstacle to effective regional policy. However, more fundamentally, both Commonwealth and State governments actively *encourage* metropolitan primacy through some of their policies.

The Commonwealth government largely refrains from explicit regional policies, but its abstention is partly illusory because many of its other policies have an implicit spatial impact. For example, the tariff policy, by which various manufacturing industries receive protection from overseas competition, influences the rural–urban balance by increasing the relative prosperity of manufacturing. Because these secondary industries tend to be concentrated in metropolitan areas, such a policy adds to metropolitan dominance. To be fair, some other policies of the Commonwealth, such as its use of specific purpose grants and, of course, the creation of a development corporation to plan the expansion of Canberra, have aided decentralization. However, on balance, the reluctance of post-war Commonwealth governments to intervene in location decisions in a primarily free enterprise economy can be regarded as buttressing the trend towards increased metropolitan primacy.

State governments, on the other hand, are sometimes said to discourage metropolitan primacy because some at least offer inducements to decentralization. New South Wales and Victoria are broadly similar in this respect; both provide low interest loans to decentralizing firms, and supplementary incentives in the form of rail freight subsidies, housing assistance and removal expenses for key employees, labour-training subsidies and various other minor forms of assistance such as subsidized transport of plant and machinery. The Victorian government has designated selected growth centres but has few 'teeth' in its policy to divert growth to them. The New South Wales government, while being generally in favour of the growth centre idea, has been hesitant and bases its policies on ad hoc bargaining with individual firms. South Australia has been virtually alone in its attitude towards the creation of new cities, first at Elizabeth and now in its plan for development at Murray Bridge. Elsewhere where the influence of the Liberal and Country parties has been stronger the new city idea has been largely ignored. The Country party may have particular fears that the creation of growth centres will cause a loss of its electoral base by bringing industrial labour into predominantly rural communities. The Liberal party seems to have a general fear of nominating growth centres, presumably because of the anticipated lack of support from the electorates in constituencies which do not contain nominated centres. The outcome is continued centralization.

Overall, the most charitable view of State government decentralization policies is to describe them as insignificant. There have been minor successes, but the 1971 census figures given in Table 2.1 show that centralization is continuing as fast as ever. Moreover, the effects of decentralization measures are outweighed by the centralizing effects of State government action.

The first and most obvious of such centralizing effects is the continuing concentration of State government offices in the capital cities. All State governments have been most reluctant to decentralize their own activities. Movement of government offices has proved quite an effective tool of regional policy in the U.K. and elsewhere, but no such initiatives have occurred in Australia.

Added to this has been the reluctance of State governments to enforce decentralization of industry where there is a possibility of losing industrial growth to other States. For example, a firm wishing to establish a new factory may be told by the N.S.W. government that it is welcome only if it selects a decentralized location. If it then threatens to go to Victoria, it is likely that the N.S.W. authorities will allow it a Sydney location. In this way, rivalry between State governments vitiates effective decentralization.

Metropolitan primacy is further reinforced by the actions of the State Planning Authorities. The current plans for Sydney and Melbourne, for example, take as *data* the projected population growth and pay little attention to possible diversionary measures. Even if half a million people are decentralized from Sydney by the end of the century (and there is little in current policies to suggest that this is likely) that still leaves over two million people to be accommodated within and around the metropolis. By making proposals to accommodate rather than redirect growth, the S.P.A. is actually adding to the pressures of metropolitan primacy.

On balance, there is little doubt that the actions of State governments are centralizing rather than decentralizing. As such the political machine can be regarded as an intrinsic element in the centre–periphery model of urban growth. Government and business have many close contacts and, as noted by Wheelwright,[29] their general alignment of interests is particularly apparent in Australia. In some ways, governments have acted as capitalists themselves (e.g. in auctioning Crown land with a view to maximizing revenue rather than minimizing speculation and otherwise controlling inflation in land prices). In other ways, they have provided the framework within which both domestic and international capital have been allowed relatively unconstrained freedom of movement. One outcome is continued pressure of metropolitan dominance. Thus, just as Frank[30] sees international capitalism as the means by which international underdevelopment is perpetuated, the particularly uneven pattern of urbanization in Australia can be seen a direct outcome of its predominantly capitalist system of economic organization.

NOTES

* I should like to express my thanks to Jill Hardwick and Michael O'Loughlin of the University of Sydney for their assistance in the preparation of this chapter.

1 II. W. Richardson, *Urban Economics*, Harmondsworth, Penguin Books, 1972.
2 E. J. Mishan, *The Costs of Economic Growth*, London, Staples Press, 1967; *idem Twenty-One Popular Economic Fallacies*, Harmondsworth, Pelican Books, 1971.
3 A. G. Frank, *Capitalism and Underdevelopment in Latin America*, New York, Monthly Review Press, 1969.
4 A. J. Rose, *Patterns of Cities*, Melbourne and Sydney, Thomas Nelson, 1967.
5 Richardson, *Urban Economics*.
6 K. E. Boulding, *Economics as a Science*, New York, McGraw-Hill, 1970.
7 T. Van Dugteren, 'A time to decentralise', *Current Affairs Bulletin*, Sydney December 1971.
8 G. J. R. Linge, 'Canberra's new allure', *Australian Financial Review*, 7 January 1972.
9 W. Bate, 'The urban sprinkle: country towns and Australian regional history', *Australian Economic History Review*, *10*, no. 2, September 1970.
10 H. S. Perloff, E. S. Dunn Jr., E. E. Lampard and R. F. Muth, *Regions, Resources and Economic Growth*, Resources for the Future Inc., Baltimore, John Hopkins Press, 1960; V. R. Fuchs, *Changes in the Location of Manufacturing in the United States since 1929*, Economic Census Studies 1, New Haven, Yale University Press, 1962; A. P. Thirlwall, 'A measure of the proper distribution of industry', *Oxford Economic Papers*, *19*, no. 1, March 1967; F. J. B. Stilwell, 'Regional growth and structural adaptation', *Urban Studies*, *6*, no. 2, June 1969.
11 R. Bunker, 'Australia since the war: a study of economic growth and physical planning', *Town Planning Review*, *35*, no. 4, January 1965.
12 E. S. Dunn Jr., 'A statistical and analytical technique for regional analysis', *The Regional Science Association, Papers and Proceedings*, *vi*, 1960.
13 F. J. B. Stilwell, 'Further thoughts on the shift and share approach', *Regional Studies*, *4*, 1970.
14 D. I. Mackay, 'Industrial structure and regional growth, a methodological problem', *Scottish Journal of Political Economy*, *15*, June 1968.
15 Richardson, *Urban Economics*.
16 F. J. B. Stilwell, *Regional Economic Policy*, London, Macmillan, 1972
17 E. L. Ullman, 'A theory of location for cities', *American Journal of Sociology*, *46*, no. 6, May 1941; B. J. L. Berry, *Geography of Market Centres and Retail Distribution*, New Jersey, Prentice-Hall, 1967.
18 J. W. McCarty, 'Australian capital cities in the nineteenth century', *Australian Economic History Review*, *10*, no. 2, September 1970.
19 R. W. Pfouts, 'Reply to Harris on testing the base theory', *Journal of the American Institute of Planners*, *24*, no. 4, 1958.
20 C. M. Tiebout, 'Exports and regional economic growth', *Journal of Political Economy*, *64*, no. 2 April 1956.
21 Richardson, *Urban Economics*.
22 J. Friedmann, *Regional Development Policy: a Case Study of Venezuela*, Cambridge, Mass., M.I.T. Press, 1966.
23 G. Myrdal, *Economic Theory and Underdeveloped Regions*, London, Methuen, 1957; Friedmann, *Regional Development Policy*.
24 J. Bird, *Seaport Gateways of Australia*, London, Oxford University Press, 1968.
25 S. Glynn, 'Approaches to urban history: the case for caution', *Australian Economic History Review*, *10*, no. 2, September 1970.

26 B. Ryan, 'A paradigm of country town development in N.S.W.', *The Australian Journal of Social Issues*, 2, no. 1, 1964.
27 K. W. Robinson, 'Processes and patterns of urbanization in Australia and New Zealand', *New Zealand Geographer*, *18*, no. 1, April 1962.
28 G. M. Neutze, 'The government and administration of metropolitan development', *Economic Papers*, no. 36, February 1971–2.
29 E. L. Wheelwright, 'Bigness in business', in V. G. Venturini (ed.), *Australia: a Survey*, Wiesbaden, Otto Harrasswitz, 1970.
30 Frank, *Capitalism and Underdevelopment in Latin America*.

Appendix 2.1

Industrial composition of the workforce 1954

	N.S.W. Metropolitan	N.S.W. Other urban	N.S.W. rural	Vic. Metropolitan	Vic. Other urban	Vic. Rural	Qld. Metropolitan	Qld. Other urban	Qld. Rural	S.A. Metropolitan	S.A. Other urban
Primary production											
fishing, hunting, trapping, forestry	674	2,032	5,343	346	1,399	3,446	309	1,422	4,039	149	365
rural industries	8,620	19,861	121,565	8,367	9,027	93,821	4,292	10,423	87,639	3,108	2,262
Mining and quarrying	1,210	25,035	4,652	1,265	1,969	1,334	332	6,591	2,346	567	328
Manufacturing											
founding, engineering, metalworking	82,763	39,362	2,521	64,362	8,725	2,078	10,803	4,895	698	23,106	5,111
ships, vehicles, parts etc.	38,881	9,757	1,492	33,122	8,550	1,467	7,736	8,353	922	15,720	2,449
textiles and fibrous materials	13,662	3,947	538	19,407	7,331	869	1,149	853	42	2,120	151
clothing and knitted goods	31,118	6,141	781	37,120	4,735	1,443	5,667	1,662	320	2,992	491
food, drink, tobacco	31,498	12,654	4,133	29,399	8,940	4,085	10,640	14,604	5,685	7,008	1,976
paper and paper products	25,264	3,244	346	20,641	3,327	643	4,763	1,722	185	4,014	455
other	75,767	16,066	8,862	68,167	10,286	6,550	15,810	7,649	5,001	15,444	1,874
Electricity, gas, sanitation, water	18,598	7,500	1,337	14,792	8,213	2,793	4,046	3,039	725	4,542	643
Building and construction	58,033	37,796	20,847	49,411	20,332	15,165	19,464	18,562	11,969	16,862	4,835
Transport and storage											
road transport	25,172	11,010	4,219	17,421	4,748	2,933	7,016	4,035	1,991	5,244	896
shipping, loading and discharging vessels	13,732	3,031	335	8,324	473	125	3,696	3,112	464	3,556	966
rail, air transport	21,107	14,113	2,880	15,874	5,288	1,944	5,521	9,671	2,075	4,816	2,810
other	499	95	14	385	61	50	148	18	7	118	17
Communication	18,244	8,997	3,467	15,270	4,676	2,851	5,645	4,171	1,843	4,443	1,094
Finance and property	29,928	8,588	1,224	23,018	4,366	1,225	7,329	4,614	788	6,412	909
Commerce											
retail trade	87,602	50,931	11,133	74,433	26,226	9,521	22,513	23,891	6,312	24,222	5,755
wholesale trade, primary produce dealing	55,213	13,954	2,617	41,839	7,228	2,233	17,612	8,193	1,273	14,807	1,679
Public authority and defence ⎱ Community and business services ⎰	108,658	45,306	13,028	88,564	20,955	14,280	33,129	22,647	6,580	25,647	3,768
Amusements, hotels, cafes, personnel services	50,833	27,098	8,961	41,208	12,619	7,239	13,481	14,019	5,650	11,757	3,090
Other industries	7,862	5,141	3,310	5,633	2,132	1,996	2,120	2,154	1,120	1,323	445
Total in workforce	804,938	371,659	223,605	678,338	182,106	178,091	203,221	176,300	147,674	197,977	42,369

Source: Commonwealth Bureau of Census and Statistics: Census of the Commonwealth of Australia, 1954.

Appendix 2.1 (*contd.*)

	S.A. Rural	W.A. Metro-politan	W.A. Other urban	W.A. Rural	Tas. Metro-politan	Tas. Other urban	Tas. Rural	A.C.T. Metro-politan	A.C.T. Rural	N.T. Other urban	N.T. Rural
Primary production											
fishing, hunting, trapping, forestry	1,522	458	861	1,263	110	194	1,237	22	102	117	27
rural industries	40,114	2,567	1,592	34,728	531	1,301	16,201	182	266	133	900
Mining and quarrying	1,686	352	5,757	3,232	111	1,514	2,046	20	—	84	887
Manufacturing											
founding, engineering, metalworking	1,806	8,172	546	976	3,813	1,458	241	93	1	47	26
ships, vehicles, parts etc.	860	5,667	861	1,011	614	1,229	184	64	8	92	4
textiles and fibrous materials	386	473	222	88	562	1,874	88	—	—	2	2
clothing and knitted goods	168	2,773	252	159	281	295	32	20	—	9	3
food, drink, tobacco	2,452	4,677	1,168	1,160	2,535	1,410	807	83	5	51	15
paper and paper products	289	2,960	310	136	806	2,538	681	297	7	36	3
other	1,806	11,047	1,824	4,812	1,494	3,149	2,352	278	16	70	20
Electricity, gas, sanitation, water	331	2,797	750	620	1,193	533	1,040	214	4	89	23
Building and construction	7,297	16,695	4,813	6,739	3,912	5,000	4,100	1,723	75	823	457
Transport and storage											
road transport	1,244	3,965	893	1,188	1,156	1,037	965	437	14	204	32
shipping, loading and discharging vessels	160	2,959	438	131	972	995	256	1	3	147	7
rail, air transport	1,616	4,223	2,730	1,829	559	1,277	432	82	7	384	42
other	41	68	13	5	16	20	12	1	—	25	1
Communication	1,400	3,072	777	1,113	1,121	1,006	734	408	12	108	50
Finance and property	695	5,007	841	691	1,471	1,052	169	156	6	83	8
Commerce											
retail trade	4,782	18,340	5,461	4,457	4,521	5,225	1,796	775	31	387	96
wholesale trade, primary produce dealing	1,620	11,844	1,783	1,589	2,173	2,262	423	114	13	145	7
Public authority and defence	4,881	22,451	4,318	5,559	6,960	5,015	2,197	6,742	216	2,020	516
Community and business services											
Amusements, hotels, cafes, personnel services	3,269	10,009	3,236	2,995	3,002	2,773	1,311	1,032	82	465	172
Other industries	759	1,062	345	584	328	441	420	46	19	81	43
Total in workforce	79,184	141,638	39,791	75,065	38,241	41,598	37,724	12,790	887	5,602	3,341

Industrial composition of the workforce 1966

	N.S.W. Metropolitan	N.S.W. Other urban	N.S.W. Rural	Vic. Metropolitan	Vic. Other urban	Vic. Rural	Qld. Metropolitan	Qld. Other urban	Qld. Rural	S.A. Metropolitan	S.A. Other Urban
Primary production											
fishing, hunting, trapping, forestry	453	2,620	3,246	349	2,018	2,168	424	1,338	3,098	189	695
rural industries	5,059	15,713	109,044	4,735	10,138	92,554	2,136	9,775	80,655	2,744	2,635
Mining and quarrying	1,935	17,429	3,920	2,229	2,111	858	2,117	6,445	2,924	941	684
Manufacturing											
founding, engineering, metalworking	122,293	57,474	5,192	95,861	12,108	4,199	17,473	7,854	2,343	34,785	8,663
ships, vehicles, parts etc.	46,617	9,914	1,917	49,268	8,900	2,530	11,163	6,155	1,504	22,437	3,561
textiles and fibrous materials	13,699	3,882	714	20,807	7,172	968	2,196	162	207	2,757	339
clothing and knitted goods	37,841	5,923	1,116	53,164	5,525	1,443	5,950	1,021	501	4,261	305
food, drink, tobacco	36,121	16,229	5,052	35,839	11,992	5,024	13,404	14,079	6,596	9,896	3,164
paper and paper products	36,538	4,718	967	29,215	3,881	860	6,616	2,443	581	5,553	1,136
other	89,426	16,939	7,647	72,720	11,362	5,629	16,609	7,045	4,607	17,737	2,984
Electricity, gas, sanitation, water	23,850	12,507	2,620	19,687	11,525	2,584	5,365	4,489	1,282	8,271	2,237
Building and construction	85,030	51,066	18,772	70,922	26,173	11,763	26,461	27,427	14,291	25,353	7,432
Transport and storage											
road transport	30,766	14,414	4,772	24,160	6,443	3,432	9,593	5,983	3,130	7,783	1,831
shipping, loading, discharging vessels	11,694	3,249	312	8,547	629	144	3,635	1,769	379	2,962	780
rail, air transport	23,407	11,443	1,962	17,122	4,549	1,621	6,441	8,043	1,736	4,292	2,470
other	809	121	15	573	92	58	341	116	44	137	20
Communication	23,507	10,269	3,539	20,639	6,119	3,075	7,335	4,989	2,097	6,411	1,982
Finance and property	56,250	14,070	2,363	41,587	6,379	2,266	13,969	7,342	1,464	13,211	1,769
Commerce											
retail trade	117,818	64,628	13,155	94,966	35,368	11,687	33,848	31,831	8,924	35,381	9,503
wholesale trade, primary produce dealing	72,135	18,123	3,713	60,163	10,132	3,659	23,943	11,547	2,822	21,313	2,586
Public authority and defence, Community and business services	181,474	69,410	22,900	149,901	39,357	17,293	59,468	31,036	10,625	52,246	7,950
Amusements, hotels, cafes, personnel services	70,995	34,364	9,037	57,483	16,436	6,584	17,780	17,753	6,047	17,323	4,354
Other industries	24,945	10,991	5,381	16,926	5,127	3,061	5,336	4,523	2,596	5,765	1,352
Total in workforce	1,113,262	465,556	227,374	946,863	244,536	183,460	291,593	213,165	158,453	301,748	68,432

Source : Commonwealth Bureau of Census and Statistics: Census of the Commonwealth of Australia, 1966.

Appendix 2.2 (contd.)

	S.A. Rural	W.A. Metro-politan	W.A. Other urban	W.A. Rural	Tas. Metro-politan	Tas. Other urban	Tas. Rural	A.C.T. Metro-politan	A.C.T. Rural	N.T. Other urban	N.T. Rural
Primary production											
fishing, hunting, trapping, forestry	1,091	636	867	1,279	100	299	1,418	49	82	44	93
rural industries	40,284	2,234	1,866	36,513	290	858	14,234	253	229	137	1,218
Mining and quarrying	1,605	893	4,534	2,897	117	2,078	1,178	80	1	230	1,038
Manufacturing											
founding, engineering, metalworking	1,392	13,303	1,652	1,432	4,122	2,513	533	568	6	205	30
ships, vehicles, parts etc.	995	6,696	1,064	932	626	1,470	278	389	7	222	14
textiles and fibrous materials	172	724	260	121	700	3,057	213	12	—	5	1
clothing and knitted goods	115	2,538	114	153	285	240	45	103	—	15	2
food, drink, tobacco	2,716	6,736	1,661	1,321	2,810	2,313	1,304	296	6	325	40
paper and paper products	381	4,387	405	207	1,100	3,799	1,119	1,234	12	76	8
other	1,682	11,066	2,673	3,377	1,475	3,321	2,634	937	17	204	56
Electricity, gas, sanitation, water	859	3,574	1,456	823	2,001	841	1,159	469	20	307	34
Building and construction	5,628	18,703	7,385	8,949	3,804	5,596	4,884	5,472	287	2,227	857
Transport and storage											
road transport	1,477	6,116	1,760	1,729	1,340	1,596	1,262	759	18	528	88
shipping, loading, discharging vessels	130	3,309	677	190	801	909	262	14	—	310	29
rail, air transport	821	4,423	2,533	1,138	528	1,076	376	219	5	598	37
other	54	143	11	12	23	22	21	4	—	16	—
Communication	1,486	4,500	1,240	1,290	1,567	1,418	906	777	11	342	88
Finance and property	910	9,346	1,472	934	2,466	1,654	446	1,418	12	315	9
Commerce											
retail trade	5,765	25,813	7,419	5,348	5,799	7,204	2,826	3,671	64	1,219	92
wholesale trade, primary produce dealing	1,634	17,471	2,657	2,338	2,972	3,303	867	995	9	397	29
Public authority and defence } Community and business services	5,621	41,170	7,699	7,143	11,322	8,406	3,255	20,624	475	4,428	1,181
Amusements, hotels, cafes, personnel services	2,813	13,174	3,958	3,397	3,297	3,431	1,551	3,471	63	1,206	222
Other industries	1,182	3,269	1,133	1,086	1,057	976	901	758	20	339	65
Total in workforce	78,813	200,224	54,496	82,609	48,602	56,380	41,672	42,572	1,344	13,695	5,231

Appendix 2.3

Algebraically we may consider the model as below:

Let $\quad E_{ij}$ = no. employed in the ith industry in region j

$\quad\quad \Sigma_i E_{ij}$ = no. employed in all industry in region j

$\quad\quad \Sigma_j E_{ij}$ = no. employed in the ith industry in all regions

$\quad\quad \Sigma_i\Sigma_j E_{ij}$ = no. employed in all industry in all regions

Let subscript o indicate the base year and subscript t denote the terminal year of the period studied. To simplify the notation, the following analysis omits the i, j subscripts which should be attached to each E. Instead, they are shown beneath the sign to indicate the range of summation.

(1) Total growth in region $j = \Sigma_i E_t - E_i E_o$

(2) Regional share $\quad = \Sigma_i E_o \left(\Sigma_i\Sigma_j E_t / \Sigma_i\Sigma_j E_o \right) - \Sigma_i E_o$

(3) Total shift $\quad = \Sigma_i E_t - \Sigma_i E_o \left(\Sigma_i\Sigma_j E_t / \Sigma_i\Sigma_j E_o \right)$

(4) Proportionality shift $\quad = \Sigma_i E_o \{ (\Sigma_j E_t / \Sigma_j E_o) - (\Sigma_i\Sigma_j E_t / \Sigma_i\Sigma_j E_o) \}$

(5) Differential shift $\quad = \Sigma_i \{ E_t - E_o (\Sigma_j E_t / \Sigma_j E_o) \}$

3

Population components in the growth of cities

C. Y. CHOI and I. H. BURNLEY

A neglected aspect of population studies in Australia has been the study of internal migration and its role in population growth in metropolitan capital cities. In fact, the isolation of the components in population growth and change in Australian cities has never been attempted although for planning purposes it is exceedingly important to separate the internal migration, natural increase and immigration components in metropolitan population growth.[1] These components also reveal the demographic character of the urbanization process and important variations between large cities in population characteristics and growth elements.

The three main measures used in the study are: natural increase, net migration of the Australian-born and net migration of the foreign-born. Net migration of the foreign-born cannot be completely equated to overseas-born immigration and net migration of the Australian-born is not quite the same as internal migration, because these measures are complicated by the movements within Australia of foreign-born persons and movements overseas of foreign-born persons and movements overseas of Australian-born persons. Nevertheless, these measures are sufficient to reveal very broad general patterns of the various components of population change in metropolitan capital cities on which further detailed case studies can be made. The great majority of the Australian-born migrants would be internal migrants while a very large proportion of the foreign-born migrants would in fact be international migrants.

A few studies have dealt with net migration and its implied effect on population growth or loss in specific regions, notably those of Johnston and Rimmer[2] and Williams and MacAulay[3] in Victoria, and Houghton in Western Australia.[4] An earlier paper by Shepherd described rural population changes (mainly decline) in New South Wales, while another paper by Fisher described some socio-economic aspects of interstate lifetime migrants, i.e. those who were enumerated outside their State of birth at censuses.[5] A recent master's thesis studied net migration in South Australia, using electoral roll transfers along with census data[6] and an article based on this work and some subsequent research is included in this volume. Little is known however of the patterns and processes of internal migration in Australia nor of the drift to the cities which became more intense from some areas in the 1966–71 period because of the rural recession, as evidenced by a more acute population decline in rural areas and small towns than recorded previously.

It is the task of this chapter then to isolate as far as possible not only the demographic components in metropolitan patterns of growth, but also the role of interstate as opposed to intrastate Australian-born migration in metropolitan population growth.

Methodology and data

Australian censuses before 1971 did not contain items pertaining to movements of persons, except the place of birth. Usual mobility questions, such as place of residence at a certain previous point in time or the length of residence at the current address, were not included. Furthermore, place of birth data were published only by State of birth and not by areas smaller than the total State. It is therefore difficult to make inferences based on census results prior to 1971 on internal migration within Australia for areas smaller than a given State.

In a similar way, vital statistics are available only as a *total* for geographic areas smaller than the total State; it is not possible, therefore, to obtain figures on deaths of Australian-born and foreign-born persons separately for the metropolitan capital cities. This lack of data presents a difficult obstacle to any accurate measurement of internal migration as distinct from international migration. Yet as noted earlier, it is important to distinguish between internal and overseas migration in the growth and loss points of total population increase and change. It will be shown below, for instance, that although net migration has been of great importance in the growth of all Australia's capital cities, the components of growth, i.e. internal versus overseas-born migration, have varied greatly between the metropolitan areas. This, of course, affects any notion of there being any one growth model common to all of Australia's capital or primate cities.

To obtain an estimate of net migration of Australian-born persons, the Life Table Survival Ratio (L.T.S.R.) has been used to estimate the number of deaths and therefore the 'expected' number of survivors by single years of age at each census. When added together for all ages, the sum represents total net migration. If age reporting at each census were accurate and if the Australian-born population were a closed population, the L.T.S.R. technique should give reasonable estimates of net internal migration of the Australian-born, provided that Australia-wide Life Table Survival Ratios are reasonable estimates of those of the different regions under study. The assumptions regarding accurate age-reporting and similar survival ratios can be made with much more confidence than that of the closed population. Detailed discussion of the technique can be found in U.N. manuals.[7]

Interstate migration of the Australian-born and metropolitan growth 1947–1966

In a previous paper which examined the role of immigration in metropolitan growth in Australia between 1947 and 1966[8] it was hypothesized
that internal migration's relative contribution to metropolitan growth may
have varied greatly between cities. The basis of this notion was that the
percentage increase and annual growth rates of the Australian-born
population differed considerably, from annual rates of 1.43 and 1.54 per
cent for metropolitan Sydney and Melbourne, compared with 1.70 per
cent for Australia as a whole and 2.67 and 2.71 per cent for Brisbane and
Perth, almost double the Sydney and Melbourne figures. The data to be
presented using the L.T.S.R. technique partially verify the original hypothesis.

At the 1947 census, age by State of birth for the Australian-born population resident in each metropolitan statistical division was not available,
but for each of the succeeding censuses these data have been made available.
In Table 3.1, it can be seen that all the State capitals gained population by

TABLE 3.1. *Net internal migration of the Australian-born to
metropolitan divisions 1947–1954*

Metropolitan division	Persons	Metropolitan division	
Sydney	−42,891	Adelaide	+10,476
Melbourne	−21,069	Perth	+ 9,263
Brisbane	+30,117	Hobart	+ 6,174

Note. Both 1947 and 1954 boundaries are adjusted to 1966 boundaries.

internal migration of the Australian-born, with the exception of Sydney
and Melbourne which had net losses of 42,891 and 21,069 respectively in
the 1947–54 period. In both Sydney and Melbourne, there was a considerable net loss of Australian-born children, particularly those aged 0–4, but
there was a substantial in-migration of persons over 10, particularly persons of 15–25. Although the State of Tasmania had a net gain of only 100
persons through internal migration of the Australian-born between 1947
and 1954, the State capital, Hobart, gained over 6,170 persons, suggesting
a high degree of out-migration from Tasmanian rural and other urban
areas.

Between 1954 and 1966, the relative contribution of internal migration
from outside a State and from within the State to the growth of its capital
city can be deduced from Tables 3.2 and 3.3. To an extent, hinterland–
primate city migration is involved, although State boundaries are only

TABLE 3.2. *Net internal migration of the Australian-born to metropolitan divisions 1954–1961*

Metropolitan division	Persons		
	Born in same state	Born in other state	Total
Sydney	+14,980	+26,961	+41,941
Melbourne	+ 3,570	+32,384	+35,954
Brisbane	+ 8,391	+21,182	+29,573
Adelaide	+ 7,882	+13,238	+21,120
Perth	+ 4,982	+ 7,316	+12,298
Hobart	+ 2,054	+ 3,166	+ 5,220

Note. Both 1954 and 1961 boundaries are adjusted to 1966 boundaries.

TABLE 3.3. *Net internal migration of the Australian-born to metropolitan divisions 1961–1966*

Metropolitan division	Persons		
	Born in same state	Born in other state	Total
Sydney	−27,718	+28,934	+ 1,216
Melbourne	−37,112	+23,666	−13,446
Brisbane	+ 9,642	+18,388	+28,030
Adelaide	+ 6,692	+14,291	+20,983
Perth	+ 4,760	+11,134	+15,894
Hobart	− 3,303	+ 1,854	− 1,449

Note. 1961 boundaries are adjusted to 1966 boundaries.

partially synonymous with hinterland boundaries, in particular those between Queensland and New South Wales, and New South Wales and Victoria.

In contrast to the 1947–54 intercensal period, Sydney gained 41,900 Australian-born through internal migration between 1954 and 1961. Once again, there was a net loss of children under 10 and born in New South Wales from Sydney, but a gain of 27,400 born in New South Wales and over 10 years of age, in particular in the age groups 15–19 and 30–34, although there were small net losses in age groups 25–29 and 60+. However, there was a heavy net loss of children, both overseas with their immigrant and Australian-born parents and elsewhere in Australia, with New South Wales-born parents moving to Queensland (Brisbane), the Australian Capital Territory (Canberra) and Victoria. Of an Australian-born gain through internal migration to Sydney of 42,000, 27,000 (64 per cent) came from outside New South Wales. In the net gain through in-migration to Sydney of persons aged 10 years and over, 27,200 out of 44,900 (61 per cent) were from outside New South Wales. The proportions born outside Victoria in the gain through internal migration to Melbourne were much higher, after allowing for the lesser out-migration of Victoria-born children.

Again Brisbane had proportionately the largest in-migration of Australian-born, with very little loss of children aged 0–4, because relatively fewer children of the small immigrant population would have been born in the city. Whereas 8,390 (28 per cent) of the in-migrants to Brisbane were born in Queensland, 21,180 (72 per cent) originated outside the State in the 1954–61 period. Although much of this latter inflow would have originated in New South Wales and Victoria, including their capital cities, some of the New South Wales migrant stream may have been hinterland–primate city migration, given Brisbane's close proximity to the northern New South Wales border and its consequent power of attraction of the rural and small town population in northern New South Wales.

Similarly, in Western Australia there was a substantial gain of 12,300 Australian-born in Perth through internal migration. Of the inflow of those over 10 years of age, 4,980 (40.5 per cent) came from within Western Australia and 59.5 per cent from the rest of Australia. In total, regardless of age, 58.3 per cent of the net gain through internal migration to Perth came from outside Western Australia.

In Hobart, the net gain through internal migration of the Australian-born was 5,200, a little less than in the previous period; but as with other capital cities, the net gain from outside its own State (Tasmania in this case) was more than half of the total gain, indicating that interstate migration was responsible for a major proportion of the net migration gain in capital cities, although rural–metropolitan migration within each State was also important.

During the 1961–6 intercensal interval, there were some interesting changes in the internal migration pattern of the Australian-born to, and presumably *between* capital cities. Melbourne in fact lost more Australian-born through out-migration (to other areas of Australia and overseas) than it gained through in-migration, and Sydney gained very little from net Australian-born migration (Table 3.3). Once again, the loss of Australian-born children of immigrants was an important factor but there was nevertheless a substantial out-migration of males over 5 years of age who were born in Victoria and New South Wales. This out-migration of persons born in the same States (and presumably the respective metropolitan areas) was substantial in age groups 20–34 and 60–69, so that even with the in-migration of persons born in other States to Sydney and Melbourne there was a net loss of Australian-born in these groups. Even in Brisbane, which gained through internal migration, there was a small net loss in the age group 20–29 despite in-migration of persons in this age group from other States.

In Adelaide, there was a net loss of Australian-born between ages 20 and 29 despite the overall gain through internal migration from other States. Similarly, in Perth there was a net loss in this age group in spite of the general gain through Australian-born in-migration from within and outside the State of Western Australia. This loss in the age groups in which it might be expected that substantial gains would occur through normal city-ward migration of the Australian-born may be in part the result of *international* migration of the Australian-born. Perth, Brisbane and Adelaide gained significantly through internal migration from within their respective States in the 1961–6 period. It appears that despite the growing concern over the growth of metropolitan Sydney and Melbourne, the Australian-born population there has begun to move to other capital cities and to smaller but rapidly growing cities such as Canberra, Geelong and Wollongong. Thus in 1970–1 (utilizing electoral roll transfers) over 50 per cent of the internal migrants to Wollongong originated in Sydney. This redistribution of the Australian-born, in particular the interstate movement, may be in part a consequence of immigration to the large cities.

In Table 3.4, the internal migration component in metropolitan population growth between 1947 and 1966 can be seen for the three intercensal intervals and for the total period.

The increasing importance of internal migration in the rapid growth of Brisbane is clearly evident as is its importance in Perth, Adelaide and Hobart. Thus the hypothesis presented in a previous paper and restated above is partially confirmed. Internal migration of the Australian-born has varied considerably in its impact on population growth of the various capital cities. The almost negligible impact on metropolitan Sydney's and Melbourne's growth was not expected although the impact on Perth's and Adelaide's population increase was less than expected. Some of the internal migration impact on growth of Brisbane, Perth and Adelaide would have been the result of rural–urban migration, but interstate internal migration, including migration from the capital cities of Sydney and Melbourne, has almost certainly taken place.

The role of the foreign-born

Australia is one of the major migrant-receiving countries in the world. During the post-war period, overseas immigration has consistently been maintained, apart from two brief recessions, at a level near 1 per cent of the total national population per year. At present (1972) there are around 2.5 million foreign-born persons in Australia (over 2 million of whom migrated to Australia in the post-war era), and they comprise about 18 per

TABLE 3.4. *The internal migration of the Australian-born component in metropolitan growth 1947–1966*

Statistical division	Australian-born gain through in-migration	Total population increase	Australian-born percentage of total growth
1947–54			
Sydney	−42,891	+239,172	−17.9
Melbourne	−21,069	+247,803	− 8.5
Brisbane	+30,117	+117,743	+25.6
Adelaide	+10,476	+106,749	+ 9.8
Perth	+ 9,263	+ 92,081	+10.1
Hobart	+ 6,174	+ 22,458	+27.5
1954–61			
Sydney	+41,941	+365,448	+11.5
Melbourne	+35,954	+395,630	+ 9.1
Brisbane	+29,573	+117,429	+25.2
Adelaide	+21,120	+142,260	+14.9
Perth	+12,298	+ 80,349	+15.3
Hobart	+ 5,221	+ 23,445	+22.3
1961–6			
Sydney	+ 1,216	+237,843	+ 0.5
Melbourne	−13,447	+245,765	− 5.5
Brisbane	+28,030	+ 85,040	+32.9
Adelaide	+20,983	+112,029	+18.7
Perth	+15,874	+ 83,423	+19.1
Hobart	− 1,449	+ 11,075	−13.1
Total 1947–66			
Sydney	+ 266	+842,463	+ 0.0
Melbourne	+ 1,438	+889,198	+ 0.2
Brisbane	+87,720	+320,212	+27.4
Adelaide	+52,579	+360,838	+14.6
Perth	+37,435	+255,853	+14.6
Hobart	+ 9,946	+ 56,978	+17.5

Source: Censuses of the Commonwealth of Australia, 1947, 1954, 1961 and 1966.

cent of the total population. An overwhelming majority of them live in major urban centres, and the six State capital cities and Canberra have over 73 per cent of the total foreign-born. Sydney and Melbourne contain the largest share, each over 25 per cent of the total, while Adelaide has over 10 per cent.

The impact of this large-scale immigration on Australian society and especially on urbanization of the population is well recognized; the immigrants' role in influencing the urban structure, social ecology and work-force characteristics is documented elsewhere in this volume. In terms of population growth in the capital city metropolitan centres this impact, while affecting the overall rates of growth, has had varying significance in different capital cities. Table 3.5 shows that in 1947–66, well over half of the total population increases in Sydney, Melbourne and Adelaide were due to increases in the immigration of foreign-born persons, while in Brisbane and Hobart the overseas immigration components of growth were a little over 30 per cent.

TABLE 3.5. *Components of metropolitan population growth in Australia 1947–1966*

Metropolitan division	Natural increase	Net migration of Australian-born	Net migration of foreign-born	Total increase
Numbers				
Sydney	378,784	266	463,413	842,463
Melbourne	365,649	1,438	522,111	889,198
Brisbane	123,672	87,720	108,820	320,212
Adelaide	104,372	52,579	203,887	360,838
Perth	103,910	37,455	114,488	255,853
Hobart	28,746	9,946	18,286	56,978
Percent				
Sydney	45.0	0.0	55.0	100.0
Melbourne	41.1	0.2	58.7	100.0
Brisbane	38.6	27.4	34.0	100.0
Adelaide	28.9	14.6	56.5	100.0
Perth	40.6	14.6	44.8	100.0
Hobart	50.4	17.5	32.1	100.0

Note. All boundaries are adjusted to the 1966 boundary.

Sources: Demography Bulletins; Censuses of the Commonwealth of Australia, 1947, 1954, 1961 and 1966.

Melbourne gained the most in net immigration of foreign-born persons, 522,000 for the nineteen years between 1947 and 1966, or 27,000 a year. Sydney came next with a net gain of 463,000 or 24,000 a year. Clearly, the growth of Melbourne and Sydney was largely the result of heavy overseas immigration and natural increase. There was very little gain through internal migration (net migration of the Australian-born). This, however, does not necessarily mean that there has been little migration from Australian rural areas to Melbourne or Sydney; in fact, this rural–urban migration has certainly taken place, but was compensated for by sizeable movements out from these two metropolises to other major urban areas, in particular Brisbane, Perth, Adelaide, Wollongong and Geelong.

In Brisbane, net migration of Australian-born has been a major factor in growth – 27 per cent of total growth in the metropolis. Together with natural increase, this was 66 per cent of total population growth. Brisbane grew from a city of 457,000 in 1947 to 777,000 in 1966, an increase of 320,000 (2.7 per cent per annum). Similarly, with strong international migration and significant internal migration, Adelaide and Perth had very rapid growth in the 1947–66 period, significantly faster (with 2.9 and 3.2 per cent annual rates) than Sydney and Melbourne which had annual rates of 2.0 and 2.6 per cent and in which gain by net migration of Australian-born was negligible.

There were some intercensal differences in migration and growth patterns of the various metropolises. Thus in the 1961–6 period the internal migration component in the growth of Brisbane, Perth and Adelaide increased, the internal migration net gain in Brisbane of 28,030 constituted 33 per cent of total population increase, while the internal migration component in total growth of both Adelaide and Perth was 19 per cent. Melbourne meanwhile had a net *loss* of Australian-born in the 1961–6 period equal to 5.5 per cent of the total metropolitan population increase, while Hobart had a net loss of 1,449 Australian-born which was equal to

TABLE 3.6. *Components of metropolitan population growth in Australia 1961–1966*

Metropolitan division	Natural increase	Net migration of overseas-born	Net migration of Australian-born	Total increase
Sydney	111,318	125,309	+ 1,216	237,843
Melbourne	118,205	141,007	−13,447	245,765
Brisbane	35,229	21,781	+28,030	85,040
Adelaide	27,792	63,254	+ 20,983	112,029
Perth	28,267	39,262	+15,894	83,423
Hobart	7,809	4,715	− 1,449	11,075
Per cent				
Sydney	46.80	52.69	+ 0.51	100.0
Melbourne	48.10	57.37	− 5.47	100.0
Brisbane	41.43	25.61	+32.96	100.0
Adelaide	24.81	56.46	+18.73	100.0
Perth	33.88	47.07	+19.05	100.0
Hobart	70.51	42.57	−13.08	100.0

Sources: Demography Bulletins; unpublished tabulations, age by birthplace by metropolitan divisions, 1961 and 1966 censuses.

13 per cent of its total population gain, as can be seen in Table 3.6. This strong net loss in Hobart was a reversal of earlier trends when Hobart gained through internal migration. This was not a movement back to rural areas or small towns in Tasmania but rather an out-migration to Victoria (Melbourne, Geelong) and New South Wales.

In the 1966–71 period the rapid growth of Adelaide, indicated by implication in Table 3.6 for the 1961–6 period, did not continue as strongly, for annual growth rates of the total population fell during this interval. The rate of growth of metropolitan Sydney on the other hand increased and although data are as yet unavailable from which Australian-born net migration can be computed, it is possible that rural–urban net migration to Sydney increased, due to the rural recession with the collapse of wool prices and fall of returns on some other primary products.

Conclusion

In the period since World War II, migration, international or internal or both, has been the dominant factor in metropolitan population growth in Australia. Thus between 1947 and 1966, migration accounted for 55 and 59 per cent of the growth of Sydney and Melbourne, and 61, 59 and 50 per cent of population increase in Brisbane, Perth and Hobart respectively. In Adelaide, migration accounted for 71 per cent of total growth, and 75 per cent of that between 1961 and 1966. However, the *type* of migration gain varied considerably between cities. Meanwhile, natural increase ranged from 50, 45 and 41 per cent of the growth of Hobart, Melbourne and Sydney to only 29 per cent of population increase in Adelaide.

An important part of the urbanization process, more especially in the development of Brisbane, Adelaide and Perth, has been internal migration, particularly interstate migration. The interstate movement is believed to consist very largely of inter-metropolitan migration, a phenomenon of increasing importance in advanced industrial economies, as Keyfitz, George and others have testified.[9] The movement of the Australian-born away from the large cities of Sydney and Melbourne to the State capitals of Brisbane, Adelaide and Perth probably reflects post-war occupational opportunities in these younger States, with newer cities benefiting from industrial establishment and building expansion as did South Australia. Expansion also occurred in the near net loss States and metropolitan centres of New South Wales and Victoria, but the large-scale influx of international immigrants may have increased job competition in these States and cities.[10] However, Adelaide, the State capital most affected by migration, has gained by both very strong international migration and significant city-ward intrastate internal migration and interstate migration, suggesting that immigrants and internal migrants have been successfully absorbed together in the rapidly expanding manufacturing and servicing labour force there.

Immigration has been the main factor in the growth of Sydney, Melbourne and Adelaide, more important than internal migration and natural increase together. The implications of the impact of international migration on their growth are discussed in detail in a later chapter. It should be realized that concealed in the net migration of the foreign-born tabulations presented above may be a significant internal migration of the overseas-born, but this is difficult to measure with data currently available. Finally, although migration in total has been the dominant factor in growth of all the large cities, because of the considerable variations in the role of the two migration components in metropolitan population growth, no one demographic model of metropolitan growth is applicable to the urbanization process in post-war Australia. Internal migration has been the dominant demographic element in the lesser cities of Canberra, Wollongong and Geelong[11] and very important in Brisbane, Adelaide and Perth's growth, but negligible in Melbourne and Sydney's growth. Exchange migration with other cities has certainly taken place between these and other cities, but net gain through internal migration there has been insignificant. With the massive flow of immigration to Sydney, Melbourne and Adelaide, and internal migration gain in the other State capitals, differential migration elements have been involved in the growth of the different city labour forces and sectors of their workforces.

NOTES

1 The components natural increase and *net migration* have, however, been separated, although the latter category, obtained as a residual, tells us nothing about the relative role of international migration or internal migration in growth.

2 R. J. Johnston, 'Components and correlates of Victorian rural population change, 1954–1961', *Australian Geographical Studies, 5,* 1967, pp. 65–81; R. J. Johnston and P. J. Rimmer, 'Population movements to nine Victorian towns', *Australian Geographer, 10,* 1968, pp. 421–4.

3 D. B. Williams and L. MacAulay, 'Changes in rural population and workforce in Victoria, 1961–1966', *Australian Geographical Studies, 2,* 1971, pp. 161–71.

4 D. S. Houghton, 'Population changes and migration in Western Australia, 1961–1966', *Australian Geographer, 11,* 1969, pp. 185–7.

5 N. W. F. Fisher, 'Some aspects of interstate migration in Australia', 41st A.N.Z.A.A.S. Congress, Brisbane, 1969.

6 D. Hugo, 'Migration in South Australia', unpublished M.A. thesis in Geography, Flinders University of South Australia, 1970.

7 United Nations, *Manuals on Methods of Estimating Population; Manual VI: Methods of Measuring Internal Migration,* New York, 1970.

8 I. H. Burnley, 'Immigration and metropolitan growth and change in Australia, 1947–1966', *Proceedings of the Sixth New Zealand Geography Conference,* 1971.

9 M. V. George, *Internal Migration in Canada, Demographic Analyses,* 1961 Census Monograph, Dominion Bureau of Statistics, Canada, 1970.

10 I. H. Burnley and C. Y. Choi, 'Internal migration in Australia 1947–1966, with special reference to interstate movements and the growth of capital cities', Institute of Australian Geographers Conference, Canberra, February 1972, p. 7.

11 Because of unavailability of census data on age by birthplace (overseas-born or Australian-born) the normal surviving or vital statistics methods of measuring migration will reveal only 'net migration' rather than Australian-born (internal migration), and therefore internal migration data for these lesser cities are not presented.

4

Patterns of urbanization in Victoria

D. T. ROWLAND

The history of urbanization in Victoria spans less than a century and a half, but it has been a history of continuing ferment. A diverse range of influences, including gold rushes, immigration schemes, droughts, technological advances and vacillations of world markets, have all left their impress on the distribution of population and settlement. Population growth has continued to be fostered in some places by the generative influence of Melbourne, while in other places a struggle for survival has been waged against the gravitational pull of the same city.

The only trend which has been unwavering, except in times of national economic crisis, has been the self-perpetuating growth of Melbourne. As in other Australian States, especially South Australia, the urbanization process is equated mainly with metropolitan growth, so much does the capital city overshadow all other urban development. In 1971, 70 per cent of the State's population of 3.5 million lived in metropolitan Melbourne, while only 19 per cent were in the other urban centres, the remaining 11 per cent being rural.[1]

This chapter is concerned with some of the demographic aspects of urbanization, partly in the static sense of the proportion living in urban places at instances in time, but more particularly in the dynamic sense of the process of urban growth or decline. Even in such a restricted interpretation, urbanization is a very complex phenomenon, and the interrelationships between town and country make a consideration of rural population trends essential to the analysis of the urban populations themselves.

Primacy of Melbourne

One of the most important preconditions for the rapid emergence of a metropolitan dominance in Victoria was the nature of the time of settlement. The first successful colony in Victoria was established in the 1830s, and the subsequent evolution of the Victorian settlement pattern coincided with the main era of urbanization in countries which had experienced the agrarian and industrial revolutions. In England, for example, the urban population rose from 16.9 per cent of the total population in 1801 to 53.7 per cent in 1891.[2] The pattern of commercial agriculture supporting large urban populations was becoming established and this pattern achieved an extreme form under Australian conditions. Victoria was settled by a technologically advanced people with the intention and the means of developing a complementary economy oriented to markets in the United Kingdom.

The founding of Melbourne in 1835, prior to the opening up of inland areas, gave the town an initial advantage which later became unassailable.[3] The absence of historical antecedents and the nature of the resource base favoured the development of a primate urban system, that is, a settlement pattern dominated by a single city. Few rural areas acquired dense populations because the main rural land uses, sheep grazing and wheat farming, did not require a large labour force. The only sizeable inland towns, Ballarat and Bendigo, grew up on gold fields. Beyond the gold fields, conditions were unfavourable for the creation of large inland towns because rural development coincided with road and rail construction which prevented isolation.[4] Although the construction of overland communications linked port and hinterland, the very nature of the communications system helped to perpetuate some forms of isolation and foster metropolitan aggrandizement. Railways were built predominantly in a radial pattern focussing on Port Phillip Bay, so that most east–west linkages were possible only via the intermediary of Melbourne. Political manoeuvering in Melbourne stifled independent regional development around other ports, notably Portland and Geelong, by cutting back funds for wharves and railways[5] and later by introducing a system of freight charges which favoured Melbourne over its rivals.[6] The isolation of inland towns from one another and from other ports was further abetted by a lack of co-ordinated planning of communications, which led to the construction of different gauge railways in Victoria, New South Wales and South Australia. This phenomenon, together with the high cost of overland transport, gave Melbourne undisputed economic hegemony throughout most of its tributary area. The settlement pattern in Victoria, as well as in other States, evolved in isolation with the result that Australia still has no unified urban hierarchy but a series of primate systems based on the States.[7]

The twentieth century concentration of population around Port Phillip Bay helped perpetuate the barrier of physical distance between Victoria and population concentrations over the border, despite continuing improvements in communications and growing economic interdependence between States. Furthermore, the greater mobility made possible by the private motor car enabled people to travel longer distances to obtain goods and services, thereby placing small towns at a disadvantage compared with regional centres and the metropolis. This trend ensured the thinning of nucleated settlement in some country districts and an increase in the gravitational pull of the cities and of Melbourne in particular.

Closely allied with the technological changes which freed industry from earlier material, energy or transport orientations has been a revolution in employment distribution which has made tertiary industry the principal employer. The implications of this trend for metropolitan growth are clear in that the largest concentration of tertiary activity is inevitably found in the main centre of population and secondary industry. While the metropolis has benefited from this trend, the countryside has continued to offer a relatively meagre number of new employment opportunities, since mechanization and advances in technology have increased production without necessitating a substantial increase in the numbers employed in agriculture.

The revolution in employment patterns favouring urban-oriented activity over rural-oriented activity has been interpreted as part of a more general tendency having profound implications, at least in theoretical terms, for the process of metropolitan growth. As an explanation for population increase in capital cities in Australia, Woolmington put forward the concept of 'Malthusian Inversion', attributing the drift of population to metropolitan centres to the converse of the relationship between population and production described by Malthus (1798).[8] Whereas Malthus believed there was a tendency for population to outgrow its food supply, Woolmington considered that the situation can arise where population capacity exceeds consumption. He argued that in 'developed' countries overproduction is increasingly common since technology has lifted agricultural productivity, thereby causing redundancy of rural labour and inefficient farms. This is the opposite of the Malthusian pattern in which farming becomes more labour intensive but yields diminishing per capita returns from expanding agricultural lands. In a 'Malthusian Inversion' situation, where agricultural employment is fairly static or declining, the excess rural population generally moves to urban centres, which are sustained by the surplus agricultural production. Urban centres achieve their own functional momentum but consumer-oriented production favours metropolitan growth rather than the expansion of rural service towns, which operate as intermediaries between the metropolis and the rural hinterland. The concept of 'Malthusian Inversion' is significant in that it is virtually the only proposition which has been offered as a general explanation of metropolitan growth and centralization in Australia.

Woolmington is not alone in proposing a 'Malthusian Inversion' and his ideas parallel some of those expressed by Galbraith in the book *The Affluent Society*. Galbraith makes a case for the existence of over-production and artificially stimulated over-consumption: 'Now goods are abundant. Although there is malnutrition, more die in the United States of too much food than of too little. Where the population was once thought to press on the food supply, now, in the affluent countries, the food supply presses on the population.'[9] He sees a surfeit existing not only in food supplies but also in manufactured goods and believes that a vicious circle is created with over-production leading to over-consumption and more over-production.[10]

Among the consequences of adherence to the myth that increased production is always beneficial Galbraith alludes to the ills of large cities[11] but he does not argue specifically that the relationship between population and production has been responsible for metropolitan growth. Yet it is easy to envisage how agglomerations of productive units and consumers, trapped in a vicious circle, could be the cause of self-reinforcing urban growth. Galbraith's economic theory possibly identifies the mainsprings of centralization in Australia.

Size of towns

Berry and Horton have suggested that primacy is the outcome of the operation of a few simple strong forces, whereas a 'rank–size' distribution, in which the largest city has only twice the population of the second city, is the result of many forces acting randomly.[12] This argument is in accord with the relatively simple set of propositions put forward above to explain the great size of Melbourne. However, while Berry and Horton's model accounts for the rise of primate cities it does not give attention to the nature of the processes affecting the smaller members of the settlement hierarchy.

In 1971, the Melbourne metropolitan area's (division) population of 2.5 million was over twenty times the size of that of the second city, Geelong. Only three other urban centres in the State had more than 20,000 people, namely Ballarat and Bendigo in central Victoria, and Moe-Yallourn in the Latrobe Valley. The four cities together contained 37.2 per cent of the State's non-metropolitan urban population, though even their combined total was dwarfed by that of Melbourne. In order to approach the rank–size pattern characteristic of urban systems in which Berry and Horton postulate that random processes are operating, Victoria in 1971 would have needed several cities larger than Geelong, including one city of about 1.2 million people. While such a city size distribution is only a theoretical proposition, rather than an ideal for Victoria, the pattern of metropolitan dominance will continue until such time as there are other large cities, distant from the metropolis, which can create a greater degree of inter-dependence in the Victorian urban system.

Commonly, settlement size is regarded as an index of the influence which towns and cities extend over the surrounding area. The fortunes and population characteristics of towns and cities are also seen as being partly related to size. Theoretical justification for this use of settlement size is found in studies of the differences between rural and urban societies[13] as well as in writing on the gravity and potential models of migration.[14] Essentially, the body of theory states that the larger the settlement, the greater the potential differentiation of its population, the larger the volume of inward and outward migration, and the more extensive the area influenced by the town. Empirical work has tested size-hypotheses of 'continuous gradation' in the population characteristics of rural and urban settlements[15] and has examined migration in terms of the 'gravitational influence' of towns. In such studies settlement size has been found to be unreliable for predictive purposes except when features associated with towns of greatly differing sizes are compared. Since the range of sizes of non-metropolitan urban centres in Victoria is relatively small it would be unjustifiable in the light of existing evidence to attribute differences in the population trends of towns mainly to the differences in their population totals. This notion is borne out by a study of towns in Victoria in which it was found, for example, that the trade area of Hamilton, which had a population of 10,062 in 1966, was greater than that of Ballarat which had a population of 56,312.[16] Size should therefore be used to account for population trends in conjunction with other explanatory items such as relative location, urban functions, employment vacancies, government policies, local enterprise and the characteristics of the rural hinterland.

Changes in the frequencies of size groupings of Victoria towns are shown in Table 4.1. The figures are areally comparable from 1947 to 1966 and conceptually comparable from 1966 to 1971. The table refers to a constant universe, only the 111 urban centres which had populations of

TABLE 4.1. *Sizes of Victorian urban centres*[a]

Population	1947	1954	1961	1966	1971[b]
Less than 1,000	24	17	10	2	9
1,000– 1,999	36	37	38	45	35
2,000– 2,999	17	17	19	21	22
3,000– 3,999	9	10	14	11	10
4,000– 4,999	7	4	1	3	4
5,000– 5,999	4	6	4	2	4
6,000– 6,999	6	6	4	2	0
7,000– 7,999	1	2	6	6	5
8,000– 8,999	0	3	2	5	4
9,000– 9,999	3	1	3	2	1
10,000–14,999	1	4	5	4	9
15,000–19,999	0	0	1	4	4
20,000 or more	3	4	4	4	4
	111	111	111	111	111

[a] Only urban centres with population of 950 or more in 1966 included. Melbourne is excluded.
[b] Includes Mornington-Balcombe and Dromana-Sorrento which became part of urban Melbourne in 1971.
Sources: Unpublished collectors' district data for 1947, 1954 and 1961; 1966 census, and 1971 census field count statement.

950 or more in 1966 being included because comparable data through time were not available for other towns. Some of the consequences of urbanization in the Australian environment are made apparent by the distribution of town sizes. Compared with New Zealand, Victoria is undersupplied with towns, but more particularly it is undersupplied with large towns. In 1966 there were 109 non-metropolitan urban centres with 1,000 or more people in Victoria compared with 137 in New Zealand which had a smaller population – 2.7 million compared with 3.2 million in Victoria. The physical environment of Victoria has not favoured dense settlement and intensive land utilization in many areas, and this situation, coupled with the other forces promoting metropolitan primacy, has acted against the proliferation of towns. Furthermore, the majority of Victorian urban centres (71 per cent) had populations below 4,000 in 1966 although their share of the non-metropolitan urban population amounted to only about 5 per cent more than the proportion in Geelong. Writers have speculated about the population size a town needs to reach before its growth becomes self-sustaining, and many have accepted that 50,000 represents the threshold, with some tendencies towards self-generation appearing around 10,000.[17] If this is correct, most towns in Victoria remain vulnerable to external influences which could impede growth if not cause decline. By the same token, external influences may have a generative effect on small towns, and Table 4.1 gives evidence that since 1947 Victorian urban centres have, on average, held their own or moved up the size hierarchy. In 1947 4 towns had over 10,000 people compared with 17 in 1971, while the number of towns in the size range 4,000–9,999 declined from 21 to 18 over the same period. These figures, together with other evidence, indicate that larger towns move up the size hierarchy more quickly than smaller towns. This is because a large initial population creates greater potential for absolute growth, although in relative terms smaller towns frequently grow faster than larger ones.

Settlement distribution

Among the items already mentioned as complementing size in accounting for population trends is location. A town's viability is partly dependent on its position in relation to other towns and the rural population. The overall pattern of population distribution may therefore be regarded as both a product of, and a conditioning factor in, the urbanization process. Settlement distribution in Victoria, and elsewhere in Australia, is strongly conditioned by the distribution of rivers and effective rainfall, which, in association with soil types, places limits upon the nature of land uses.

Relatively high rural population densities occur in parts of a 40 kilometre wide coastal zone extending from Warrnambool to Sale. Densities are highest in close proximity to Melbourne, and remain high in the south-east between Melbourne and Traralgon. In the north, pockets of dense rural population occur along the Murray Valley, with further high densities extending southwards adjacent to the Goulburn River and the Ovens River, which are tributaries of the Murray. Eastern Victoria is extensively forested and sparsely settled, while central and western Victoria have widely dispersed rural populations except in the vicinity of Bendigo and Ballarat and some smaller towns.

Similarly, most of the large towns occur in the coastal zone or in the river valleys of the north. The main exceptions are Bendigo and Ballarat, whose original raison d'être was servicing the gold fields, and Horsham, which is a good example of a central place serving an extensive rural district. When details of the size and spacing of Victorian towns are considered, however, the pattern is not readily explained. Fairbairn has made a study of Victorian towns using central place theory as a basis for interpretation. He found many anomalies in the distribution pattern which could not be accounted for by the theory, and showed that the sizes of towns and the extent of their trade were in many instances due to the nature of isolated resources, historical background, and other local rather than regional influences.[18]

Rural population changes

Victorian towns derive a proportion of their income by providing goods and services to the population of their hinterlands. Consequently urban population trends are partly dependent upon trends in the surrounding rural areas. Large towns are fairly well insulated against changes in rural areas because of their functional diversity, while small rural servicing centres are exposed to the full impact of rural changes because of their dependence on income from retail sales, primary processing or financial transactions with the rural population.

In order to analyse population change through time it was necessary to obtain comparable data for the censuses of 1947, 1954, 1961, 1966 and 1971. Published figures for Victoria are frequently not comparable from one census to the next because of boundary changes. To overcome this problem, unpublished population totals for collectors' districts, the smallest census units, were re-aggregated so that the 1947, 1954 and 1961 totals referred to the rural and urban areas defined in the 1966 census.

Published census figures were used for 1966 and 1971 without any adjustments because more realistic definitions had been applied in fixing the boundaries of rural areas and urban centres.

Annual rates of population change were calculated for each of the 137 rural areas for which comparable data could be obtained. This gave four sets of figures referring to the two seven year and the two five year intercensal periods. The data were then grouped by means of a cluster analysis which linked areas having similar annual rates of population change over the four intercensal periods.[19] The cluster analysis yielded eight main groups whose average population trends are shown in Table 4.2 and in the graphs in Fig. 4.1.

TABLE 4.2. *Mean rates of population change in rural areas*

Group	f	Annual growth rate per cent[a]			
		1947–54	1954–61	1961–6	1966–71
1	7	1.77	3.79	4.32	6.16
2	9	2.51	0.22	1.16	2.52
3	4	0.49	0.17	−2.35	0.84
4	13	1.81	1.83	1.74	0.11
5	67	1.13	0.22	−0.55	−1.69
6	15	0.31	−1.85	−1.16	−1.55
7	6	3.82	4.33	0.80	−4.17
8	6	4.97	1.53	4.93	−1.49
Ungrouped	10				
Total	137				

[a] From 'compound interest' formula.

The analysis enabled areas to be classified according to their population trends over a twenty-four year period, and permitted complex information to be represented on a single map.

Rural depopulation is a familiar phenomenon in Australia and its occurrence is much in evidence in Fig. 4.1; extensive areas of rural Victoria in the period 1947–71 being characterized by a slowing of growth followed by absolute decline. The decline, however, has begun at different times and has proceeded at different rates, and in the short term is scarcely very serious. Nearly all the shires where sudden declines in rates of population change have occurred are adjacent to expanding urban centres, especially Melbourne and Geelong. Elsewhere rural decline has been a gradual process.

Shires belonging to group 1 had an average annual rate of increase of 1.8 per cent from 1947 to 1954, rising to 6.2 per cent between 1966 and 1971. Many of the areas of group 2, which have also experienced continuous growth, although with a u-shaped trend rather than a linear one, are found in association with those of the first group. They occur in a circular zone around Melbourne and Geelong as well as adjacent to the cities of Mildura, Ballarat and Moe-Yallourn. Although part of the population growth in these areas is attributable to the intensification of farming and the extension of market gardening, the suburbanization process enlarging dormitory towns on the outskirts of cities has also played a role.

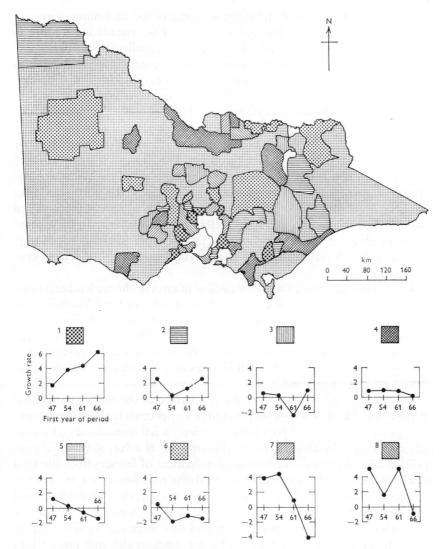

Figure 4.1. Rural Victoria population trends 1947–71

Most of the shires in group 4 are found beyond the Port Phillip Bay core area, especially adjacent to Echuca and Shepparton in northern Victoria, as well as in proximity to other towns such as Wangaratta, Ballarat and Sale. Between 1947 and 1966 the shires had an annual average population increase of about 1.8 per cent but in the following five years population change almost ceased. The primary industries of these areas are diverse and although fluctuations in the prices of primary produce accompanied by rising overheads may be responsible for some of the slackening of growth in the shires, changes in the age structures of the population leading to increased out-migration to urban areas may be equally responsible.

Only 33 of the 137 Victorian shires belong to groups 1 to 4 where population growth or stability is the rule rather than decline. In groups 5 and 6, however, into which 82 areas fall, the demographic effects of rural recessions and the circumscribed nature of rural life are most in evidence. Much of western Victoria, together with parts of central and eastern Victoria, were characterized by falling population growth rates from 1947 to 1961 followed by ten years of decline (group 5). Places more strongly affected by rural population decline (group 6) were portions of the Wimmera and Mallee districts north of Horsham, three shires in the north-east near Wodonga, and several shires in central Victoria adjoining the areas of sustained population growth near Melbourne and Ballarat. In these areas the population grew at the low rate of 0.3 per cent per annum between 1947 and 1954 and thereafter declined at an average annual rate of 1.5 per cent (Table 4.2).

In 12 shires (groups 7 and 8) the decline in rates of change has been rapid and sudden rather than slow as is typical of most of rural Victoria. It is significant that nearly all these areas are located around Melbourne and Geelong as well as in the Murray Valley north of Shepparton. The extension of urban boundaries into former rural areas between 1966 and 1971 largely accounts for the rapid fall in rates of population change in shires belonging to groups 7 and 8.

Over the period 1947 to 1971 the percentage of the State's population living in rural areas fell from 29 per cent to 12 per cent. In the same twenty-four years the total rural population of Victoria fell from about 593,000 to 427,000, that is by 28 per cent.[20] Although this is a very substantial proportion an exaggerated impression of movement of farmers from the land can be arrived at if the components of rural depopulation are not recognized. In a study of rural population change in Victoria 1954–61, Johnston showed that the decline in the rural workforce did not account for a substantial proportion of total population change and that there was no single causal factor influencing rural change.[21] This was because although proportions employed in primary occupations tended to decline in most shires, the total population either decreased at a slower rate or increased. Another factor which may disguise the nature of rural population change is the practice of 'town farming'. In 1966, 7.8 per cent of the farmers and farm workers in Victoria lived in Melbourne, and 10.1 per cent lived in other urban centres. In a survey by Williams of town farming in the Mallee lands of South Australia and Victoria it was found that 29 out of 70 town farmers travelled daily to their farms, 33 were people who had moved to town and allowed a relative to live on the holding and take over part of all of the farm operations, and 8 were people who worked in town and either share-farmed or worked the land themselves on a part-time basis.[22] The main reasons for becoming town farmers were: approaching retirement, a desire for urban services such as schools and shops, and the belief that, in face of a need to replace an ageing rural dwelling, a house in town was a better investment. Finally, a most important factor in rural depopulation is the entry of the children of rural dwellers into the working age groups. The shortage of employment opportunities and the lack of tertiary educational institutions within access of most rural areas makes this outward migration inevitable. It must be concluded that while the impact of changes in the organization of rural industry on rural population numbers is an important public issue, its effects have yet to be accurately gauged and compared with the effects of other social and economic processes.

Urban population changes

Urban population trends have also been analysed by means of the clustering technique. Fig. 4.2 shows the distribution of Victorian urban centres and their population trends through time.

Comparison of Figs. 4.1 and 4.2 reveals some association between rural and urban population trends. In general, the majority of urban centres situated within the two discontinuous zones of rural population increase have experienced sustained population growth since 1947, especially those close to Melbourne and Geelong and in the north near Shepparton. Urban centres located in rural areas where increase has been superseded by decline (group 5) have also been characterized by a slowing of growth which, between 1966 and 1971, gave way on average to zero growth or slight decline. The main exceptions to this pattern are a number of larger urban centres such as Swan Hill, Horsham and Warrnambool which have continued to grow, though at falling rates, despite unfavourable demographic trends in the surrounding countryside. A similar tendency was observed by Fairbairn in his remarks on Victorian population change in the 1961–6 period. He suggested that the wider economic base of larger towns, together with their self-generating properties and their better commercial exploitation of rural areas, made them less vulnerable than small towns to adverse rural trends.[23]

When urban population changes are considered in detail, however, the influence of location and settlement size on population trends becomes less clear as a complex of causal factors appear to be operating. Rapid linear increase in annual growth rates from 1947 to 1971 occurred only in the five urban centres belonging to group 1 (Fig. 4.2). All five were located on the outskirts of Melbourne in 1966 and their growth is related particularly to the suburbanization process, involving industry as well as homes, and the attractions of the country and the seaside.

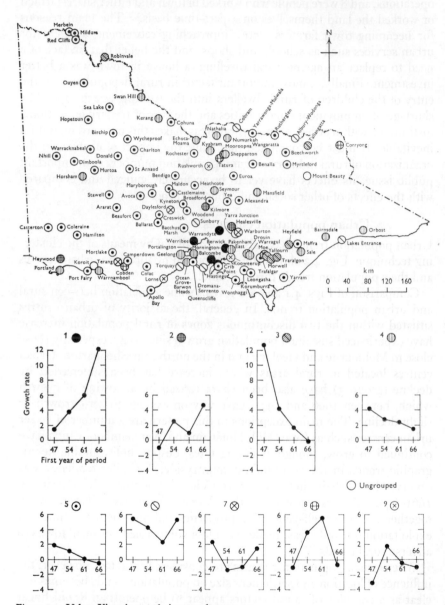

Figure 4.2. Urban Victoria population trends 1947–71

Towns in group 2 were also characterized by increasing growth rates except that the range of values was lower (Table 4.3) and on average there was a slight reversal of the upward trend between 1961 and 1966. They are among the few urban centres which have experienced a long phase of accelerating growth in the post-war period, thus proving their viability despite their being in an urban system where decelerating growth is the principal tendency.

TABLE 4.3. *Mean rates of population change in urban centres*

| Group | f | Annual growth rate per cent[a] | | | |
		1947–54	1954–61	1961–6	1966–71
1	5	1.45	3.81	5.99	12.16
2	4	− 1.08	2.51	0.93	5.60
3	6	12.71	4.18	1.66	− 0.25
4	22	4.16	2.69	2.31	1.46
5	56	1.89	1.09	0.05	− 0.54
6	6	5.43	4.22	2.23	5.31
7	3	2.26	−1.43	−1.10	1.52
8	3	− 1.16	3.60	5.59	− 0.69
9	3	− 3.23	1.80	−0.54	− 1.10
Ungrouped	3				
Total	111				

[a] From 'compound interest' formula.

Towns belonging to group 3 display a pattern of linear decrease which is the antithesis of the population trends in towns of group 1. All the group 3 urban centres had relatively small population bases in 1947 and subsequently underwent very rapid growth, most notably the Latrobe Valley towns whose raison d'être is electricity generation using local brown coal. Since the 1960s the older coalfield settlements have lost their impetus as new generating plants and associated urban development, such as the town of Churchill, have been built on sites which do not overlie exploitable coal deposits.

Other towns in Gippsland and most of the remaining urban centres in the Port Phillip Bay area, including Geelong, belong to group 4, which was characterized by a downward trend in growth rates ranging from 4.2 per cent to 1.5 per cent over the twenty-four year period (Table 4.3). Many other urban centres to the east of Melbourne and in north-eastern Victoria exhibit a similar pattern of change, as do some of the larger towns in the central and western parts of the State. For Geelong, the reduction in the growth rate is partly a function of the increasing size of the city, a feature which is also illustrated by the rate for metropolitan Melbourne which was 2.7 per cent in 1961–6 and 2.5 per cent in 1966–71. Yet the slowing down of growth in the urban centres of group 3 is more generally attributable to factors such as the completion of major economic development within towns and their hinterlands, economic recession, the maturing of age structures, and the difficulties which towns face in retaining and attracting population in competition with Melbourne and expanding areas in other States.

Linear decline in growth rates is also characteristic of the very large number of towns belonging to group 5 but in these urban centres the average pattern has been a reduction in growth rates between 1947 and 1966, followed by an annual decline of 0.5 per cent from 1966 to 1971 (Table 4.3).

The annual growth rates for both Ballarat and Bendigo remained near 1 per cent in the later years instead of declining, thus giving the two cities relatively constant growth rates since 1947. Despite departures from the mean, the deceleration of growth remains the most widespread pattern of urban population change in the State. Members of groups 4 and 5 combined account for 70 per cent of the total Victorian urban centres. Size and location of settlement have offered little immunity against this trend as towns of many different sizes have been affected in locations throughout the state.

In a number of towns a reversal of the downward trend has occurred (groups 6 and 7) owing to developments which in some instances have had a regional effect while in others the effect has been localized. In towns belonging to group 6, the rate of population change did not fall below 2.2 per cent before the fall was checked and growth accelerated, while in the three towns of group 7 rejuvenation took place after a phase of absolute decline. For the urban centres situated near Melbourne and Geelong the rejuvenation is to some extent attributable to their location, the impact of suburbanization or resource development being delayed because of distance from the centres of growth. Whereas the trend in these towns may be regarded as a result of the widening of Melbourne's regional influence, rejuvenation of population expansion in towns such as Wodonga and Lakes Entrance can be related to purely local factors such as the expansion of industry, or, in the case of Lakes Entrance, to tourism and the acquisition of service functions for the Gippsland oilfields.

Pattern and process

Patterns of urban growth and decline are the net results of the operation of the processes of migration, fertility and mortality. These processes in turn are the manifestations of other forces which in specific places may be readily recognized, but at a larger regional or State scale are often obscure.

Closure of a mine or factory can have obvious repercussions on the population size of an individual town, but the mainsprings of change, which account for general tendencies in the urban system as a whole, still remain matters of conjecture.

Urban growth and decline may be seen as the balance between natural increase and net migration. Yet recognition of these two components of changes does not fully illustrate the operation of demographic processes, and a comprehensive analysis would need to investigate the components of net migration, including overseas immigration and emigration and the movement of people within Australia, that is, internal migration. In addition, natural increase differentials would need to be accounted for particularly through the study of fertility.[24]

Between 1966 and 1971 the population of the Melbourne statistical division, which comprises the metropolitan area together with adjacent rural areas, grew by 267,200, the increase being fairly evenly divided between natural increase (54 per cent) and net migration (46 per cent) as

TABLE 4.4. *Total population change and net migration[a] in statistical divisions*

Statistical division	1961–6		1966–71	
	Total change	Net migration	Total change	Net migration
Melbourne	245,765	123,444	267,200	122,778
West Central[b]	17,841	8,819	14,350	5,202
North Central[b]	1,039	−2,176	−2,003	− 4,665
Western	5,328	−7,209	−3,601	−13,512
Wimmera	1,190	−2,702	−4,444	− 7,217
Mallee	2,015	−4,445	−1,258	− 5,852
Northern[b]	10,916	−1,095	4,576	− 6,158
North Eastern	305	−4,884	− 748	− 6,049
Gippsland	6,505	−5,818	2,086	− 9,287
East Central	130	−2,272	514	− 1,345
Migratory	−1,621	−1,621	− 728	− 728
Total Victoria	289,413	100,041	275,944	73,167

[a] From vital statistics.
[b] Small boundary changes affected the division between 1966 and 1971. The 1961–6 figures have not been adjusted.
Sources: 1961–6: Wilson, 'Demographic trends and characteristics in rural Victoria', Table II. 1966–71: Bureau of Census, Melbourne.

shown in Table 4.4. Similarly, between 1961 and 1966 net migration accounted for over half of the population increase in the same statistical division. However, in both 1961–6 and 1966–71 only one other statistical division, West Central, which contains Geelong, experienced net inward migration, all other divisions having lost population through migration. Rates of outward migration were highest in the Wimmera and Mallee districts in north-western Victoria, but also exceeded 1 per cent per annum in all other areas except the Northern division centred on Euchuca. Despite the net outward movement the total populations of all divisions continued to grow slightly during 1961–6 because of natural increase, but during the next five years natural increase failed to compensate fully for outward migration. From 1966 to 1971, absolute decline occurred throughout the western half of the State as well as in the North Central division north of Melbourne and the North Eastern division centred on Wodonga (Table 4.4).[25]

In view of the widespread occurrence of outward migration in Victoria, juxtaposed with the continuing expansion of the metropolis, it is tempting to assume that Melbourne is exerting an irresistible attraction on the population of the rest of the State, and is the prime influence on rural and urban population trends. Yet the link between the pattern of change and the processes responsible for it remains indeterminate.

During the post-war period, Melbourne has not been greatly dependent upon the rest of the State as a source of population, natural increase and immigration from overseas having played a more important role. Between 1947 and 1966 about half of Melbourne's population increase was contributed by the arrival of immigrants from overseas.[26] Also, Victoria has lost population by departures both to other States and overseas. Between 1961 and 1966 Victoria experienced a net loss of 20,220 Australian-born people through departures to other States, and Australia as a whole had a net loss of over 200,000 Australian-born people through emigration between 1947 and 1970.[27] If these types of losses were experienced by places other than the metropolis they could represent an important component of the net outward migrations shown in Table 4.4. Yet the fact that Melbourne has absorbed the bulk of Victoria's overseas immigrants means that if Melbourne is not exerting profound depopulating influences elsewhere in the State, it is at least debilitating non-metropolitan development by absorbing labour force increases and continuing its self-reinforcing growth at an accelerated pace.

NOTES

1 'Metropolitan Melbourne' was termed 'urban Melbourne' in the 1971 census. An urban centre is generally defined as a settlement with 1,000 or more people. 'Rural area' and 'urban centre' are not synonymous with 'shire' and 'municipality' since the latter are local government areas which often do not correspond to discrete areas of dispersed and nucleated settlement.

2 Peter Hall, *The World Cities*, World University Library, London, 1968, p. 17.

3 A. J. Rose, 'Dissent from down under: metropolitan primacy as the normal state', *Pacific Viewpoint*, 7, 1966.

4 K. W. Robinson, 'Processes and patterns of urbanization in Australia and New Zealand', *New Zealand Geographer*, *18*, 1962; M. I. Logan, 'Capital city development in Australia', in G. H. Dury and M. I. Logan (eds.), *Studies in Australian Geography*, Melbourne, 1968, pp. 245–301.

5 I. A. H. Turner, 'The growth of Melbourne: an historical account', in P. N. Troy (ed.), *Urban Redevelopment in Australia*, Canberra, 1967, pp. 24–7.

6 Geoffrey Blainey, *The Tyranny of Distance*, Melbourne, 1971, pp. 264–5.

7 Rose, 'Dissent from down under'; R. J. Johnston, 'Population changes in Australian small towns 1961–1966', *Rural Sociology*, *34*, 1969, p. 213.

8 E. R. Woolmington, 'Government policy and decentralisation', in G. J. R. Linge and P. J. Rimmer (eds.), *Government Influence and the Location of Economic Activity*, Canberra, 1971, p. 281; E. R. Woolmington, 'Theoretical implications of the Malthusian inversion', *Proceedings of the Sixth New Zealand and Geography Conference*, vol. 1, Christchurch, 1971, pp. 19–25.

9 John Kenneth Galbraith, *The Affluent Society*, second ed. revised, Victoria, 1971, pp. 125–6.

10 Ibid. pp. 152–3.

11 Ibid. pp. 18–19.

12 Brian J. L. Berry and Frank E. Horton, *Geographic Perspectives on Urban Systems*, New Jersey, 1970, p. 73.

13 Louis Wirth, 'Urbanism as a way of life', *American Journal of Sociology*, *44*, 1938, pp. 1–24.

14 John Q. Stewart. 'Empirical mathematical rules concerning the distribution and equilibrium of population', *Geographical Review*, *37*, 1947, pp. 461–85; George K. Zipf, 'The P1 P2/D hypothesis: on the intercity movement of persons', *American Sociological Review*, *11*, 1946, pp. 677–86.

15 O. D. Duncan and A. J. Reiss, *Social Characteristics of Urban and Rural Communities*, New York, 1956.

16 K. J. Fairbairn and A. D. May, *Geography of Central Places*, Adelaide, 1971, p. 48.

17 K. J. Fairbairn, 'Victorian towns as service centres', Ph.D. thesis, University of Melbourne, 1968, p. 261.

18 Fairbairn and May, *Geography of Central Places*, pp. 47–8.

19 P. M. Mather, *Cluster Analysis, Computer Applications in the Natural and Socia Sciences*, no. 1, cyclostyled Nottingham University, 1969. The author is very grateful to Mr L. J. Hobba, Department of Geography, Monash University, for advice on this technique.

20 Comparable estimates by Dr C. Y. Choi, Department of Demography, Australian National University.

21 R. J. Johnston, 'Components and correlates of Victorian rural population change', *Australian Geographical Studies*, *5*, 1967, pp. 165–81.

22 M. Williams, 'Town-farming in the mallee lands of South Australia and Victoria', *Australian Geographical Studies*, *8*, 1970, pp. 173–91.

23 Fairbairn, 'Victorian towns as service centres', p. 249.

24 M. G. A. Wilson, 'Alternate measures of human reproduction – some geographic implications', *New Zealand Geographer*, *27*, 1971, pp. 195–6; M. G. A. Wilson, 'The spatial dimension of human reproduction in Victoria', *Proceedings of the Sixth New Zealand Geography Conference*, vol. 1, Christchurch, 1971, pp. 258–64.

25 M. G. A. Wilson, 'Demographic trends and characteristics in rural Victoria', *The Church in Rural Victoria*, Melbourne, 1969.

26 I. H. Burnley, 'Immigration and metropolitan growth and change in Australia, 1947–1966', *Proceedings of the Sixth New Zealand Geography Conference*, vol. 1, Christchurch, 1971, pp. 63–72.

27 I. H. Burnley and C. Y. Choi, 'Internal migration in Australia 1947–1966, with special reference to interstate movements and growth of capital cities', Institute of Australian Geographers Conference, Canberra, 1972.

5
Internal migration and urbanization in South Australia

G. J. HUGO

The period between 1947 and 1971 has seen an unprecedented growth in the urban population[1] of South Australia from 470,916 to 992,300 persons, while the rural population increased only slightly from 173,456 to 178,733 persons despite a considerable extension of the area under close agricultural settlement. Thus the proportion of the State's population residing in urban centres has increased from 72.9 per cent to 84.6 per cent. The most striking feature of this rapid intrastate urbanization has been the increasing dominance of metropolitan Adelaide, the population of which has more than doubled while the proportion of all South Australian residents living in the capital has risen sharply from 59.2 per cent to 71 per cent.

The pattern of population growth in South Australia before World War II has been comprehensively surveyed by Fenner[2] and Lawton,[3] while Williams[4] has discussed and broadly explained the overall changing growth and distribution of the State's population during the post-war period. There has, however, been little examination of the major demographic processes by which these changes have occurred.

In this chapter an attempt is made to assess the contribution of intrastate population movements to the post-World War II growth of South Australia's urban centres, particularly Metropolitan Adelaide. The broad patterns of internal migration are outlined and some of the characteristics of persons participating in this movement are indicated. The extent to which the migrant population differs from that in their places of origin and destination is also considered. The main causes of the internal redistribution of population are then discussed.

Sources of data

Although internal migration throughout the entire post-war era is to be considered, special attention will be focussed on the 1961–6 intercensal period, which a recent study has examined [5] Estimates of net migration were obtained for all South Australian local government areas using the Life Table Survival Ratio and Vital Statistics Methods.[6] This is supplemented for the 1961–6 period with a set of gross migration data – transfers to and from the electoral rolls of South Australian non-metropolitan subdivisions.

Internal migration 1947–71: an overview

The overall tendency for the State's population to concentrate in urban centres and the dominant position of Metropolitan Adelaide in the pattern are apparent in Table 5.1. The accelerated growth of Adelaide has been

TABLE 5.1. *South Australia: population in metropolitan, other urban and rural sectors at post-war census enumerations*

Year	Adelaide		Other urban		Rural		Migratory	
	No.	%	No.	%	No.	%	No.	%
1947	382,454	59.2	88,462	13.7	173,456	26.9	1,701	0.3
1954	483,508	60.7	110,107	13.8	210,133	25.2	2,346	0.3
1961	587,957	60.7	117,380	18.3	200,065	20.6	3,938	0.4
1966	728,279	66.5	174,964	16.0	190,167	17.4	1,574	0.1
1971	809,466	69.0	182,834	15.6	178,733	15.2	1,741	0.2

Note. A significant proportion of Adelaide's growth between 1947 and 1961 occurred outside the metropolitan boundaries then recognized for census purposes and was thus included in the 'other urban' category. The figures used vary somewhat from those used by Burnley and Choi in the present volume, for they used metropolitan statistical divisions standardized to 1966 division boundaries.

facilitated by the creation of many thousands of job opportunities as a result of a rapid post-war growth of secondary industry and the associated tertiary activities in the city.[7] In Chapter 6 it is shown that the major component of this growth during the 1947–66 period was net migration gains of overseas-born persons. The influx of immigrants, particularly from the United Kingdom and southern Europe, resulted in the proportion of foreign-born persons in Adelaide's population increasing from 8.4 per cent to 27 per cent in that period. Although comprising a smaller share of the net in-migration, intrastate gains experienced by the capital had a significant influence on the growth and development of Adelaide. Moreover, between 1966 and 1971 there was a stepping up of out-migration from rural areas – much of which would have been directed towards Adelaide.

The population of the State's non-metropolitan urban sector[8] has also more than doubled in the post-war period (see Table 5.1). However, individual urban centres experienced widely divergent patterns of growth according to differences in their economic base, size, location and historical development.

The largest concentration of urban population outside of metropolitan Adelaide is found in the three industrial cities on the northern coastline of Spencer Gulf. The smelting steel manufacturing and ship building centre of Whyalla is by far the largest and fastest growing of the State's non-metropolitan urban centres. Between 1947 and 1971 Whyalla's population

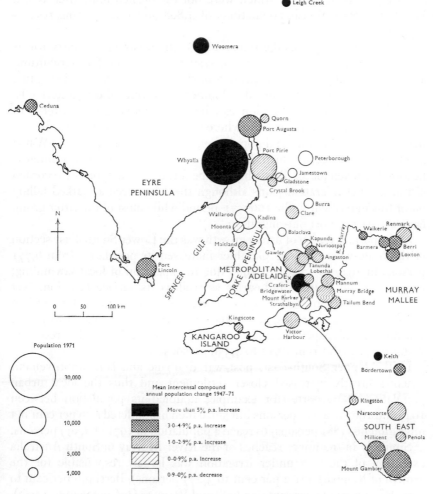

Figure 5.1. South Australia: growth of major non-metropolitan towns 1947-71

increased from 7,845 to 32,085, with 64.7 per cent of the increment being attributable to net migration gains. The majority of in-migrants were overseas-born persons, and the foreign-born component of the city's population increased from 417 persons (5.3 per cent) in 1947 to 8,521 (38.5 per cent) in 1966. Of the other Spencer Gulf towns Port Augusta has grown the most rapidly – increasing its population by 178 per cent to 12,095 between 1947 and 1971 while that of Port Pirie grew from 12,019 persons to 15,506.

Further north, net in-migration has obviously been the dominant component in the growth of the specialized function townships of Woomera and Leigh Creek, both of which were not established until after World War II and reached peak populations of 4,808 and 1,021 persons respectively in 1961.

With a few exceptions the remaining South Australian country towns are predominantly service and processing centres for the agricultural areas surrounding them. The growth of these centres has thus been, to a large extent, dependent on developments[9] within their hinterlands. Accordingly a broad distinction can be made between the patterns of growth in towns located in areas where closer agricultural settlement, and hence an increase in the rural population, has occurred since World War II and those in districts in which little or no agricultural expansion or intensification has taken place. Townships in the former group typically recorded significant net migration gains although there has been a marked falling off of this movement in the 1966–71 period while most of the latter group have experienced net out-migration.

An important region of urban growth was the Lower South-East section of the State where Mount Gambier increased its population from 6,771 persons in 1947 to 17,261 in 1966 due to expansion of local sawmilling, processing and tourism industries as well as its service function. Net migration gains (comprising approximately equal proportions of Australian and overseas-born persons) accounted for 49 per cent of this growth. The sawmilling and paper manufacturing centre of Millicent also recorded sustained growth (from 1,912 to 4,539 persons).

In the Upper South-East, post-war drainage and land improvement schemes greatly increased closer settlement and thus the local urban population. Naracoorte, for example, doubled its population between 1947 and 1961 to 4,410 persons but since then has suffered a 20 per cent net migration loss (881 persons) to reach a population in 1971 of 4,399 persons.

Similarly in the upper reaches of the River Murray in South Australia extension of the area under irrigation was largely responsible for the growth of Renmark (71.2 per cent to 3,277 persons), Berri (96 per cent to 2,712), Loxton (144 per cent to 2,658) and Barmera (106 per cent to 1,683). Net migration gains have been an important component of this growth, being responsible, for example, for 51.8 per cent of their combined population increase from 7,770 persons in 1971 to 9,188 in 1966. In the Lower Murray region, Murray Bridge doubled its population from 3,690 to 7,400 persons during the post-war era. Net migration was responsible for 36.8 per cent of the 1954–71 population increase (of 3,038 persons).

Expansion of viticulture and wine production in the Barossa Valley was responsible for the post-war growth of Nurioopta (126 per cent to 2,467 persons), Tanunda (32 per cent to 1,956) and Angaston (34 per cent to 1,887). Only Nuriootpa, however, has recorded net migration gains in recent years.

Other regions of post-war agricultural expansion were Eyre Peninsula and Kangaroo Island. In the former region the most important growth occurred at Port Lincoln (from 3,972 persons in 1947 to 8,912 in 1966) due to expansion of the town's service function together with the establishment of fish processing and fertilizer manufacturing industries. For the 1954–66 period, 40.6 per cent (1,236 persons) of Port Lincoln's population increase was due to net migration gains but a 4.7 per cent (416 persons) net loss was recorded between 1966 and 1971 although the total population increased to 9,158 persons.

An examination of Fig. 5.1 indicates that a different pattern of town growth characterized the long-established agricultural areas of the Adelaide Hills, Yorke Peninsula and Upper and Lower North. The population of these towns has increased slightly due to the in-movement of retiring rural folk, increased town-farming and the extension of the service areas of larger towns at the expense of smaller central places, which has been facilitated by the greater personal mobility afforded by high rates of motor vehicle ownership and improvement of country roads.

In the Lower North, Clare has increased its population from 1,454 to 2,105 persons during the post-war period but recorded a net migration loss of 134 persons (9.7 per cent) between 1954 and 1966. Balaclava and Kapunda also experienced minor population increases but net out-migration. The former mining townships of Kadina, Wallaroo and Burra have all suffered absolute population losses since 1947 and between 1954 and 1966 recorded net out-migrations of 496 persons (16.1 per cent), 625 persons (26 per cent) and 225 persons (15.8 per cent) respectively.

The situation was somewhat different in the long-established agricultural areas of the Adelaide Hills where intensification of cultivation, in-movement of Adelaide people and acceptance by local people of commuting as an alternative to migration has resulted in some urban growth. Thus between 1954 and 1971 Crafers-Bridgewater increased its population by 85.6 per cent to 5,301 persons and 55 per cent of this increment was due to net in-movement. Mount Barker grew only slightly from 1,609 to 1,872 persons between 1947 and 1966 but increased its population by 25 per cent to 2,340 in 1971. Victor Harbour, although an important service centre, owes much of its post-war growth (from 1,798 to 3,533 persons) to its increasing popularity as a resort and retirement centre.

The diversity of population trends within the South Australian non-metropolitan urban sector is concealed in Table 5.2, but the figures do show an overall pattern of population growth and in some places significant net migration gains. The rural areas on the other hand have experienced substantial population losses and have been important source areas for the net migration gains of the State's urban centres. Expansion of rural settlement in several parts of the State resulted in an overall gain of rural

TABLE 5.2. *South Australia : growth of the non-metropolitan urban and rural population 1947–1971*

	Urban			Rural		
Period	Population No.	Change % p.a.	Net migration No. % p.a.	Population No.	Change % p.a.	Net migration No. % p.a.
1947–54	88,462 to 104,588	+2.6	n.a.	173,456 to 201,133	+2.3	n.a.
1954–61	104,588 to 129,442	+3.4	+9,987 +1.9	201,133 to 215,328	+1.0	−10,511 −1.0
1961–6	143,499 to 161,813	+2.6	+5,126 +0.7	200,065 to 188,590	−1.1	−19,479 −1.9
1966–71	163,130 to 182,834	+2.4	n.a.	190,167 to 178,733	−1.2	n.a.

Note. Census definitions of 'urban' as at 1954, 1966 and 1971 are used for the 1947–61, 1961–6 and 1966–71 periods respectively, except that Salisbury urban area is considered metropolitan for the 1947–61 period, as is Noarlunga in the 1961–6 period; sufficient data were not available to calculate net migration in the 1947–54 and 1966–71 periods.

population between 1947 and 1961 but subsequent intercensal periods have seen an increasing rate of population loss and out-movement. Although the data necessary to estimate rural net out-migration between 1966 and 1971 were not available at the time of writing, the 6 per cent absolute loss of rural population and net migration estimates for the State's non-munici-pal local government areas indicate that heavy net migration losses have been experienced by the South Australian rural sector. High rates of net out-migration were recorded in the Murray Mallee (20.4 per cent), Yorke Peninsula (14.6 per cent), Northern Agricultural Areas (10.8 per cent, 4,436 persons), Kangaroo Island (14.3 per cent), Lower Eyre Peninsula (11.6 per cent), and Upper South-East (9.4 per cent).

Internal migration: a two-way movement

The net migration figures indicate that the general tendency for South Australia's population to concentrate in a few favoured urban localities, particularly Adelaide, is indeed a strong one. The ratio of rural to urban population within the State has widened from 37:100 in 1947 to 18:100 in 1971. An analysis of the electoral roll data, however, reveals that although movements from rural areas and smaller country towns toward larger centres are dominant there are less strong but nevertheless substantial movements in the opposite direction.

The focal position of the Adelaide metropolitan region in the State's migration pattern is confirmed in Table 5.3, but it also indicates that the

TABLE 5.3. *South Australia non-metropolitan Commonwealth electoral subdivisions: moves made by registered voters to and from metropolitan Adelaide 1961–1966*

	Outgoing moves	Incoming moves
No. of moves	25,106	15,262
Percentage of all moves	28.9	22.1
Percentage of non-metropolitan registered voters in 1961	15.8	9.6

migration relationship between Adelaide and the rest of the State is a reciprocal one. The importance of recognizing that net migration figures represent only the 'tip of the iceberg' of a complex pattern of in- and out-movements is further indicated in Table 5.4, which shows that the gross rate movements recorded by various non-metropolitan settlement cate-gories were several times larger than net gains or losses of voters. This is of critical importance when the composition of the migration stream and its counterstream are markedly different. Between 1966 and 1971, for example,

TABLE 5.4. *South Australian non-metropolitan Commonwealth electoral subdivisions: classification of residence locations of incoming voters and of former place of residence of outgoing voters 1961–1966*

Settlement category	Outgoing moves		Incoming moves	
	No.	%	No.	%
Less than 1,000 persons	25,931	44.5	19,761	41.8
1,000– 4,999 persons	19,900	34.5	15,960	33.8
5,000– 9,999 persons	2,515	4.3	2,692	5.7
10,000–29,000 persons	9,822	16.8	8,777	18.5
Total	58,168	100.1	47,190	99.8

Renmark municipality experienced a net out-migration of 368 persons, but the number of families in which the household head was born in Greece more than doubled to approximately 200.

The composition of migration streams

Migrants rarely constitute a representative cross-section of the resident population in their districts of origin and destination. Thus the demographic and social structure of those communities will be changed to a greater or lesser extent as a result of any migration that occurs. An analysis of migration differentials gives insights into the underlying causes of population movements and into changes being wrought by them.

TABLE 5.5. *South Australia: estimates of net migration for metropolitan, other urban and rural areas 1961–1966*

	Net migration			Net migration as a percentage of the 1961 population		
	Males	Females	Total	Males	Females	Total
Metropolitan	+33,599	+36,127	+69,726	+11.6	+12.1	+11.9
Other urban	+ 2,010	+ 3,116	+ 5,126	+ 2.2	+ 3.6	+ 2.9
Rural	− 9,078	−10,401	−19,479	− 8.5	−11.1	− 9.7

The net migration estimates recorded for the 1961–6 period by the 'metropolitan', 'other urban' and 'rural' sectors of the State (Table 5.5) all have an unbalanced sex composition. In both urban sectors the volume and rate of net in-migration tends to be greater for females while net out-movements from rural districts were also selective of females. Females outnumbered males in the estimates recorded by urban places experiencing net migration gains,[10] while males predominated where towns recorded net migration losses.[11] There are, however, important exceptions in towns whose economic base is such that employment opportunities for females are greatly outnumbered by those for males. In Whyalla, for example, migration selectivity between 1954 and 1966 preserved the marked masculinity of the city's population, which was associated with the bulk of employment opportunities being in the rapidly expanding heavy industrial sector. As a result the sex ratio (females per hundred males) fell from 92.2 to 81.6, but predominance of females in the 1966–71 net migration gains has resulted in an improvement of the sex ratio to 88.4.

There is insufficient space here to examine age–sex differentials in the net migration estimates recorded by the metropolitan, other urban and rural sections of the State, so attention will be focussed on the latter, since it constitutes the main source of intrastate net migration gains experienced by the urban areas and it is much less affected by the direct in-movement of people from overseas and from other States.

The pattern is one of deficits of varying intensity with the only significant gains being recorded in the age 20–24 female cohort, and important differentials are apparent from a visual inspection of Fig. 5.2. These

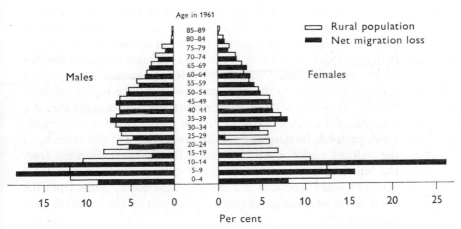

Figure 5.2. South Australia: age pyramid of 1961 rural population and net out-migration from rural areas 1961–6

differences in the distribution of ages between the net migration and resident populations were found to be statistically significant (at the 0.01 level) using the one-sample case of the Kolmogorov–Smirnov test. Some of the major characteristics of this selectivity are indicated below.

1. The net loss of children in the infant and early school ages (0–4 in 1961) is under-representative of that group in the resident rural population.

2. Net migration was particularly selective of the later school years age group (5–9) in which the high positive differential for males (6.4 per cent) was twice as large as that for females. This differential is indicative not only of the movement of children from country districts to Adelaide as dependents within family units, but also singly to attend educational institutions in the city. South Australia's only boys' agricultural high school and the major prestigious private schools are located in Adelaide. Moreover, a recent survey by the South Australian Institute of Teachers[12] indicated that students in rural areas were considerably restricted in the choice of schools and subjects available to them.

3. A sharp interchange of male and female trends occurs in the 10–14 cohort. Although strong positive differentials are maintained for males (6.3 per cent) that for female net out-movement was twice as large (15.5 per cent). The 'other urban' sector also experienced net losses of persons in this age group but this loss was representative of males and highly unrepresentative of females (negative differentials of 0.8 per cent and 7.24 per cent respectively). The main reasons for the adolescent net migration loss are twofold:

(i) The absence of tertiary educational institutions outside of Adelaide.
(ii) The cohort also contains large numbers of persons who entered the workforce for the first time between 1961 and 1966 since they were the group who reached the minimum school-leaving age (15) in that period. Undoubtedly the lack of a sufficient range and number of job opportunities[13] outside of Adelaide caused many school leavers to migrate to the metropolitan area. The highly selective female net out-movement from rural areas is to a large extent a function of the lack of scope for female participation in the agricultural, pastoral, forestry and mining industries. On the other hand the marked under-representation of female out-movement from the 'other urban' sector indicates that much movement in these centres toward Adelaide was compensated for by gains from the rural sector of females seeking employment as clerical staff, shop assistants etc.

4. In the younger working age cohorts of persons aged 15–34 in 1961 another major reversal of trends occurs. Fig. 5.2 above shows that here net migration loss is under-representative of the resident rural population and that the under-representation is more marked for females than males. In fact there was a net gain of females aged from 18 to 21. Some of the reasons for these trends can be listed as follows:

(i) A substantial backflow of females from urban areas as a result of marriage migration.[14]

(ii) The backflow of the children of rural and country town dwellers on completion of their education to take up occupations in primary industry and local businesses.

(iii) A flow of newly trained persons in tertiary service occupations to non-metropolitan areas, largely on transfer or to acquire experience for later promotion. This is apparent, for example, in a recent survey[15] which found that approximately half the staff of non-metropolitan schools were in their first three years of teaching, while the proportions of staff with that level of experience in Adelaide's infant, primary and high schools were 28 per cent, 24 per cent and 32 per cent respectively.

Although these cohorts are under-representative of the rural population it is clear from Fig. 5.2 that there was a substantial out-movement of established numbers of the workforce in rural areas and their families.

5. Migration differentials for the remaining, older age cohorts are much less marked.

It is clear, then, that the net migration losses experienced by rural communities are highly selective of females and of the school-leaving age groups. As a result the population of many rural areas is characterized by an increasing sex imbalance and general ageing compared to the State's urban areas. The ageing of the rural population structure is evident in the age structure of the male workforce at the 1966 census. Some 31.5 per cent of the primary industry workforce were aged 50 years and over compared to 25.5 per cent of males employed in all other industries, while the proportions for the highly economically active 20–49 age group were 58.5 per cent and 66 per cent respectively.

The out-movement of young people has been a feature of the State's rural areas for a long time, as can be seen from the following statements made in the 1920s: 'The city, with its up to date facilities, attractions and variety of occupations draws the younger generation to its centre.'[16] However during the 1961–6 period there was an overall net loss of established members of the rural workforce and their families.

The occupations of adult migrants

Some information regarding the occupations of migrants who are also members of the workforce can be obtained from electoral roll transfers. The utility of the data is limited by a failure to take account of overseas immigrants, new enrolments and minors entering the workforce, but they do allow the occupational composition of both in and out voter migration streams to be determined. Moreover the relative mobility of voters in different occupation groups can be obtained by comparing the proportion of all transfers into or out of non-metropolitan subdivisions made up of voters in particular occupation categories with the representation of those categories in the non-metropolitan workforce as a whole. Some brief observations regarding the mobility of a selection of occupation groups are given below.

1. Workforce in primary industry: out-migrant voters in this category (7,261) heavily outnumbered in-migrants (5,636). Although the primary sector accounted for 33.8 per cent of the State's non-metropolitan workforce in 1961 it employed only 22.4 per cent of outgoing voters and 22.1 per cent of incoming voters. The low mobility rates are due partly to the substantial fixed capital investments of many employed in primary industry.

2. Skilled and unskilled manual workers: manual workers employed in manufacturing, utility and building and construction industries also tended to have a comparatively low level of mobility. These industries employed 30.6 per cent of the 1961 non-metropolitan workforce but only 21.1 per cent and 24.2 per cent respectively of the in- and out-migrating voters.

3. White collar and professional groups: in 1961 these groups constituted 8.1 per cent of the workforce living outside of Adelaide but comprised 27.7 per cent of incoming and 25.8 per cent of the outgoing voter transfers between 1961 and 1966. The reasons for this high mobility are readily apparent. It is accepted practice of certain government departments, banks and private firms to transfer newly trained staff to non-metropolitan appointments to allow them to gain experience.

There seem to be two important aspects to this movement.

(i) The electoral transfer data indicate that many small country towns are suffering net losses of persons within this occupation group. The loss of qualified, well-educated persons who often tend to possess leadership qualities must have some depressing effect on the vitality of social life within communities already hard hit by selective out-movement of younger people.

(ii) The high mobility of this group means that their presence in a country town is often not seen as permanent. As a result their local investments – both financial and social – may be restricted. Some indirect evidence of the former is that the proportion of people owning or purchasing the dwelling in which they live is significantly greater in the metropolitan area than in the State's other urban centres and to a lesser extent the rural districts. Frequently, community projects initiated by members of the 'floating population' may lapse when the leaders are transferred elsewhere.

The scale of population turnover in South Australian country towns can be seen from the example of Renmark, where a recent survey[17] found that 24.6 per cent of the resident population had definite intentions of moving out of the town within five years. Slightly more than half of these nominated Adelaide as their destination.

Causes of internal migration

The most important factor impelling migration from South Australian country towns and rural districts toward the major urban centres is undoubtedly the greater number, variety and type of educational, economic and social opportunities in Adelaide and, to a lesser degree, other cities. The opportunities gap between the rural and metropolitan sector has been widened in the last fifty years by structural changes in the State's workforce. The substitution of capital and scientific inputs for labour inputs on farms has greatly increased production per capita in primary industry. Demand for agricultural products has not kept pace with this increase so that demand for labour has been reduced.

The existence of a static employment situation is certainly not new in South Australian rural areas. It has been shown[18] that once a section of the State was taken up for initial close agricultural settlement there tended to be a shortage of work in that area for the next generation, thus forcing some out-migration to occur. Much of this out-movement, however, was absorbed in districts recently opened up for closer settlement. This close settlement continued into the 1950s when large tracts of the South-East, Upper and Lower Murray, Kangaroo Island and Eyre Peninsula regions were developed. However, for persons entering the workforce in the 1960s few job opportunities were available in primary industry in any part of the State. Moreover, in the long-established agricultural areas amalgamation of holdings and replacement of labour by capital investment has produced a situation in which opportunities are not only static but declining, so that established members of the rural workforce have been made redundant. In fact there was a strong positive correlation between the rate of out-migration from South Australian non-metropolitan districts between 1961 and 1966 and the proportion of the male workforce in those areas at the beginning of the migration period who were employed in primary industry.[19]

The out-movement of the rural primary population has had an inevitable debilitating effect on the numbers of secondary population providing goods and services for them. Smailes[20] has pointed out that the ageing of the rural population and net migration losses of rural dwellers have eroded the basis of support for fourth order central places (1966 population range from 310 to 3,116 persons). The decline in the numbers of merchants, tradesmen, business and professional people in these centres is being further hastened by the growing ability and tendency of rural residents to bypass smaller centres and seek goods and services in the larger provincial towns and Adelaide. In another paper Smailes[21] has demonstrated the presence of a metropolitan trade shadow over extensive parts of the State, in which rural residents carry out more than half of their trade in Adelaide.

This decline of employment opportunities in rural areas has been concurrent with an unprecedented expansion of secondary and tertiary industries in the Adelaide metropolitan area and to a lesser extent in provincial urban centres. In addition all of the State's major tertiary education institutions are located in Adelaide. Thus the urban sector has absorbed much of the drift from the rural districts.

The mere existence of interregional differences such as these is not sufficient in itself to cause population movement. Potential migrants must be aware of them and this knowledge is a function of the nature of their communications with Adelaide and other urban centres. The post-war period has seen a substantial lessening of the friction of distance within the State. Smailes[22] has convincingly demonstrated that both the time and real money costs of personal travel were dramatically reduced between 1933 and 1969. This has resulted in an increase in the frequency of shopping and social visits made to Adelaide by rural folk which, together with the extension of Adelaide's newspaper, radio and television media into most parts of the State, has meant that the level of information concerning the opportunities available in Adelaide is high and accurate.

It is necessary to distinguish between persons (together with families) transferred by their employers, and others moving toward the State's largest urban centres. Although the factors discussed above undoubtedly have some effect on their decision to migrate, the addition of the fourth and often most important force of their employer's priorities, administrative and promotional procedures sets them apart as a special case.

Although the main gradient of intrastate migration is toward the large urban centres, predominantly Adelaide, it is important to remember that there is a weaker migration stream operating in the opposite direction. The main causes here appear to be return movement of former residents after schooling or marriage and of persons transferred by their employers.

Conclusion

This chapter has examined one aspect of the post-war operation of the urbanization process in South Australia – the intrastate redistribution of population. It is clear that the pattern has been one of increasing concentration of population at two levels. Firstly, the Adelaide metropolitan area recorded large net in-movements from all parts of the State, which together with its even larger net gains of overseas immigrants resulted in its primacy within South Australia being increased. In addition the migration data indicate that several of the State's major regional centres experienced growth due to migration gains from surrounding rural areas. The inevitable corollary of urban migration gains has been widespread movement out of long-established rural districts. In regions where post-war developments have resulted in intensification or expansion of the area under cultivation migration gains were experienced up to 1966, but there are indications that the last intercensal period has seen migration losses even in those areas.

The population movements and migration differentials recognized here are of sufficient magnitude to have significant social, economic and demographic implications for policy makers in both the areas that are 'sending' migrants and those receiving them. The effect of intrastate population movements into metropolitan Adelaide (although not the largest component of its growth) on the quality of life and economic efficiency of the city certainly needs further study. The growth of Adelaide beyond some threshold level may well result in the city being subject to some diseconomies, so that a solution to some of the major urbanization problems may lie in a policy of decentralization to a favoured locality elsewhere in the State.

It has been shown[23] that heavy emigration also has important social effects on the communities which the migrants leave behind. In South Australia the age–sex selectivity of the rural net migration loss has resulted in an ageing of the rural population and a lowering of its sex ratio. This, together with a reduction in both the primary and secondary population, has produced an accelerating diminution of the social and economic potential of many rural areas. It is clearly unrealistic to think in terms of developing most rural communities to stop the drain of population from the countryside. However, the quality of life in rural areas with declining populations could be greatly improved by judicious consolidation of communities, so that economies of scale can be achieved and basic social and economic services provided.

A third policy area is one that is often overlooked – the migrants themselves. With the present depressed market situation for many primary products and increased application of technology in primary industry it is inevitable that the flow of persons from rural areas will continue. Major difficulties are faced not so much by school leavers but by those who were previously employed in rural areas and often have fixed capital investments in those areas. Heady[24] has argued (in the American context) that the movement of many persons in the latter group toward cities is a necessary adjustment, and hence 'we must provide appropriate compensation, training opportunities, mobility endowments and other conditions for all relevant population strata of adjusting regions and communities.' Such a programme would seem to be applicable in Australia, where many rural dwellers with heavy local capital investments and skills which are not readily transferable to the urban context are forced to remain in rural areas and accept a declining real income or to migrate to the city suffering financial loss and often confronting difficulties in adjusting to urban life. In several European countries, programmes initiated to ease the transfer of persons from one type of employment to another (particularly from rural to urban jobs) have resulted in a substantial reduction in costs, personal hardship and social damage resulting from the change.[25]

There is, then, a need for a co-ordinated regional planning policy which minimizes the total community costs incurred in the increasing concentration of population and maximizes the benefits to be obtained from it. Such a plan would need to take into account the existing pattern of internal migration and thus it is imperative that more research be undertaken to increase our knowledge of its nature, causes and effects.

NOTES

1 Based on definitions of urban areas used in the 1954 and 1971 census enumerations respectively.
2 C. Fenner, 'A geographical enquiry into the growth, distribution and movement of population in South Australia 1836–1927', *Royal Society of South Australia, Transactions and Proceedings, 53,* 1929, pp. 79–145.
3 G. H. Lawton, 'The growth and distribution of population', in R. J. Best (ed.), *Introducing South Australia,* Adelaide, 1958, pp. 58–47.
4 M. Williams, 'The changing face of South Australia', in M. Williams (ed.), *South Australia from the Air,* Adelaide, 1969, pp. 1–17.
5 G. J. Hugo, 'Internal migration in South Australia 1961–66', unpublished M.A. thesis, Flinders University, 1971.
6 See United Nations, *Manuals on Methods of Estimating Population, Manual VI: Methods of Measuring Internal Migration,* Department of Economic and Social Affairs, Population Studies no. 47, United Nations, New York, 1970.
7 Discussed in detail by the South Australian Town Planning Committee's *Report on the Metropolitan Area of Adelaide,* Adelaide, 1962, and Williams, 'The changing face of South Australia', pp. 2–5.
8 Townships outside Adelaide with a population of 1,000 persons or more.
9 Williams, 'The changing face of South Australia', pp. 5–13.
10 E.g. Mount Gambier – male net in-migration 163 persons (2.1%), female 268 (3.6%); Berri – male 170 (20.1%), female 193 (23.1%).
11 E.g. Naracoorte – male net out-migration 259 persons (11.3%), female 140 (6.6%); Port Augusta – male 318 (6.1%), female 158 (3.5%).
12 Reported in *The Advertiser,* daily newspaper, Adelaide, 2 April 1970.
13 See R. K. Hefford, 'Decentralization in South Australia', *Australian Geographic Studies, 3,* 1965, pp. 79–96.
14 Mean age at first marriage for South Australian females fell from 22.4 in 1961 to 21.8 years in 1966.
15 South Australian Institute of Teachers, *Survey into Conditions in Schools,* Adelaide, 1970, p. 15.
16 Fenner, 'A geographical enquiry into the growth, distribution and movement of population in South Australia 1836–1927', p. 138.
17 G. J. Hugo, 'The growth and structure of the population of Renmark, South Australia', unpublished paper, Flinders University, 1971, p. 7.
18 Hugo, 'Internal migration in South Australia 1961–66', pp. 21–68.
19 $r = + 0.52$ significant at the 0.0001 level (138 df).
20 P. J. Smailes, 'Some aspects of the South Australian urban system', *Australian Geographer, 11,* 1969, p. 39.
21 P. J. Smailes, 'A metropolitan trade shadow: the case of Adelaide, South Australia', *Tijdschrift voor Economische en Sociale Geografie, 60,* 1969, pp. 329–45.

22 P. J. Smailes, 'Some aspects of the South Australian urban system: a reply', *Australian Geographer*, *11*, 1970, pp. 397–8.
23 E.g. D. Lowenthal and L. Comitas, 'Emigration and depopulation: some neglected aspects of population geography', *Geographical Review*, *52*, 1962, pp. 195–210.
24 E. O. Heady, 'Sociological aspects and implications of u.s. farm policies', *Sociologia Ruralis*, *8*, 1968, pp. 368–9.
25 Organization for Economic Co-operation and Development, *Adaptation of Rural and Foreign Workers to Industry*, Paris, 1965, p. 9.

6

International migration and metropolitan growth in Australia

I. H. BURNLEY

It has been shown how post-war immigration has been of considerable significance in the growth of the Australian population, and particularly important in the growth of the southern metropolitan State capitals. In this chapter, the variations in impact on metropolitan areas are further reviewed, along with the role of immigration in population character and change within sub areas of the large cities.

Even in 1947, most of the overseas-born population was more urbanized than the Australian-born: 31.8 per cent of the latter in rural areas, 24.3 per cent of the former. However, Yugoslavs, Italians and Maltese were relatively more numerous in rural areas than in the total population. But several of the rural migrations of these groups tapered off after an initial upsurge in the first post-war decade.[1] By 1966, all of the overseas-born groups were more urbanized than the Australian-born and more concentrated in the metropolitan cities. In 1966, 73.1 per cent of the overseas born population was located in the State capitals compared with 54.8 per cent of the Australian-born.

The majority of immigrants preferred urban life and especially large city life, because there have been consistently more jobs available in metropolitan and industrial centres than in smaller centres and rural areas.[2] For decades, the demand for labour in the country areas has declined in response to the impact of increasing mechanization; traditional specialized craftsmen servicing farmers have no longer been required with technological change and small towns have also lost in the competition with larger centres in the provision of services.

The post-war immigrants arrived when most new employment opportunities arose in manufacturing in the southern metropolitan centres of Sydney, Melbourne and Adelaide and the fast growing larger cities of Wollongong and Geelong. In Melbourne in 1966, for example, 45.5 per cent of male workers employed in manufacturing were born overseas, as were 41.5 per cent of those in building and construction, compared with 36 per cent of the whole labour force. Migrants from southern Europe, Yugoslavia and Poland were predominantly unskilled on arrival, in contrast to migrants from north-west Europe. Of a sample of Displaced Persons shipping lists, 66.5 per cent of Yugoslavs were unskilled and semi-skilled on arrival.[3] In the years 1967–8, which are indicative of trends in the period under study, 64 per cent of the Yugoslavs and 75.9, 49.7 and 49.6 per cent of the Greeks, Italians and Maltese respectively were unskilled on arrival, compared with only 10.6 per cent of the British and 26.6 per cent of all overseas-born.[4] The magnets for such migrants have been the large centres with rapidly expanding mass production assembly type or heavy manufacturing industry. However, chain migration and kinship networks have been major factors in southern European immigration to Australia. These are discussed in detail in a later chapter.

Immigration and metropolitan population growth

Three possible techniques can be utilized in the assessment of the role of international migration and metropolitan growth in Australia. These are the 'residual' method already used in the discussion of the various demographic components in urbanization in Chapter 3 above, the simple increase technique, which has certain advantages but which tends to understate the role of immigration, and the Life Table Survival Ratio method, whereby the overseas-born population in the capital cities is extrapolated through time using the Australian Life Tables. However, because the overseas-born population has a different age structure on arrival, which varies because of the differential role of the different ethnic groups between cities, and because the mortality pattern varies, the total Australian Life Table was not used for the foreign-born populations in the cities. Thus the 'residual' and 'simple increase' methods are used in this chapter. The advantage of the 'simple increase' technique is that comparison can be made between trends in different local government areas within cities, an analysis which cannot be undertaken with the other two methods. In the following discussion, the simple increase method is used with L.G.A.s and total metropolitan areas, while the residual technique is used with the larger metropolitan statistical divisions. Period of residence data are not utilized because they are a 'survival' measure which cannot be meaningfully compared with an increase measure.[5] With both methods and areal units, the outer boundaries were standardized backwards through time to approximately equal the 1966 boundaries. In Table 6.1, both methods are utilized to illustrate the impact of immigration on metropolitan and larger city growth in Australia between 1947 and 1966.

In Sydney, Melbourne and Adelaide, immigration was more important than the other two demographic components – natural increase and internal migration – in metropolitan population growth. If the children born to immigrants in Australia (included in the natural increase figures) are included in the number of persons in the three cities being present directly or indirectly due to immigration, it is estimated that over two-thirds of

TABLE 6.1. *The role of immigration in large city growth in Australia 1947–1966*

City	Simple increase method, Metropolitan areas		Residual method, metropolitan statistical divisions	
	Overseas-born increase	% Total population increase	Net migration of overseas-born	% Total population growth
Sydney	329,321	42.28	463,413	55.00
Melbourne	409,724	51.11	522,111	58.70
Brisbane	58,265	18.62	108,820	34.00
Adelaide	164,736	47.89	203,877	56.50
Perth	83,056	35.63	114,488	44.80
Hobart	10,661	24.83	18,286	32.10
Canberra	22,843	29.60	29,002	35.60
Major non-metropolitan				
Newcastle	10,881	16.87	19,748	20.99
Wollongong	40,097	37.77	44,578	40.86
Geelong	22,470	31.84	27,020	43.32

Source: Censuses of the Commonwealth of Australia, 1947 and 1966.

Note. Net migration figures for Newcastle, Wollongong and Geelong calculated on the basis that deaths among the overseas-born are proportional to their components in the 1966 city populations.

post-war population growth in Sydney, Melbourne and Adelaide was the result of immigration.

In Perth immigration was the most important of the three demographic elements in growth, while in Newcastle and Geelong it was the second most important. It was only in Brisbane that immigration was less important or only equal to either natural increase or internal migration of the Australian-born in population growth. In the two industrial cities on the urbanizing New South Wales coast, Wollongong and Newcastle, immigration played very different roles in growth. In rapidly growing Wollongong migrants entered the fast developing iron and steel industry at Port Kembla, whereas in Newcastle immigrants took a more peripheral role in manufacturing in which expansion was comparatively sluggish in the post World War II period.

Birthplace components in metropolitan growth

Certain groups played a conspicuous part in the strong overseas-born contribution to growth in Sydney, Melbourne and Adelaide. In Melbourne, the Italian increase accounted for 10.8 per cent of total increase, the British Isles 10.7 and the Greek 7.3. The three main southern European groups (Greeks, Italians and Maltese) accounted for 21 per cent of the growth of Melbourne, 13.5 per cent in Sydney and 11.4 per cent in Adelaide. The British Isles component in growth was most significant in Adelaide, where the South Australian State government had its own policy of incentives for migrants from the British Isles.

Variations occurred among the metropolitan centres in the contribution of different birthplace groups to the overseas-born increase, with differing implications for the population ecology of the cities. Thus the three main southern European groups contributed 41.3 per cent of the overseas-born increase in Melbourne, 31.9 and 23.8 per cent in Sydney and Adelaide, and only 14.5 per cent in Brisbane. The British Isles-born, on the other hand, were responsible for only 21 and 17 per cent of the overseas-born increase in Melbourne and Sydney, but their contributions in Adelaide, Perth and Brisbane were much greater, being 44, 36 and 34 per cent respectively.

Immigration and intra-metropolitan growth and change

Immigration to the major southern State capitals of Australia has been of such volume since 1947 that it has profoundly affected population composition within the metropolitan areas. The impact on the internal metropolitan demographic structure has of course varied in relation to variations in the contribution of immigration to metropolitan population growth and also inter-city contrasts in ethnic composition of the immigrant streams.

Five areal categories within each mainland capital city have been delineated in terms of population growth, change and the impact of immigration for the period under study. In four of these ecological areas, immigration has profoundly influenced population change and structure. Regrettably, local government areas had to be used rather than the more reliable aggregated collector's districts, because birthplace statistics by C.D. were not available for censuses prior to 1961.

The ecological categories were:

(1) An inner area with a steeply declining Australian-born population but with substantial 'replacement' by immigrants. This process of replacement was one of ecological succession, which Burgess and others found in United States cities with the great migration to the U.S.A. from Europe in the years prior to World War I.[6]

(2) Areas adjacent to category 1 with a moderately declining Australian-born population but with an overseas-born increase offsetting this decline and resulting in a total population increase of moderate dimensions (see Figs. 6.1 and 6.2).

(3) Areas of moderate Australian-born and total population increase, where immigration has contributed substantially to the total population increase in areas of mainly pre-war residential development.

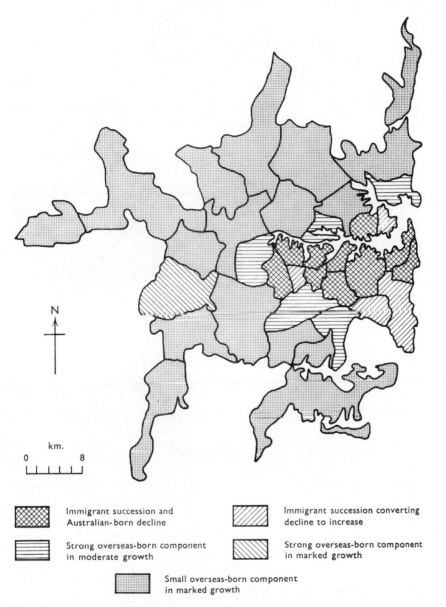

Figure 6.1. Immigration and growth, Sydney 1947–66

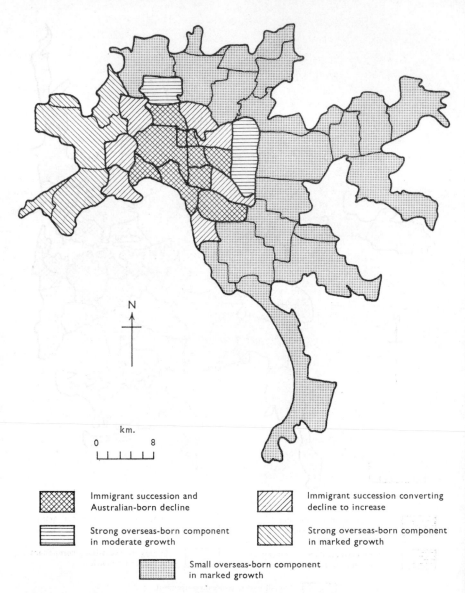

N

km.
0   8

Immigrant succession and
Australian-born decline

Immigrant succession converting
decline to increase

Strong overseas-born component
in moderate growth

Strong overseas-born component
in marked growth

Small overseas-born component
in marked growth

Figure 6.2. Immigration and growth, Melbourne 1947–66

(4) Certain industrial suburbs on the metropolitan perimeter where there has been marked total population increase and a strong immigrant contribution to growth.

(5) Residential suburbs on the metropolitan periphery, where there has been marked population increase but a relatively slight influence of immigration in these areas of largely post-war built housing.

Inner areas of total population decline

Burgess's term 'ecological succession' is used rather than 'replacement' in order to avoid identification with the notion of replacement used in demography, which is concerned with births replacing deaths. The concern here is the extent to which a declining inner city population (declining due to mortality and out-migration) is being 'replaced' due to international migration. The bottom line of Table 6.2 is a succession index, whereby overseas-born increases in the areas of population decline during 1947–66 are converted to a percentage of the decrease of the declining birthplaces in the same period. In most L.G.A.s where the Australian-born numbers fell, the British Isles- and New Zealand-born declined also. The extent of the Australian-born decline would have been greater had the children born to migrants in Australia not been included in the Australian-born figures, but instead added to the overseas-born increase.

Immigrant succession in the areas of declining population was greatest in Melbourne out of the three metropolitan areas where immigration has been the largest component of post-war population increase. Taking the areas of total decline in aggregate, the succession indices for Sydney, Melbourne and Adelaide were 46.1, 59.7 and 42.3 (per cent), while the percentage decreases of the declining birthplace groups were 31.5, 37.5 and 36.6 per cent respectively. In Brisbane, the metropolitan area whose 1947–66 growth was least affected by immigration, the declining birthplace groups decreased by 28.7 per cent while the overseas-born succession score was only 32.4. These figures must be used with caution because L.G.A. boundaries and size vary between metropolitan areas and do not necessarily conform with 'natural' ecological areas. It appears, however, that the greater volume of international migration to Melbourne resulted in a greater degree of ecological succession than in cities in which immigration was less important in growth.

One factor in the more marked arresting of population decline within inner Melbourne was the greater southern European element in the overseas-born increase, evident in a comparison of Tables 6.2 and 6.3. With mainly unskilled occupations, southern Europeans had little initial economic choice in standard of housing, and older semi-detached and terrace dwellings in inner suburbs attracted new immigrants into declining Australian-born working class areas. Greeks and Italians were often

TABLE 6.2. *Birthplace components in overseas-born increase in areas of Australian-born and total population decline;
Melbourne 1947–1966*

Major overseas birthplaces	L.G.A.s										
	Melbourne	Fitzroy	Collingwood	Richmond	Port Melbourne	South Melbourne	Brunswick	Hawthorn	Caulfield	St Kilda	Prahran
United Kingdom and Ireland	—	—	—	—	19.25	—	—	11.77	7.60	21.49	—
Italy	47.26	38.71	20.78	20.66	13.85	11.58	55.07	18.83	8.49	5.70	7.03
Greece	13.95	36.71	63.95	51.94	46.14	51.04	25.61	23.88	9.92	8.13	48.74
Malta	13.05	6.47	5.88	3.79	8.55	7.27	6.20	1.12	1.06	0.82	0.81
Total main southern European birthplaces	74.26	81.89	90.61	76.39	68.54	69.89	86.88	43.93	19.47	14.65	56.58
Yugoslavia	6.57	7.42	5.95	6.33	1.35	4.16	2.74	5.53	3.73	5.33	4.70
Poland	—	0.47	1.15	2.07	1.65	2.75	0.21	3.66	22.44	14.00	5.86
Germany	2.01	0.95	0.87	2.39	1.68	3.31	1.35	6.59	9.53	7.77	5.11
Netherlands	1.60	0.58	0.58	0.76	1.13	1.52	0.41	3.99	3.38	2.82	2.80
Total overseas-born increase	14,082	10,896	8,074	10,968	2,722	5,885	18,004	6,411	11,366	14,220	10,911
Total Australian-born and other birthplaces undergoing decline	−37,946	−16,057	−15,373	−17,828	−4,336	−19,104	−23,521	−10,147	−15,160	−14,409	−16,038
Percentage decline	−40.24	−51.86	−52.33	−45.98	−32.73	−44.71	−41.61	−27.61	−21.07	−29.53	−30.68
Percentage decline total population	−23.90	−15.94	−24.53	−17.42	−11.36	−30.42	−9.59	−9.23	−4.74	−0.32	−8.73
Overseas-born increase as percentage Australian-born and other decrease	37.11	67.86	52.52	61.52	62.78	30.80	76.54	63.18	74.97	98.68	69.03

Note. — denotes declining birthplace group.

Source: Censuses of the Commonwealth of Australia, 1947 and 1966.

TABLE 6.3. *Population change in areas of Australian-born and total population decline, metropolitan Sydney 1947–1966*

L.G.A.s	Sydney	Marrick- ville	Leichhardt	Drum- moyne	Ashfield	Strathfield	Concord	North Sydney	Waverly	Woollahra
Southern European percentage in overseas-born increase	56.30	67.12	71.90	74.29	43.40	28.34	44.15	15.11	17.20	10.58
Total overseas-born increase	29,762	19,852	11,167	4,505	7,278	2,737	3,230	4,765	8,950	4,519
Total Australian-born and other birthplaces undergoing decline	−84,474	−31,808	−22,098	−6,860	−19,105	−3,899	−5,514	−13,395	−20,143	−11,453
Percentage decline	−41.54	−36.31	−32.04	−21.06	−22.95	−14.20	−19.20	−26.24	−28.54	−22.62
Total population percentage decline	−25.58	−13.48	−15.56	−7.14	−6.32	−4.17	−8.04	−14.29	−14.96	−12.78
Overseas-born increase as percentage Australian-born and other decrease	35.23	62.41	50.53	65.57	72.02	70.19	57.74	35.57	44.43	39.45

Source: Censuses of the Commonwealth of Australia, 1947 and 1966.

joined by kinsfolk from the same region of origin and ethnic neighbourhoods developed, e.g. migrants from Viggiano in Carlton (Melbourne)[7]
and Levkas in part of Redfern (Sydney).[8]

In Table 6.2, it can be seen how the three main southern European
groups constituted three-quarters or more of the overseas-born increase
in Melbourne, Fitzroy, Collingwood and Richmond local government areas,
all L.G.A.s in central Melbourne with relatively steep Australian-born
declines in the 1947–66 period and considerable immigrant ecological
succession. Thus in 1966, all four had overseas-born proportions of the
population in excess of 40 per cent, while that of Fitzroy was 48 per cent.
Fitzroy then had the greatest degree of ecological succession, considering
its very steep Australian-born population decrease of almost 52 per cent
and 68 per cent 'replacement' through ecological succession, of which 82
per cent was due to southern European immigration.

By comparison, in Sydney the degree of ecological succession of the
overseas-born, although considerable, was not as great and the southern
European component, although the major element in immigrant population growth, was not as marked as in Melbourne. Whereas in central
Melbourne there were four local government areas with over 40 per cent
of the population born overseas in 1966, in Sydney the overseas-born
proportion of the inner city population in the areas of maximum ecological
succession was at least 10 per cent lower.

There were other L.G.A.s in central Sydney and Melbourne where a
considerable decline in Australian-born numbers took place, with an
invasion and succession by groups other than southern Europeans, such
as St Kilda and Caulfield (Melbourne) and Woollahra and Waverly
(Sydney). St Kilda in particular had an Australian-born decline of almost
30 per cent but with almost comparable succession in which British Isles-
and Polish-born figured prominently. Originally a higher status area,
St Kilda declined with out-movement of Australian-born, although housing
quality and costs were still significantly higher than in suburbs already
described, as F. L. Jones has observed in conjunction with areal socio-
economic status.[9]

In Adelaide, there were similar trends in the inner city as in Sydney and
Melbourne in the 1947–66 period. In Adelaide L.G.A., the declining birthplace groups (Australian-, British Isles- and New Zealand-born) lost by
18,764 or 56.09 per cent, while the overseas-born increase compensated
for this decline by only 12.53 per cent, of whom 45 per cent were southern
Europeans. But in adjacent inner metropolitan L.G.A.s, there was more
substantial population succession. In Hindmarsh, the host society population decreased by 6,143 or 42.65 per cent, while the succession index was
55.4. Over 60 per cent of this succession consisted of Greeks, Italians and
Maltese. In Thebarton L.G.A., the Australian-born and British Isles-born

populations declined by 43 per cent, with 63.18 per cent of this decrease replaced by invasion of migrant populations, 78 per cent of which were Greeks and Italians. Similar trends occurred in other L.G.A.s within central Adelaide, particularly in Kensington and Norwood L.G.A.s (with a large influx of Italians) as well as in St Peters, Unley, Walkerville, Prospect and Colonel Light Gardens. Walkerville, Prospect and Colonel Light Gardens had relatively small (under 20 per cent) Australian-born losses in the 1947–66 period and comparatively limited succession, but with continued strong migration to Adelaide along with ageing of housing, areas of intense ecological succession may move out to include these and other adjacent suburbs.

In Sydney, Melbourne and Adelaide, the Greek concentrations in inner suburbs continued to grow with heavy migration during 1961–6, but Italian numbers fell in central suburbs (excepting Brunswick in Melbourne and Drummoyne, Annandale and Leichhardt in Sydney) with movement to middle distance and outer suburbs. Greeks were substantially replacing Italians in southern Fitzroy (Melbourne) and Redfern, southern Leichhardt and northern Marrickville in Sydney. Between 1966 and 1971, Yugoslav and Turkish migrants arriving under newly formulated governmental agreements began to form settlement clusters in these long-term migrant-receiving areas, replacing the Italians in several areas and even Greeks in some street blocks. By 1971, the impact of immigration on the inner suburbs had been such that it had indirectly arrested population decline in some areas which between 1947 and 1966 had lost population heavily, through the children being born to relatively recent arrivals (particularly the Greeks). Thus immigration resulted in the beginning of a new demographic cycle in areas which had long been typified by out-migration of persons between 25 and 45 and by an ageing residual population. By 1971, new accommodation and population stresses were being felt by pre-school centres and schools in the inner city, as well as by hospitals and other welfare services and institutions, and it was evident that such pressures would increase in the immediate future.

Although considerable population succession occurred in inner city declining areas, tenement neighbourhoods, such as occurred in large United States cities with the great immigration prior to World War I, did not form.[10] In 1966, whereas 69.9 per cent of Australian-born household heads in private dwellings owned or were buying their own homes, 82 per cent of Italians and 73 and 76 per cent of Greeks and Maltese household heads were owners and buyers.[11]

> *Areas of declining Australian-born population but total*
> *increase due to immigration*

Fringeing the inner suburbs of Australian-born decrease and ecological succession in all five mainland metropolitan areas were areas of moderately declining Australian-born population, but with immigrant invasion from the central suburbs and direct succession movement from overseas, resulting in total population increase (Figs. 6.1 and 6.2). These areas were most extensive in Melbourne, as Table 6.4 indicates.

Many factors were involved, such as partitioning of old homes into smaller units, and a higher density due to larger family size, with a higher proportion of secondary family unit members in households with primary families. In unpublished census tabulations at the State level, a higher number of secondary family unit members were in households with primary (simple family) family member heads in the southern European birthplace groups. Certainly in Sydney, Greek, Italian and Maltese heads of house-holds had more persons per dwelling unit (4.80, 4.09 and 4.66 respectively) than the Australian-born (3.29) in 1966 (as ascertained from unpublished cross-tabulations of birthplace of household head by persons per room and number of rooms). In contrast to the inner suburbs of total population decline, the British Isles-born were significant in the overseas-born increase in the Melbourne L.G.A.s, Williamstown and Brighton, and in the North Shore Sydney L.G.A. of Mosman. Comparable areas of total increase due to immigration in areas of Australian-born decline in other cities were Glenelg in Adelaide, Mosman Park and Freemantle in Perth, and Fernberg and Toowong in Brisbane.

Outer areas of Australian-born and total population increase

The overseas-born component in the growth of outer suburban areas of Australian-born and total population increase was less than the equivalent element in total metropolitan growth. In Melbourne, 27.7 per cent of the 850,941 total population increase in these areas was overseas-born compared with 51 per cent of the metropolitan total increase. In Sydney, the overseas-born constituted 24.4 per cent of the 872,080 total increase in comparable areas, compared with a contribution to total metropolitan growth of 42 per cent. Table 6.5 indicates by implication that the British Isles-, German- and Netherlands-born components in overseas-born increase were much greater than in the inner suburbs and greater also than for the metropolitan areas as a whole. The British Isles-born increases, however, undoubtedly included pre-war migrants who moved from inner suburbs to outer areas between 1947 and 1966.

In the outer suburbs developed mainly before World War II, and thus having relatively moderate population increases since 1947 (generally under 40 per cent), the overseas-born contribution to growth was greater than in the newer areas developed mainly since 1947. It can be seen from Figs. 6.1 and 6.2 that these slower growing areas tended to be arranged con-centrically around the inner areas already described, so that the movement

TABLE 6.4. *Population change in areas of Australian-born decline with total population increase, Sydney and Melbourne 1947–1966*

Melbourne	L.G.A.s						
	Northcote	Kew	Essendon	Williamstown	Footscray	Malvern	Brighton
Southern European percentage in overseas-born increase	77.71	37.23	68.80	34.45	56.00	37.96	17.29
Total overseas-born increase	14,099	4,437	10,867	5,960	14,223	5,504	3,313
Total Australian-born and other birthplaces	− 2,846	− 2,480	− 8,005	− 1,982	− 8,859	− 4,559	− 2,465
Percentage decline	− 6.36	− 8.30	−15.56	− 8.36	−18.10	−10.35	− 6.97
Total population percentage increase	+25.04	+ 6.34	+ 5.17	+15.03	+10.03	+ 1.92	+ 2.13

Sydney	L.G.A.s			
	Mosman	Botany	Randwick	Burwood
Southern European percentage in overseas-born increase	10.04	41.64	31.03	34.31
Total overseas-born increase	2,233	6,548	16,104	5,244
Total Australian-born and other birthplaces undergoing decline	− 1,669	− 1,862	− 3,401	− 3,750
Percentage decline	− 7.16	− 6.33	− 3.79	−13.81
Total population percentage increase	+ 2.05	+17.28	+12.59	+ 4.92

Source: Censuses of the Commonwealth of Australia, 1947 and 1966.

TABLE 6.5. *Overseas-born component of total population increase in outer areas, Sydney and Melbourne 1966*

Areas of moderate total population increase (below 40 per cent). Mainly pre-war residential development

L.G.A.S	Southern European percentage of overseas-born increase	Total overseas-born increase	Overseas-born percentage of total increase
Canterbury	49.21	12,777	77.88
Rockdale	47.51	7,076	96.79
Auburn	40.12	3,794	58.39
Hunter's Hill	20.25	976	35.67
Lane Cove	10.25	2,204	41.65
Camberwell	22.00	8,485	35.53
Coburg	67.77	13,611	71.75
Preston	60.68	14,464	33.64
Heidelberg-Dandenong Valley	17.61	8,431	18.13

Areas of marked population increase (over 80 per cent). Post-war residential development

L.G.A.S	Southern European percentage of overseas-born increase	Total overseas-born increase	Overseas-born percentage of total increase
Sydney			
Parramatta	22.11	11,252	23.29
Blacktown	20.12	19,813	23.78
Fairfield	24.94	25,400	35.79
Holroyd	44.58	10,237	24.55
Bankstown	16.57	23,731	20.24
Ryde	29.07	7,235	17.78
Other metropolitan	11.59	85,408	20.01
Melbourne			
Moorabin	16.63	14,675	19.68
Broadmeadows	34.55	21,733	27.85
Keilor	33.49	15,173	40.80
Sunshine	37.40	23,824	44.11
Other metropolitan	15.70	115,254	25.62

Source: Censuses of the Commonwealth of Australia, 1947 and 1966.

Note. The areas in this table are bounded by official metropolitan area boundaries as at 1966 and 1947 figures are adjusted to conform with the 1966 boundaries.

into these districts was one of invasion from contiguous inner areas as well as direct migration from overseas.

In the rapidly growing, *residential* non-industrial outer suburbs, the impact of immigration on growth was due mainly to British Isles-born and north-west European settlers, although the importance in growth, as noted earlier, was significantly less than its role in total metropolitan growth. But in the industrial outer suburbs, such as Fairfield in Sydney, and Keilor, Altona and Sunshine on the western perimeter of Melbourne, immigration was exceedingly important in growth, in particular immigration of Maltese and Italians, but also British Isles-born and east Europeans. In Adelaide, immigrants accounted for over 65 per cent of the growth of the satellite new town of Elizabeth, which includes industry; seven-tenths of the immigrant flow consisting of British Isles-born.

Between 1961 and 1966, the role of the overseas-born in the growth of rapidly expanding outer Melbourne areas such as Moorabin remained insignificant, but in other new suburbs, such as Knox-Sherbrooke and Dandenong to the east, migrants, including Italians, were beginning to make an impact, 'leapfrogging' the belt of high-rent suburbs in between. Between 1966 and 1971, there was evidence of continued immigration of the overseas-born to these relatively low-cost eastern fringe suburbs.[12] Furthermore, the sheer volume of Italian migration to Melbourne resulted in a radial wedge-shaped movement of Italian settlement from inner areas through Brunswick to modest new housing areas in Broadmeadows and Heidelberg on the northern periphery.[13] Different aspirations of ethnic and cultural groups might be involved, for in contrast to the Italians the Greeks, despite similar socio-economic status and considerable migration to the cities, made a negligible impact on outer surburban development.

The impact of immigration on metropolitan age and sex structure

The characteristic pattern of immigration to Australia during the post-war period has been a movement of persons mainly in the 20–40 age range, with relatively few older and younger persons. Southern and eastern Europeans migrated with comparatively few children or aged persons, the southern Europeans in particular preferring to start their families in Australia. However, the British Isles-born age structure on arrival, like that of the Dutch and Germans, was more balanced than those of the other immigrant groups.

The resultant age structure of the overseas-born population in Melbourne and Sydney as at 1966 was the main reason why the overseas-born contribution to the labour force was significantly greater than that to the total population. The overseas-born contributed little directly to the under 14 and over 70 age groups, the greatest impact occurring in the 20–24 age range in both Melbourne and Sydney in 1966. In Sydney, however, the overseas-born contribution to the aged population over 65 was proportionately greater than in Melbourne, due most likely to the larger long-resident British Isles-born population.

In Melbourne, 43.0 per cent of the 25–29 year old males were overseas-born at the 1966 census, compared with almost 40 per cent of the females. Almost 46 per cent of the 30–34 year old males in Melbourne were born overseas compared with 37 per cent of the females in the same age group. Almost 22 per cent of males aged 30–34 were born in the three southern European countries of Italy, Greece and Malta, compared with only 8.9 per cent born in the British Isles.

In both Sydney and Melbourne, the British Isles contributions to the aged and age group 0–9 were the most significant of the overseas-born groups, reflecting family migration made possible by the assisted passage scheme. By contrast, with southern Europeans in particular, children aged 0–9 were proportionately less significant. Masculinity was greater with Italians and Greeks than with most other groups, especially in the age range 30–45, but below these ages numbers tended to be more balanced, with a female surplus of Greeks and Italians in the 15–24 age range, reflecting chain migration of wives and other female relatives of older male cohorts who migrated earlier to Australia.

In the inner suburbs, the immigrant impact on the age structure was profound. By utilizing special cross-tabulations of age by birthplace at the local government area and collector's district level, it was evident that in 1966, 84 per cent of the 30–34 male age group in Fitzroy, Melbourne, was born overseas, while 60 per cent were from southern Europe. At the collector's district level percentages of southern Europeans in the 30–39 age group in northern Fitzroy reached 70 per cent in four C.D.s, an area encompassing fourteen street blocks. Most of the migrants here were Italians, but in Richmond, south-east of the central business district, 73 per cent of the 30–39 age group were overseas-born, and in five collectors' districts 62 per cent of males in the same age group were born in Greece or Cyprus (ethnically Greek). This area corresponded to approximately twelve residential street blocks.

The implications of these figures are, first, that few persons in age groups which contribute most strongly to community leadership and to membership in parent and teacher and other grass roots organizations were available from Australian-born persons, while language difficulties and cultural differences impeded participation by migrant parents and persons in these institutions and secondary groups. Second, in inner city electorates, in part because of low naturalization rates among southern Europeans, little participation in the political process at the State or Federal level through the ballot box takes place, with the migrant population contributing a disproportionate segment of the 20–45 age groups. This reinforces the pattern of inequality discussed in subsequent chapters. The trends discussed for Melbourne have been replicated in inner Sydney and Adelaide and some industrial outer suburbs such as Altona and Sunshine (Melbourne), Fairfield (Sydney) and Cringila (Wollongong).

Immigration and the labour force

Because of the age structure characteristics of the immigrant stream to Australia, the migrant contribution to the labour force composition and growth was significantly greater between 1947 and 1966 than the overall immigrant percentage of the population. Thus in 1966 the overseas-born constituted 26 per cent of the male labour force of Australia, compared with 18 per cent of the population.

The impact of immigration on labour force growth was of course even more pronounced. Between 1947 and 1966, the total *male* workforce of Australia increased from 2,479,269 in 1947 to 3,421,808 in 1966, a gain of 942,539. Of this increase, 549,480 or 59 per cent consisted of the growth of the overseas-born in the labour force. Meanwhile, 293,760 or 41 per cent of the increase in the female workforce consisted of the overseas-born.

The role of immigration in the growth of the urban, non-farm workforce was even more important, in particular in the manufacturing and building and construction sectors. Over 65 per cent of the growth of the male urban labour force in the 1947–66 period was the direct result of immigration through the increase of the overseas-born at work.

Concomitant with the role of immigration in metropolitan growth being most important in Melbourne of all the capital cities, immigration contributed most to labour force growth in that city, constituting 70 per cent of the increase in size of the labour force and over three-quarters of the increase in the manufacturing and building and construction sectors of the workforce.

By 1966, the overseas-born constituted 36 per cent of the male labour force of metropolitan Melbourne, compared with the percentage in the total population in that city of 25.7 per cent. It was possible at the 1966 census to reclassify occupations for metropolitan areas in terms of degree of skill, in order to study the role of immigrants in the occupational stratification system of Australia.[14] Thus the overseas-born males in Melbourne contributed almost 50 per cent of all the unskilled workers within the metropolitan area. Almost 27 per cent of all unskilled male workers in Melbourne were born in Italy, Greece and Malta. It is evident then that the residential succession of these southern European groups into poorer inner city areas has been paralleled by their movement into unskilled occupations. In the inner suburbs of total population decline, but with immigrant succession partially replacing the declining host society population, the overseas-born constituted over 76 per cent of the unskilled manual workers (males) in 1966. Hence class and ethnicity were clearly becoming related in Melbourne.

In Sydney, where immigration was important in growth, but less so than in Melbourne, the overseas-born contributed 30 per cent of the total male workforce, compared with 22 per cent of the total population. Almost 39 per cent of the unskilled manual workers in 1966 were born overseas, 14 per cent of the total being southern Europeans. In both Sydney and Melbourne, the overseas-born contribution to the expansion of the professional, managerial and clerical sections of the workforce was less than the foreign-born contribution to the growth of the manual occupational groups.

Conclusion

Immigration has been of great but varying significance in metropolitan growth in post-war Australia. The greatest impact was on Sydney, Melbourne and Adelaide, where immigration was considerably more important than either urban natural increase or internal migration in growth. The impact on growth was perhaps comparable to that of international migration on world cities such as São Paulo, Buenos Aires or Toronto in the post-war period and New York, Boston and Pittsburg before World War I. In the metropolitan centres, immigration substantially arrested the decline of population in inner city areas and in some suburbs fringing the central districts converted declining populations to increasing numbers or contributed greatly to overall growth. The influence of immigration on urban sprawl in peripheral suburbs was significant, although less important than its role in total metropolitan (or Australian) population growth, except for low-rent/cost housing areas in industrial outer suburbs.

It is likely that in the future (assuming high immigration rates and similar ethnic composition as with 1947–66 immigrants) the impact of immigration on outer suburbs will increase as immigrants directly join relatives who have dispersed to new housing areas, rather than settling in the inner suburbs. The inner areas of population succession may continue, however, to take southern Europeans of limited means, and newcomers, such as Turks and Yugoslavs, arriving under recently concluded migration agreements, but who have started chain migration processes similar to those which have operated with Greeks, Italians and Maltese.

The importance of immigration in the growth of the national labour force and in the growth of the manufacturing and building and construction industries in particular has been noted: the motor assembly, textiles, building and transport industries in particular in Melbourne and Sydney and the iron and steel industry in Wollongong have been cited. The age selectivity of the migration stream has been the major factor in the significantly larger role of migrants in the labour force than in overall population composition. Migrants have played a very important part in key industries, notably the petrochemical industries in areas such as Kwinana on the metropolitan periphery of Perth, and in ship building, while they have supplied the manual labour without which the heavy industrial expansion in Sydney, Melbourne and Adelaide, so evident in the post-war period, could not have been undertaken.

Finally, the age selectivity of immigration, with many southern and some north-western and eastern European migrants starting families in Australia, has exerted considerable pressure on social facilities, crèches, schools, hospitals and housing, all essential elements of the urban fabric. This pressure has been felt in particular parts of the large cities but these social costs have at least in part been ameliorated by rapid growth of a consumer market, the easing of an initial chronic labour shortage and the creation of an urban cultural pluralism and diversity – the addition of a cosmopolitan dimension to the Australian urbanization process.

NOTES

1 C. A. Price, *Southern Europeans in Australia*, Oxford University Press, 1963.
2 A. J. Rose, 'Some social aspects of Australia's immigrant population', *Australian Quarterly*, *30*, 1958, p. 65.
3 C. A. Price, 'International migration – Australia and New Zealand, 1947–1968', International Union for the Scientific Study of Population General Conference, September 1969, 9.1.12.
4 J. Zubrzycki, 'Some aspects of the structural assimilation of immigrants in Australia', *International Migration*, 6, 1968, pp. 106–7.
5 With period of residence data, it is survivors present at the later census who are considered, whereas with total population increase, the components which we are interested in, it is not survivors present at the later census who are counted but the growth in numbers between two censuses. Use of 'period of residence of the overseas-born' data considerably overstates the role of immigration in growth.
6 E. W. Burgess, 'The growth of the city: an introduction to a research project', *Publication of the American Sociological Society*, 1924, pp. 85–97.
7 F. Lancaster Jones, 'The Italian population of Carlton', unpublished Ph.D. dissertation, Australian National University, 1962.
8 A. Jakubowicz, 'Changing patterns of community organisation', Honours thesis in Government, University of Sydney, 1969.
9 F. Lancaster Jones, *Dimensions of Urban Social Structure*, A.N.U. Press, 1969.
10 Report of Immigration Commission, *Immigrants in Cities*, United States Government, 1911.
11 Unpublished 1966 census cross-tabulations of birthplace of household head by nature of occupancy.
12 Lois Bryson and Faith Thompson, *An Australian Newton. Life and Leadership in a New Housing Suburb*, Penguin, Ringwood, Victoria, 1972.
13 R. J. Johnston, 'Zonal and sectoral patterns in Melbourne's residential structure', *Land Economics*, *45*, 1969, pp. 463–7.
14 Part of a nationwide stratification study undertaken by F. Lancaster Jones, J. Zubrzycki and L. Broom of Australian National University.

7

Future population patterns of Australian cities

C. Y. CHOI and I. H. BURNLEY

In the previous chapters the various demographic elements in the growth of Australia's largest cities and the processes of urbanization in the post-war era have been discussed. The importance of the large metropolitan cities, developing on a variant of the western model with relatively low population densities but relatively rapid growth rates, has been stressed, and the population projections outlined below indicate that such trends should continue, although the critical variable, migration, is an uncertain factor. Speculation concerning the future of urbanization is as hazardous as that concerning any other aspect of human society, as Kingsley Davis has noted.[1] Following the direction of trends in the post-war era involving great industrial expansion in Australia, one may however conclude that urbanization there has reached a stage from which there may be no return, given the substantial mineral resources of the continent. Nevertheless, redistribution of population for both economic and 'quality of life' reasons may take place.

Projections up to the year 2000 have been carried out under varying assumptions to be discussed shortly and tables are presented of estimated populations of the ten largest cities on a five year basis to the year 2000 A.D., after which tabulations to the year 2050 are outlined on a ten year basis, although the method used was a direct continuation of the techniques applied to the 1970–2000 period. The tables differ on the basis of the assumptions used about relative strength of components in population growth and it must be stressed that no *absolute* answers can be given as to the ultimate population size or population characteristics of metropolitan area *x* at any point in time. Institutional decisions are of critical importance here. Large companies or government may decide to develop particular industries and plants in city *A* rather than metropolitan area *B* and this will generate quite different city growth rates and migration volumes than hitherto experienced. Concepts of the residential desirability of cities of various sizes may also change.

Methodology and assumptions

The following were the assumptions concerning fertility, mortality, age structure and amount and type of migration; the units used were the metropolitan or urban statistical divisions with boundaries as at 1966, which included at that time almost if not all of the urban growth areas functionally related to the main centre. Queanbeyan was included with Canberra because of the obvious symbiotic relationship between the two cities, which may ultimately join as one conurbation.

Fertility and mortality

There were two fertility assumptions: the 1968–70 Australian fertility level remaining constant through time, and fertility decline beginning at the 1968–70 level and diminishing to a net reproduction rate (N.R.R.) of 1 by the year 1990, or from the base year of 1966 declining to replacement level in 24 years. For mortality, the 1968–70 Australian mortality was utilized and has been assumed to remain constant through time.

Migration

(*a*) The age structure of overseas net migration to Sydney and Melbourne was assumed to remain relatively constant as at the 1968–70 period, while no internal migration gain was assumed (based on the analysis and findings presented in Chapter 3). In Brisbane, Adelaide and Perth, the 1968–70 overseas-born migration age structure[2] and the 1961–6 age structure of Australian-born (internal migrants) estimated by the present authors for each city were utilized, while in Hobart, the 1968–70 net overseas-born migration age structure only was adopted. As discussed in Chapter 3, migration estimates for Geelong, Wollongong and Newcastle could not be developed separately for the Australian-born and foreign-born. Estimates based on the vital statistics method are split into proportions based on approximations of the internal migration and foreign-born international migration to these lesser cities between 1968 and 1970 (Table 7.1).

(*b*) The second migration assumption was that although the internal migration number would be the same as in assumption (*a*) there would be little or no gain through immigration.

Where immigration was assumed to continue, the *net gain* to the country as a whole was assumed to be as in 1968–70, i.e. approximately 100,000 per year, although the excess of arrivals over departures was greater. The estimate was based on the wotk of C. A. Price of the Australian National University.[3] The sex ratio of immigrants was assumed to be 0.49451 for Brisbane, 0.51369 for Adelaide and 0.50235 for Perth, while for all other State capitals it was taken as being 0.53908 (based on the 1968–70 figures for net migration to Australia). Brisbane, Perth and Adelaide figures include internal migration as well.

Thus there are two basic projections, the first based on fertility constant at the 1968–70 level and the second with progressively declining fertility until replacement level is reached in 1990 For each projection there are

TABLE 7.1. *Estimated annual number of overseas immigrants and internal migrants to Australia's ten largest cities as base for population projections*

Metropolitan or urban division	Overseas immigrants	Internal migrants
Sydney	27,000	0
Melbourne	27,400	0
Brisbane	5,000	5,000
Adelaide	12,000	4,000
Perth	7,000	3,000
Hobart	600	0
Canberra-Queanbeyan	1,450	4,250
Wollongong	2,800	2,000
Newcastle	0	0
Geelong	1,200	500

Notes.
(1) The *overseas-born immigrant* numbers were estimated on the basis of a *net gain* of not more than 100,000 immigrants per year into Australia. The proportion settling in each city was estimated by the *1966* census proportion of those with a period of residence of less than five years.
(2) The internal migration estimates for the capital cities (except Canberra) are derived from the estimates presented in Chapter 3.

two different migration assumptions, the first being immigration at the 1968–70 rate, which has been fairly typical of the post-war immigrant gain to the Australian population in general, and the second being no immigration but with internal migration to the cities at the 1961–6 level. Hence there are four projections for Australia's large cities set out in Tables 7.2–7.5.

It is difficult to say which of the four somewhat arbitrary combinations (or alternatives) will be the more accurate projection or estimate of future events. For instance, although one assumption assumes no immigration it is unlikely that absolutely no immigration will take place unless the Australian public become convinced that immigration is harmful in some way to the Australian 'quality of life' or to the Australian city. At the same time, the 100,000 net gain to Australian population is not excessive, as it was a common level experienced throughout much of the 1947–71 period when official targets were that annual immigration should result directly in a 1 per cent increase[4] in total population. In fact if this number continues, as has been assumed in the projections of the city populations, the net percentage gain through immigration will actually decline as the base population increases, for the assumption is of a fixed figure. Given the increased prosperity in Europe with the growing strength of the European Economic Community, it is unlikely that high rates of immigration from that source will continue indefinitely, so that unless new source areas are found and immigration selection policies (and philosophies) are radically altered, the flow of immigration to Australia is highly unlikely to increase beyond the (net gain) levels taken as a base in these projections.

TABLE 7.2. *Projection of capital city populations on the assumption o*

Year	Sydney (1)	Sydney (2)	Melbourne (1)	Melbourne (2)	Brisbane (1)	Brisbane (2)
1966	2,541,300	2,541,300	2,230,800	2,230,800	777,700	777,700
1970	2,773,200	2,659,700	2,453,300	2,337,800	852,100	831,100
1975	3,089,000	2,817,900	2,758,200	2,483,600	960,400	910,500
1980	3,420,500	2,975,900	3,082,300	2,630,400	1,080,500	998,300
1985	3,765,000	3,131,500	3,424,500	2,780,600	1,208,300	1,090,400
1990	4,127,300	3,288,500	3,786,800	2,934,100	1,342,100	1,185,700
1995	4,520,500	3,459,000	4,175,900	3,096,900	1,484,500	1,285,300
2000	4,950,400	3,648,900	4,596,800	3,273,900	1,640,600	1,396,000
2010	5,898,500	4,069,500	5,525,200	3,665,000	1,993,400	1,647,800
2020	6,963,500	4,547,400	4,565,100	4,108,100	2,386,500	1,936,500
2030	8,168,500	5,101,000	7,729,400	4,611,300	2,823,300	2,235,300
2040	9,515,800	5,719,000	9,027,300	5,170,900	3,311,200	2,579,400
2050	11,021,600	6,413,600	10,482,600	5,848,600	3,857,900	2,964,400

TABLE 7.3. *Projection of populations of Wollongong, Newcastle and Geelong on the assumption of fertility remaining constant at 1968–70 level: total population*

Year	Newcastle (1)	Newcastle (2)	Wollongong (1)	Wollongong (2)	Geelong (1)	Geelong (2)
1966	(same as (2) because	327,478	177,400	177,400	111,200	111,200
1970	little or no	340,700	207,500	195,800	123,500	118,400
1975	immigra-	360,600	248,900	220,700	141,000	128,900
1980	tion)	283,600	294,500	248,400	160,800	141,000
1985		407,700	344,000	278,200	182,100	153,900
1990		431,400	396,300	309,200	204,100	166,800
1995		454,900	450,800	240,600	226,800	179,600
2000		480,500	508,300	396,700	251,200	193,900
2010		541,400	635,900	471,400	306,300	224,900
2020		609,900	778,800	528,100	367,400	259,900
2030		684,900	936,600	618,300	434,900	297,900
2040		768,600	1,113,300	719,700	509,300	340,400
2050		861,700	1,311,100	832,900	593,100	388,200

Notes.
(1) Immigration at 1968–70 level; 100,000 net gain to Australia distributed.
(2) No immigration but internal migration at 1961–6 level.

rtility remaining constant at 1968–70 level: total population

elaide		Perth		Hobart		Canberra-Queanbeyan	
	(2)	(1)	(2)	(1)	(2)	(1)	(2)
769,500	769,500	558,800	558,800	141,300	141,300	105,800	105,800
71,900	820,800	628,200	597,100	150,400	147,900	137,900	131,800
17,200	895,300	728,900	554,300	164,100	158,100	181,500	167,000
77,800	944,400	842,300	718,900	179,700	169,800	228,700	204,800
49,400	820,900	963,400	796,200	197,100	182,000	279,700	245,600
29,300	1,151,200	1,089,900	853,700	212,500	193,900	334,200	289,100
20,300	1,241,600	1,224,800	924,300	229,200	105,600	392,100	335,000
49,200	1,340,900	1,372,900	1,002,900	247,300	218,300	453,600	383,600
95,000	1,567,700	1,708,400	1,183,200	288,800	248,100	587,300	488,900
15,800	1,431,800	2,081,000	1,379,900	334,100	280,400	736,100	606,300
95,000	2,098,000	2,496,300	1,597,900	383,300	315,900	900,900	736,100
42,100	2,408,900	2,961,700	1,841,100	438,200	253,800	1,085,100	881,200
66,600	2,765,100	3,483,300	2,112,600	499,100	396,600	1,291,600	1,043,800

tes.

Immigration at 1968–70 level; 100,000 net gain to Australia distributed.
No immigration but internal migration at 1961–6 level.

Similarly it is unlikely (although not impossible) that fertility levels in the future will be higher than those on which the higher fertility assumptions were based for the first projections (Tables 7.2–7.3).

Although evidence at present (up to August 1972) indicates a recent rise in Australian fertility levels in contrast to a downtrend in comparable countries such as the United States, it is possible that a decline in fertility in Australia may occur later with increasing education of the population, desire for higher family living standards, education costs, concern for the quality of life and its relation to population size. However, as the threat of a large population may be felt less in Australia than in the United States, it is probable (although by no means certain) that fertility decline will not fall until replacement level is reached, but will even out at some intermediate level, should significant decline occur at all.

Turning to Table 7.2, the State capital and Canberra populations have been projected forwards in a five year basis until the year 2000 with decennial estimates thereafter, using the 1968–70 fertility level assumption. By 2000, Sydney's population with continued immigration and current fertility levels would reach almost 5 million, while that of Melbourne would reach 4,600,000 approximately. These figures assume little or no internal migration net gain based on post-war trends, for reasons outlined in Chapter 3. Should internal migration patterns change, as is quite possible, then the growth of these two cities could well be greater. It should

TABLE 7.4. *Projection of capital city populations on the assumptio rate of 1 (replacement level) by 1990*

	Sydney		Melbourne		Brisbane	
Year	(1)	(2)	(1)	(2)	(1)	(2)
1966	2,541,300	2,541,300	2,230,800	2,230,800	777,700	771,700
1970	2,769,300	2,655,900	2,449,800	2,334,600	850,900	830,000
1975	3,063,400	2,794,300	235,300	2,461,700	952,200	892,700
1980	3,351,800	2,915,900	3,020,200	2,575,900	1,057,700	977,000
1985	3,628,800	3,014,800	3,299,400	2,675,200	1,162,200	1,048,200
1990	3,893,800	3,094,700	3,570,400	2,758,100	1,262,700	1,113,700
1995	4,163,100	3,170,100	3,844,400	2,834,900	1,363,600	1,178,200
2000	4,443,400	3,246,900	4,127,700	2,910,700	1,469,400	1,245,600
2010	4,999,000	3,379,300	4,688,900	3,042,400	1,688,500	1,382,500
2020	5,522,000	3,475,200	5,219,400	3,138,800	1,892,500	1,505,000
2030	6,017,100	3,537,800	5,747,800	3,204,800	2,073,900	1,626,300
2040	6,472,200	3,577,900	6,176,900	3,234,800	2,260,700	1,707,900
2050	6,897,100	3,585,800	6,608,300	3,214,300	2,428,700	1,793,100

TABLE 7.5. *Projection of populations of Wollongong, Newcastle and Geelong on the assumption of fertility decline beginning at 1968–70 level but declining to a net reproduction rate of 1 (replacement level) by 1990*

	Newcastle		Wollongong		Geelong	
Year	(1)	(2)	(1)	(2)	(1)	(2)
1966	(same as (2) because	327,500	177,400	177,400	111,200	111,200
1970	little or no	340,300	207,300	195,500	123,300	118,300
1975	immigra-	357,600	246,900	218,900	139,900	127,900
1980	tion)	375,500	288,700	243,300	157,500	138,000
1985		391,800	331,600	267,800	175,200	147,900
1990		404,800	374,000	291,100	192,200	156,600
1995		415,800	416,200	313,100	208,700	164,600
2000		426,700	459,000	334,800	225,700	172,500
2010		448,500	545,900	377,800	260,400	188,400
2020		465,300	629,600	418,200	293,300	202,200
2030		475,900	711,700	555,100	323,500	213,500
2040		480,400	789,100	488,700	351,300	222,600
2050		482,000	863,700	520,000	377,800	230,500

Notes.

(1) Immigration at 1968–70 level; 100,000 net gain to Australia distributed.
(2) No immigration but internal migration at 1961–6 level.

f fertility decline beginning at 1968–70 level but declining to a net reproduction

Adelaide		Perth		Hobart		Canberra-Queanbeyan	
1)	(2)	(1)	(2)	(1)	(2)	(1)	(2)
769,500	769,500	558,800	558,800	141,300	141,300	105,800	105,800
870,700	819,600	627,300	596,200	150,200	147,700	137,700	131,600
,008,700	887,700	722,800	648,600	162,700	156,700	180,000	165,500
,153,500	957,100	824,300	703,300	175,800	166,000	224,200	200,700
,299,300	1,103,000	926,300	755,100	188,500	174,600	269,900	236,900
,441,500	1,081,900	1,025,400	801,400	199,400	181,600	316,100	273,100
,585,100	1,138,200	1,125,800	846,400	209,700	187,500	362,200	309,800
,735,000	1,196,400	1,231,600	893,900	220,200	193,500	411,400	347,100
,043,900	1,313,700	1,451,400	990,600	241,300	205,200	508,900	412,900
,343,200	1,418,800	1,662,900	1,075,600	259,300	213,800	604,800	494,800
,628,700	1,507,900	1,864,600	1,139,300	279,900	218,900	698,000	565,300
,899,000	1,583,200	2,056,000	1,212,100	285,400	221,100	788,800	633,300
,159,500	1,650,100	2,240,800	1,268,800	295,200	221,600	877,500	699,500

otes.

1) Immigration at 1968–70 level; 100,000 net gain to Australia distributed.
2) No immigration but internal migration at 1961–6 level.

be noted also how Adelaide, growing rapidly from *both* international and internal migration, will have reached well over 2 million by the year 2000, while Perth will have grown very rapidly to a true metropolitan size of 1,373,000. Even without immigration and in part because of a continued strong interstate net internal migration gain, Perth would still reach over 1 million if relatively recent fertility trends continue. It must be stressed that these figures are not unreal and it is the authors' contention the figures based on current fertility trends and immigration may be nearer reality, although only time will tell. Thus it is almost certain that Australia will maintain its lead among world regions as already asserted by Kingsley Davis and Hilda Hertz,[5] in both degree of urbanization and degree of metropolitanization.

For Sydney and Melbourne, differences in size, depending on continued strong immigration or little or no immigration, are clearly evident and this is particularly so if one takes a futuristic glance at the figures for 2050 with differences of 11,022,000 and 6,414,000 for metropolitan Sydney and 10,483,000 and 5,849,000 for Melbourne, depending on the presence or not of immigration. The differences are equally marked with the second set of projections based on a lowered fertility (Table 7.4), so that immigration will be a crucial factor determining metropolitan centre size in the future. It should be noted from Table 7.4 that even with significant

decline in fertility with continued immigration, the population of metropolitan Sydney will reach 4,443,000 by 2000, compared with 4,950,000
with a continuing fertility rate at current levels. Thus for Australia's two
largest cities, Sydney and Melbourne, migration differentials will be of
much greater importance in growth than fertility differentials, in particular
international migration.

With little or no immigration but with fertility differences – a con-
tinuance of the 1968–70 rate or a decline to replacement level by 1990 –
the population of Brisbane would vary by only 150,000 by 2000 with the
two projections and only 144,000 in Adelaide by the same date. With
fertility remaining constant but with the two different migration assumptions, the population of Adelaide would vary by 710,000 in 2000 for
comparison, while with declining fertility the difference would be approximately 540,000. Both these differences are very great, considering the
size of the city. Given constant fertility, Adelaide would be 53 per cent
larger in population by 2000 with immigration at the 1968–70 level, and
with declining fertility it would be 46 per cent larger with immigration
than without immigration.

In Tables 7.3 and 7.5, the populations of the lesser cities of Newcastle,
Wollongong and Geelong are projected on the basis of the two fertility
levels and migration assumptions. Because Newcastle sustained hardly any
net gain through internal migration in the post-war period and little
increase through immigration, only one migration assumption is applied,
most of its population increase, unlike that of the other two cities (and the
metropolitan centres), coming from natural increase. However, the recent
decision by Broken Hill Proprietary to increase substantially its plant and
capital investment in Newcastle will almost certainly result in an attraction
of population to that city and thus the population size in 2000 will be
larger in all probability than either projection estimates. Migration is
expected to remain critically important in Wollongong's growth as in
Geelong. Assuming constant fertility at recent rates and migration (international and internal annual numbers of 2,800 and 2,000 respectively),
Wollongong's population is expected to grow to over 508,000 in 2000,
almost tripling its size in 35 years. With no immigration but with internal
migration and constant fertility Wollongong would still grow to 397,000
by 2000, while with declining fertility its population without immigration
would reach *only* 333,000 by the same date.

The great importance of migration and the relative unimportance of
fertility differences in the expected growth of Wollongong can be seen by
comparing Tables 7.3 and 7.5, for with constant fertility and continuing
immigration the expected total population in 2000 is 508,000, whereas
with continued immigration and fertility decline to replacement level by
1990, Wollongong's population would be 459,000, a difference of only

49,000. Wollongong, Newcastle and Sydney are however, part of one urbanizing region as indicated by Clarke[6] and also in the first chapter of this book, and with immigration and the constant fertility level, the population of what may become a conurbation should reach almost 6 million by 2000. Similarly Geelong and Melbourne may ultimately link and there has been considerable and increasing interaction between these centres in the post-war era. By 2000 they should approach a population of 4,850,000 with continued immigration and constant fertility.

By the mid twenty-first century, if current migration and fertility trends continue, the urbanizing region along the east central New South Wales coast could total over 13,200,000 and that based on Melbourne around Port Phillip could reach over 11,070,000 people, although projections become highly speculative this far ahead. Compared to the growth of other conurbations in the western world this growth pattern would be quite rapid[7] and growth could well be greater given greater immigration, higher fertility and a different internal migration pattern. Thus the future of the urbanizing process in Australia may be fraught with urban and social planning, social segregation problems and concentrated demand on local water and recreational resources.

NOTES

1 Kingsley Davis, 'The origin and growth of urbanization in the world', *American Journal of Sociology*, 60, March 1955, pp. 429–37.
2 Calculated from annual immigration tabulations.
3 C. A. Price, 'Overseas migration to Australia: 1947–1970', in C. A. Price (ed.), *Australian Immigration; a bibliography and Digest*, no. 2, A.N.U. Press, 1970, pp. A1–23.
4 R. T. Appleyard, 'The population', in A. F. Davies and S. Encel (eds.), *Australian Society, a Sociological Introduction*, second ed., Cheshire, 1970, pp. 3–15.
5 Kingsley Davis and Hilda Hertz, 'The world distribution of urbanization', *Bulletin of the International Statistical Institute*, 13, part IV, p. 230.
6 G. Clarke, 'Urban Australia', in A. F. Davies and S. Encel (eds.), *Australian Society, a Sociological Introduction*, second ed., Cheshire, 1970, pp. 31–83.
7 Kingsley Davis, 'The urbanization of the human population', *Scientific American*, special issue on World Urbanization, 1965; Leonard Reissman, *The Urban Process*, Free Press, New York, 1964, pp. 160–2.

PART II

The impact and consequences of urbanization: urban residential and social structure

8

Urbanization and social segregation

I. H. BURNLEY

A feature of urbanization in contemporary Australia has been the development of large metropolises on the world scale, with metropolitan Sydney approaching a population of 3 million by 1975 and Melbourne over 2.8 million if post-war trends continue. All the State capitals with the exception of Hobart are of true metropolitan size, and as previously noted there are only five intermediate sized urban centres, three of which are growing rapidly. Melbourne and Sydney had already taken on a metropolitan character before the turn of the century, with areal differentiation of suburbs into working class, middle class and high status areas. In fact, the areal differentiation of suburbs into different housing quality and status districts can be regarded as attributes of the western metropolitan centres in which free market forces favour the agglomeration of like land uses and social types.

Although only limited research has been undertaken on residential differentiation in Australian cities, with the notable exception of F. Lancaster Jones's[1] Melbourne study, some generalizations can be made on variations in residential structure of the large Australian city, as a background to the discussion of social segregation in the urbanization process. A finer analysis of residential differentiation is discussed in R. J. Stimson's chapter, with particular reference to Adelaide. Briefly it can be stated that ethnicity, social status and familism have been found to be three of the more important differentiating factors in Melbourne's[2] and Adelaide's residential structure, following the patterns found in several North American industrial cities, notably Los Angeles.[3] These differences have a spatial pattern as population sub-groups, differentiated in terms of degrees of occupational skill and levels of education and income, will exhibit differences in choice of residential location in the metropolitan residential system. Further, groups at different stages of the life cycle requiring specific housing and social service facilities tend to group together in various types of household composition.

It is probable that areal differentiation (and in effect social segregation) is more acute in the two large metropolitan centres of Sydney and Melbourne and in Adelaide than in smaller cities such as Wollongong, Geelong and Newcastle, although it is difficult to find empirical measures which can be used to contrast segregation between cities, and especially between cities of greatly different sizes. This of course makes empirical comparisons between cities and social systems of different countries doubly difficult. However, even in cities such as Wollongong and Geelong, there are significant spatial variations seen at the collector's district level in terms of ethnicity and occupational status, although 60 per cent of collectors' districts were relatively heterogeneous in occupational status and in proportions of self-employed versus employees. At one end of the scale in Wollongong were collectors' districts in hill suburbs such as Mt Pleasant and Austinmer with high proportions of persons in professional–technical and managerial occupations and of self-employed occupational status, these areas constituting approximately 8 per cent of the Wollongong population. At the other end of the scale were the industrial suburbs of Port Kembla, Cringila and Warrawong adjacent to the large steel works and linked industries complex. Here there was a considerable Yugoslav, Italian and mixed ethnic population along with Australian-born, plus a high proportion of industrial workers, in particular unskilled workers and labourers. In the high status suburbs mentioned, average house prices for properties on sale in March 1972 were $30,500, with over 40 per cent over $35,000, while in Cringila-Port Kembla, average prices were $14,500 at the same date, with 28 per cent under $12,500.[4] This was not merely a contrast due to relative prestige of areas but reflected also house quality, from split-level and architect-designed homes in the former to fibro and even plywood dwellings of modest size in the latter. Not only were there considerable status variations between areas, but there were also spatial variations between suburbs in high school retention rates (i.e. children staying on in school in age groups 16–18 beyond the minimum legal age limits for leaving), reflecting possibly unequal opportunities between areas but also social class values as to the worth of education. Ethnic and cultural attributes of suburban populations were also possibly factors here.

In Geelong, significant variations were also evident in occupational type and occupational status (self-employed, employee or helper etc.) between collectors' districts, although very few districts were very homogeneous (e.g. over 90 per cent white collar or 90 per cent blue collar). Over 45 per cent of collectors' districts were in fact quite heterogeneous in occupational type and occupational status characteristics. There was also a tendency towards ethnic concentration in some low status collectors' districts in the older parts of the city, although these areas were polyethnic in make up without segregated ethnic neighbourhood formation.

Even in the national capital Canberra, still a small to medium sized city (162,000 with Queanbeyan) in 1972, socio-economic status variations certainly developed in the post-war period, despite the strong role of urban planning in the city's development at all stages.[5] Unskilled manual workers were proportionately few in the Canberra occupational structure, in that most industry consisted of service industries associated with government, but they tended to concentrate in the satellite city (in New South Wales) of Queanbeyan or in the older low-cost housing suburb of Narrabundah. Certainly the inter-suburb and intra-suburb variations which developed in Canberra (whose growth has been largely post-war with consequently better overall housing) are much less than in the great cities of Sydney and Melbourne, or even Adelaide, Wollongong and Geelong. Some suburbs in Canberra were designed and built as definite prestige areas, such as Aranda and Belconnen, along with Red Hill (Mugga Way), the home of diplomats, but the general pattern which developed was one of government houses along with private dwellings grouped around neighbourhood community and shopping centres. In many Woden Valley suburbs, the highest streets on the adjacent slopes tended to be of high priced housing, prestigious and much sought after, where senior executive civil servants, senior academics and professionals took up residence. On the valley floor, housing was more modest. Even in Canberra there were segregative trends in some ethnic group distributions: in 1966 almost one-third of the Italians in the city resided in Narrabundah, while small concentrations of Italian- and Yugoslav-born formed in the satellite town, Queanbeyan. Again, retention rates in high schools varied moderately between suburbs, but much higher proportions for the whole city stayed on in high school than the New South Wales or national averages. It is nevertheless evident that as a planned national capital, less social segregation, as expressed by spatial variations in socio-economic characteristics, developed in Canberra than in other special function national New World capitals, such as Ottawa, Washington D.C. or Brazilia.

A generalization which emerges from the above discussion, and also from that to follow, is that although significant ecological variations exist in small to intermediate sized cities in Australia such as Hobart, Geelong, Wollongong, Canberra and even the Latrobe Valley (Victoria), the contrasts are more acute within the large metropolitan centres of Sydney, Melbourne and Adelaide. City size is undoubtedly an important determinant of social segregation in urban Australia. Contrasts between cities are also important, for the ten largest urban centres in Australia vary somewhat in economic function. Thus, industrial Wollongong has school retention rates well below the New South Wales (and national) averages while Canberra with its white collar and tertiary base has significantly higher rates. But it is the large metropolises that have real and highly significant contrasts in status, housing, living conditions and schools, as the following discussion testifies.

Social segregation in metropolitan urbanizing centres
Demographic and socio-economic differences

Within Sydney and Melbourne, similar patterns of demographic, ethnic and social status differentiation evolved in the 1947–66 period although, as indicated in the two chapters dealing with immigrants in Australian cities, immigration was greater to Melbourne. The similarities in terms of socio-economic differentiation are that both cities have (i) inner cores of nineteenth century terrace and semi-detached housing, with the population working in manual occupations, (ii) outer western industrial suburbs of modest and low-cost pre-war and post-war housing development, (iii) intervening areas of mixed land uses and socio-economic status, and (iv) middle distance high status suburbs such as Vaucluse in Sydney, Toorak and Caulfield in Melbourne. Melbourne developed additional industrial suburbs in the south-eastern urban fringe, while Sydney extended its higher status residential areas on the North Shore.

Along with these socio-economic gradations there were demographic areal contrasts with the metropolitan areas, elements of which have already been described for the earlier half of the post-war period of evolution of metropolitan Sydney by Scott[6] and Rose.[7] It can tentatively be stated that within Sydney three broad areas of demographic differentiation evolved in the post-war period and were evident at the 1966 census: (i) the older and inner city areas with higher proportions of flats, older age groups, low dependency and fertility ratios, fairly high proportions of males and females in the workforce and relatively large numbers of pensioners; (ii) the rapidly developing outer suburban areas with high concentrations of their population in the 0–14 age group, relatively large numbers in the 30–39 age group (young parents), lower percentages of women in the workforce, high proportions of married women in home duties, and high child dependency and fertility ratios; (iii) between these two types of area there are suburbs where the single family home predominates but the 40–50 age group is prominent and the dependency and fertility ratios are less than average.

There was a general conformity between these areas and the socio-economic and housing areas described above. However, more especially in the outer suburbs but also in the middle distance suburbs, there was an additional differentiation in terms of socio-economic status within areas of relatively homogeneous demographic character. Thus in the outer suburbs there evolved both high status, high fertility and low status, high fertility suburbs, although there are few high status areas with young parents, reflecting the fact that high status in managerial occupations is more frequently attained at higher ages. Most areas of high ethnicity in Sydney were areas of low to medium fertility, although this is expected to change towards high fertility when children are born to recent arrivals, particularly those from southern Europe. This would in part reverse the tendency for low familism to be characteristic of the old inner suburbs, for distinct areas (at the collector's district level) of Greek and Italian young married couples have been identified, in Marrickville and Drummoyne respectively. Other areas of high familism appearing in the inner suburbs which are associated with low socio-economic status have been those connected with Commission housing (public high-rise apartment blocks), where an income ceiling is applied so that low socio-economic status is linked with family status through giving preference to persons with children as tenants. Thus institutional factors have operated to maintain social segregation, more especially in the high-rise low-rent apartments in Redfern and Waterloo within inner Sydney and in Carlton and Fitzroy in central Melbourne. In outer suburbs such as Green Valley and Mt Druitt in western Sydney, Commission housing consisting of bungalows and small apartment blocks was developed, where the income ceiling was also applied, so that social segregation with homogeneous social status and demographic characteristics has again resulted, with young to middle aged married residents with two or more children. Such suburbs have also been developed as part of the suburbanization process on Melbourne's urban periphery and their social patterns have been described in a recent study by Bryson and Thompson.[8] They found that many families were basically poor, being financially heavily committed to hire-purchase contracts. However, most of the people were generally satisfied with their living conditions, which was not surprising since the State Housing Commission offers cheaper accommodation of a higher standard than most of the families could find elsewhere in Melbourne (or Sydney) outside similar Commission estates.

It was also found that as the inhabitants of public housing estates were predominately working class they had working class values and few sought upward social mobility. There were nevertheless social problems, such as financial commitments, higher than average incidence of psychological disturbance and juvenile delinquency, problems which also developed in the Mt Druitt and Green Valley areas west of Sydney.

The highest densities of housing which developed during the 1947–71 post-war period of urbanization in Australia have been in accommodation erected to house two extremes of the socio-economic scale – the high-rise Commission housing blocks of the inner city with densities of up to 200 persons per acre, discussed above, and high income tenanted and owner-occupied blocks of flats located both in better and most residentially desirable inner and middle distance suburbs, more especially in locations with favourable aspect near the harbour in Sydney and also in South Yarra, and parts of Toorak and Caulfield in Melbourne. This form of urban residential development was proportionately and absolutely greatest in Sydney out of all the capital cities.

Associated with the urbanization process in the large metropolitan centres of Australia since World War II has been the growth in popularity and social acceptance of flats as a form of residential accommodation at both ends of the socio-economic scale. In 1921, houses (excluding flats and tenements) comprised almost 97 per cent of Australian dwellings. Even by 1947, when large-scale Continental European immigration was getting under way, detached houses (excluding flats and tenements) still comprised more than 92 per cent of dwellings in Australia.[9] However, the proportion of flats was somewhat higher in Sydney and Melbourne, while home ownership was greater in some small towns and medium sized cities. By 1966, after two decades of immigration, flats alone (excluding tenements which were still relatively limited in comparison with metropolitan centres in Canada and the United States of America) had risen to over 14 per cent of dwellings in Australia.[10] Between 1966 and 1971, 50 per cent of the dwellings erected in metropolitan Sydney consisted of flats, although flat *ownership*, following the tradition of private ownership of detached homes in urban Australia, was common. However, it may well be that for economic reasons, including the soaring cost of land, private ownership (owner-buying) of dwellings may become less possible for the lower socio-economic groups in Australian society. Home ownership may thus become an additional socio-economic status differentiating factor, whereas in the initial stages of post-war urbanization and in previous generations property (dwelling) ownership cut across class lines.

The measurement of occupational segregation

So far in the present discussion, high and low status areas and their association with familism and other demographic attributes have been reviewed. It is possible to assess the residential stratification of occupational groups in Australian cities by use of the Index of Dissimilarity. Thus the distribution of occupational groups by collectors' districts can be compared. Because there were over 2,500 collectors' districts in metropolitan Sydney in 1966, only broad occupational groups were utilized in Tables 8.1 and 8.2, to avoid the artificial inflating of segregation scores. As with residential concentration, indexes below 20 on a scale 0 (no dissimilarity) to 100 (complete dissimilarity or segregation) are regarded as being of low segregation, 20–40 moderate segregation, 40–60 high segregation and above 60 very high segregation. Although 100 is the theoretical maximum on this index, in practice scores above 80 are exceedingly rare for any sets of variables.

In Table 8.1 it is clearly evident that professional–technical and craftsmen and labourer groups were quite strongly dissimilar in their residential distributions. Furthermore, managerial–executive workers were strongly segregated from craftsmen, production process workers and labourers.

TABLE 8.1. *Spatial segregation of occupational groups in metropolitan Sydney 1966, by collectors' districts*

Distributions compared	Indexes of dissimilarity	
	Males	Females
Professional–technical *and* craftsmen, production process workers and labourers	49	44
Clerical and sales workers *and* craftsmen, production process workers and labourers	38	33
Managerial–executive workers *and* craftsmen, production process workers and labourers	51	66

Source: Census of the Commonwealth of Australia, 1966.

TABLE 8.2. *Spatial segregation between occupational groups based on level of skill in metropolitan Sydney 1966, by collectors' districts*

Distribution compared	Indexes of dissimilarity	
	Males	Females
Upper professional *and* craftsmen, production process workers and labourers	56	44
Upper professional *and* skilled manual workers	57	44
Upper professional *and* unskilled manual workers	60	51

Source: Census of the Commonwealth of Australia, 1966.

However, when the distributions of clerical and sales workers (lower status white collar workers in effect) and craftsmen, process workers and labourers were compared, the index of dissimilarity between them was more moderate, indicating some overlap between these distributions. In fact at the collector's district level in Sydney (and Melbourne) there were relatively few districts which did not contain some blue collar workers in areas of lower white collar status dominance. The very high index of dissimilarity between female managerial–executive workers and craftsmen, process workers and labourers may reflect the relatively small numbers involved.

Because the broad occupational categories within Table 8.1 include a wide range of statuses within each occupational group, the professional–technical and related worker categories were split into 'higher professional' (doctors, lawyers, research scientists, architects etc.), and lower professional (teachers etc.), while the large heterogeneous manual workers categories were split into skilled manual and unskilled workers. The results are tabulated in Table 8.2. It is obvious that when the higher professional and total manual worker distributions were compared, the dissimilarity index was higher than that of all professionals against all manual workers. And when higher professional and unskilled manual worker distributions by collectors' districts were compared, the index of dissimilarity score for males (60) indicated very high segregation between highest and lowest status groups. These differences existed within the major ethnic groups as well, as discussed in Chapter 10. Thus there is evidence of a high degree of residential stratification in Sydney (and Melbourne where similar tendencies are recorded in Tables 8.3–8.4), despite the egalitarian image of Australian society held by many.

TABLE 8.3. *Spatial segregation of occupational groups in metropolitan Melbourne 1966, by collectors' districts*

Distributions compared	Indexes of dissimilarity	
	Males	Females
Professional–technical *and* craftsmen, production process workers and labourers	50	52
Clerical and sales workers *and* craftsmen, production process workers and labourers	39	33
Managerial–executive workers *and* craftsmen, production process workers and labourers	51	51

Source: Census of the Commonwealth of Australia, 1966.

TABLE 8.4. *Spatial segregation between occupational groups based on level of skills in metropolitan Melbourne 1966, by collectors' districts*

Distributions compared	Indexes of dissimilarity	
	Males	Females
Upper professional *and* craftsmen, production process workers and labourers	55	69
Upper professional *and* skilled manual workers	55	68
Upper professional *and* unskilled manual workers	60	72

Source: Census of the Commonwealth of Australia, 1966.

The evolution of high status and problem areas in Sydney and Melbourne

Contrary to views held by some, many of the problem and depressed areas in Australia's large cities do not have themselves to blame for their conditions and circumstances. According to Bernard Barrett, 'some of these areas were doomed from the beginning and were in fact set apart by the somewhat cynical reasoning of 19th Century commerce, to be slums from the outset'.[11] In fact in Melbourne and Sydney, the ten suburbs ranked as being of lowest status by F. Lancaster Jones and Athol Congalton[12] were developed largely as working class areas in the nineteenth century close to their cities' central business districts. Those included in the Sydney study (in descending order of rank) were Zetland, Erskineville, Alexandria, Macdonaldtown, Ultimo, Waterloo, Pyrmont, Woolloomooloo, Surry Hills and part of Redfern. In Melbourne, they included North Melbourne, Carlton, Fitzroy, Collingwood, Richmond, South Melbourne and Port Melbourne. Conventional theories as to the origins of depressed areas often suggest that originally the poor areas were genteel, but decayed as the gentry moved out to create new suburbs (a form of social segregation) and as the poor replaced them. Solid homes were subdivided into apartments, flats or boarding houses. Barrett argues that factories then attracted more poor people to the districts, which became not merely senile in the modern period but were 'crippled from birth' – spoilt from the outset, with noxious industries often concerned with animal products (Collingwood and Richmond), and with associated pollution. In the 1930s, disproportionate numbers of the unemployed resided in these suburbs, as in those of south Sydney. Much bad housing in the inner suburbs survived to the middle of the twentieth century, despite several public investigations. In the inter-war years some tenements did exist in Richmond and Collingwood in Melbourne and in Paddington, Redfern and Newtown in south Sydney with absentee landlordism. The State Housing Commissions intervened, so that by the beginning of the post-war era the tenement system had been largely although not entirely broken up. Cottages were built by the State Housing Commissions in the outer suburbs for low income families, as already noted. This, together with improvements in economic circumstances which began to make new private housing available, resulted in an exodus from the inner suburbs (which was itself in part a desire for social segregation) after World War II. The vacancies in the inner suburbs were filled in part by industrial expansion and car storage facilities but mainly by European immigrants, as discussed elsewhere in this book, in particular Italians and Maltese, who began to move out after 1961 when massive Greek- and later Yugoslav-born and Turkish immigration to these suburbs took place.

The extent of social segregation in some of these inner suburbs into low social status districts coupled with high ethnicity is indicated by the following figures. In Fitzroy L.G.A. (Melbourne) in 1966, in two collectors' districts covering nine street blocks containing 1,794 persons, 465 (26 per cent) of whom were born in Italy, only 13 per cent were white collar, while almost 87 per cent were blue collar and less than 1 per cent (of the male labour force) had attended university. In an adjacent area corresponding to six street blocks in Fitzroy, and containing 304 Greeks (27.5 per cent) in a population of 1,106, only 7 per cent were in white collar occupations, while there were no persons who had attended university and 79 per cent of males (in the labour force) were unskilled manual workers, compared with 15 per cent of the metropolitan workforce. Meanwhile, in Carlton, in a more densely populated group of collectors' districts comprising ten street blocks, and where 800 of the 2,540 persons resident were born in Italy, 88 per cent were blue collar workers and 69 per cent unskilled manual workers, while only 1.8 per cent had attended university. In a further section of North Melbourne, also a polyethnic area where Greeks, Italians, Yugoslavs and Maltese constituted over 65 per cent of the population of 1,620 persons, white collar workers comprised only 4 per cent of the male labour force, blue collar 96 per cent and unskilled manual workers 77 per cent, while there were no university-trained persons. There were many other such areas within inner Melbourne, most of which had a male unemployment rate of over 2 per cent, well above the 1966 average, while in one area 12 per cent of the male labour force of 670 was unemployed.

In Sydney, there were similar segregated areas. Thus in three inner city collectors' districts where there were 312 Maltese-born in 1966, only 12 per cent were white collar workers and 64 per cent were unskilled manual workers, compared with 15 per cent of all male workers in the metropolitan area. In the peak Greek concentration in Redfern, 214 out of 713 persons in three blocks were Greek-born and only 8 per cent were white collar workers, 71 per cent were unskilled manual workers and less than 1 per cent had attended university. Furthermore, in the district within Leichhardt which contained Sydney's main Italian concentration, less than 9 per cent were white collar workers, 72 per cent were unskilled manual employees and there were no persons who had attended university.

At the upper end of the socio-economic scale, segregated high status areas evolved in Sydney and Melbourne, often from well-favoured districts already emerging as elite areas in the late nineteenth century. Thus in Toorak (within Prahran L.G.A.) in a group of five collectors' districts, involving twenty-five street blocks and 4,000 people, 70 per cent of the male labour force were in professional–technical, managerial and executive occupations, while 88 per cent were in white collar occupations (excluding sales workers) and 40 per cent had attended university or other tertiary educational institutions in 1966. Over 60 per cent were self-employed.[13]

In the adjacent local government area of Caulfield there was another high status district, this time in association with an ethnic concentration, that of Jewish persons, more especially of people from central and eastern Europe. In an area of twelve collectors' districts with almost 9,000 people, 72 per cent were white collar, 40 per cent self-employed and 44 per cent in professional and managerial–executive occupations. In particular street blocks, proportions in these latter categories reached 80 per cent, as estimated from street directories and electoral rolls. Parts of nearby St Kilda local government area, an inner residential district, also had high status concentrations with home values averaging $45,000–$50,000 compared with a metropolitan average of $17,000 in 1972. However, high status families were beginning to move out into the prestigious areas of Caulfield and even further out by the 1966 census.

Although low status segregated areas evolved mainly in the older inner suburbs of Sydney and Melbourne, problem areas also developed in many outer suburbs, especially those to the west of both cities. Thus in Broadmeadows (Melbourne) over 86 per cent of the male labour force were in blue collar occupations and 68 per cent in unskilled manual work in an area of twelve adjacent street blocks in 1966. Other such segregated areas of low socio-economic status evolved in Sunshine, Keilor and Altona west of Melbourne in the post-war period, and in Fairfield and parts of Blacktown and Bankstown in western Sydney, most of which were developed in the post-war era with the erection of low-cost fibro, weatherboard or brick veneer housing. Some of these areas were associated with ethnic concentrations, as in Broadmeadows, where Maltese constituted between 10 and 15 per cent of the population of five large collectors' districts (twenty-five street blocks), and 72 per cent of the male labour force consisted of unskilled manual workers. Similar patterns of segregation occurred with Italians in Sunshine, Yugoslav-born in parts of Keilor and Sunshine, and Maltese in one section of Altona, all outer suburbs of Melbourne.

Associated with these patterns of concentration of low socio-economic status groups in particular areas has been the incidence of poverty. At the outset it can be stated that the incidence of poverty in Australia is lower than in other western industrial societies; one major survey into living conditions of people in Melbourne estimated that up to 7 per cent of 'income units' were in poverty in 1966, and 4 per cent very much in need.[14] These figures should be compared with estimates of 14 per cent of the United Kingdom population and 20 per cent of families in the United States which have been found to be in poverty. The incidence of poverty in Melbourne and by inference in urban Australia is less than in those two countries. Only New Zealand and Scandinavia, with which countries Australia enjoys roughly comparable living standards, are likely to have as little poverty. The reasons for this lower incidence of poverty are a high degree of literacy, relative absence of discrimination and enough pressure on demand to make employment available to almost everyone capable of earning a living (at least until the 1971–2 recession). However, for a small segment of the Australian population poverty has been a real experience.

In the survey of living conditions in Melbourne carried out by the Institute of Applied Economic and Social Research, University of Melbourne, in 1966 some 4,000 randomly selected households were surveyed. On the basis of census data on population at the collector's district level, differing sampling ratios were applied to six strata, the more intense sampling being undertaken in the inner suburbs where poverty was known (through contacts of State and voluntary welfare agencies) to be more common. The data were then 'grossed up' by different formulae to give estimates for the total population.[15] Groups among whom a disproportionate amount of poverty was found were old age pensioners, fatherless families, elderly migrants, recently arrived migrants (especially from southern Europe), the sick and the unemployed. Large families of low socio-economic status had a higher incidence of poverty, and this finding has been confirmed in another enquiry in Sydney.[16]

It is true that the aged, fatherless families and recent southern European migrants concentrated in the inner ring of suburbs around the Melbourne central business district and that there was a much greater incidence of poverty in these inner suburbs, particularly in Richmond, Collingwood, Prahran, South Melbourne and Port Melbourne. The criterion of poverty was an income (in 1966) for a standard family of a man, wife and two children equal only to the basic wage plus child endowment. This amounted to $32.00, so it was assumed that $33.00 was a reasonable figure to use as a poverty line. An adjustment was also made in order to measure poverty in terms of 'adjusted income after housing costs', as it was a common assumption that housing costs for low income families should represent not more than 20 per cent of income. The poverty line of $27.00 per week was adopted for 'adjusted income after housing costs'.

Utilizing the adult income unit adjusted incomes (for income unit definitions, see note 18 to Chapter 10), 4.2 per cent were classed as being very poor (an estimated number of 32,594 income units) and a further 3.5 per cent had adjusted incomes between $27 and $33. In addition 5.2 per cent (40,462 estimated income units) were classified as being marginally poor, so that 87 per cent were found to be distinctly not poor and almost 13 per cent were either poor or marginally poor. The marginally poor were less than $6 per week (under 20 per cent) above the poverty line, were often quite vulnerable, and in many cases only a slight change in their circumstances would result in their falling below the poverty line.

In terms of social segregation between areas, and by implication differences in the life chances of children between districts the breakdown of poverty and the marginally poor by sub areas makes graphic reading. Taking the 'very poor' and 'poor' categories described above, which together account for over 7 per cent of all income units in metropolitan Melbourne, over 22 per cent of income units in Richmond and over 20 per cent of those in Prahran, South Melbourne and Port Melbourne were below the poverty line in 1966. When those with marginal incomes are included, over 33 per cent were either poor or highly vulnerable in Richmond and over 30 per cent in Prahran, Collingwood, South Melbourne and Port Melbourne.

Recently arrived migrants contributed to this pattern in the inner suburbs, for 15.3 per cent and 16.2 per cent respectively of Greek and Italian post-1960 arrivals were below the poverty line compared with 7.7 per cent of the population as a whole. In Richmond, recently arrived migrants (mainly Greek) constituted over 45 per cent of those below the poverty line and over 52 per cent of the poor and marginally so.

Finally, the relationship between spatial variations in socio-economic characteristics and educational participation rates and school facilities is discussed. In theory, education is available in Australian cities and towns up to matriculation level at State schools which charge no tuition fees. In Australia, as in most countries, nominally free education involves quite high costs for books and school amenities as well as the cost of keeping the children. These factors often force many children of poor families to leave school as soon as they reach the legal minimum age. Moreover the quality of State schools (which 77 per cent of Australian children attend) varies greatly, usually in direct ratio to the economic and social status of the areas in which the schools are located, in a pattern similar to the variations in motivation of children to acquire education, which are strongly related to the economic and social status of their families.

Scholarships are awarded on a competitive basis, by both State and Commonwealth governments, to encourage students to continue past the minimum school-leaving age with secondary and tertiary education. These awards tend to be won by students at better schools and from backgrounds sympathetic to education. They are thus not often enjoyed by the children of poor families.

Hence in 1964, for every one student entering university from the industrial western suburbs of Melbourne, four came from the higher status south-eastern suburbs and only one from the poorer inner suburbs.[17] More recent figures have reinforced the trends indicated.[18] In the western industrial suburbs, there were 16.4 per cent of the appropriate age groups staying on beyond the minimum school leaving of 15, compared with an estimate of 12 per cent for the inner suburbs and 35.4 per cent of the south-eastern L.G.A.S. – St Kilda, Caulfield in particular and the other municipalities between Port Phillip and the eastern periphery. In Kew,

Camberwell and Caulfield over 40 per cent of the age group had matriculated and applied for university entry.[19]

There were also considerable variations in the incidence of pre-school and child care facilities and the percentages of 3–4 year olds attending centres between the western and central suburbs and the suburbs south and east of the River Yarra. The Victorian Education Department stated that 2,586 children in these age groups in the western suburbs were enrolled (17 per cent) out of a total of 14,580. Caulfield and Kew in the east have had up to 80 per cent participation, while in Footscray and South Melbourne attendance was little more than 10 per cent.

Despite the nominal free education available, parent contributions provide most of the day-to-day buying power and represent far greater inequality than any subsidy scheme devised. These small fees have normally been levied at the beginning of each year and are used by the headmaster for such things as text books, typing paper, phone bills, library books and the like. The principal of a school in a more affluent area can afford to set a $20 fee and often does so. Although its payment cannot be enforced, almost every parent pays. In a school in a relatively poor area the fee is set at $10 and only 60 per cent may pay. The result of this system is that headmasters of affluent area schools frequently have more than $10,000 extra to spend.[20] Until recently the amount of subsidies would be directly proportional to the amounts raised through parents. At the tertiary level (technical institutes, universities, colleges of advanced education), fees pose additional problems, unless the student is lucky enough to win a much sought after Commonwealth scholarship. Thus it can be seen that in Australia's cities, social segregation between areas has been reflected in the pattern of inequality between schools and in school environments.

Conclusion

A descriptive approach has been used in this essay to show that social segregation patterns have evolved in the Australian metropolis in the contemporary era, and that high and low status areas had begun to develop by the end of the nineteenth century. Clearly the highest and lowest status groups in the urban social structure have become the most residentially segregated, while those more similar in status were less spatially dissimilar in residence, this pattern following that described for Chicago by Duncan and Duncan.[21] There is a linkage between this study and those elsewhere in this volume on the impact of immigration on large cities and minority groups in the Australian metropolis, in that immigrant distributions are part of the residential stratification system and segregative process. The very flow of the Australian-born population from declining inner city areas to outer areas, while reflecting preferences for low residential densities and new housing, also indicates, as Harris found in America, a desire for class segregation.[22] There have been distinct areal variations in demographic and family composition and some social status and occupational segregation within areas relatively homogeneous in demographic composition. However, as Beshers noted for cities in the United States[23] familism and demographic characteristics may not be as meaningful as occupational rank in the analysis of segregation within the urban *social* structure. In so far as the ethnic groups can be regarded as a demographic factor, the ethnic dimension has become an important factor in social segregation, at once contributing to areal differentiation and at the same time reflecting socio-economic differences between areas.

Institutional factors have also been involved in the segregation process, if unwittingly. In the relocation of inner city families in high-rise Commission housing blocks or in State housing areas in new outer suburbs, social segregation exists because of the application of an income ceiling as well as selection of groups with particular family attributes. In the subsidy and supplementary fund-raising schemes for schools, as well as in provision of pre-school facilities, because of the self-help ethos implicit in these arrangements, social inequality and inequality of opportunity between areas have been maintained. In some outer suburban districts, individual and group developers have aimed at selective, higher status and cost-prohibitive new neighbourhoods.

Although in Sydney and Melbourne very broad geographical areas of different housing costs, status desirability and opportunity have evolved – as between the North Shore, south of the harbour and eastern suburbs in Sydney and east and west of the River Yarra in Melbourne – the areal social differentiation pattern is a mosaic in reality. But the areas of relative homogeneity are large enough in all probability to affect the life chances of the individual within them. Rich areas and slum areas have developed, but the gradient between these and their size relative to the whole urban social system are almost certainly less than in the United States or Canada. The incidence of poverty is also less, although in the Melbourne study reported upon, insufficient weight was given to the low socio-economic status outer western suburbs in the sampling scheme, so that the relative incidence of poverty in Australian cities may be greater than the figures suggest. Yet Australian society is a mobile one and residential and social mobility are common; the work of Allingham[24] and others indicates that opportunities and mobility are greater than in contemporary Europe and at least comparable with those in Anglo-America.

NOTES

1 F. Lancaster Jones, *Dimensions of Urban Social Structure*, A.N.U. Press, 1969.
2 F. Lancaster Jones, 'Social area analysis: some theoretical and methodological comments illustrated with Australian data', *British Journal of Sociology, 19*, 1968, pp. 424–4; F. Lancaster Jones, 'A social ranking of Melbourne suburbs', *Australian and New Zealand Journal of Sociology, 3*, 1967, pp. 93–110.
3 E. Shevky and M. Williams, *The Social Areas of Los Angeles*, Berkeley and Los Angeles, University of California Press, 1949.
4 Survey of properties offered for sale through real estate agents, Wollongong, March 1972.
5 Hugh Stretton, *Ideas for Australian Cities*, The Author, 1970.
6 P. Scott, 'Population structure of Australian cities', *Geographical Journal, 131*, 1965, pp. 463–81.
7 A. J. Rose, *Patterns of Cities*, Nelson, 1967.
8 Lois Bryson and Faith Thompson, *An Australian Newton. Life and Leadership in a New Housing Suburb*, Penguin, Ringwood, Victoria, 1972.
9 George Clarke, 'Urban Australia', in A. F. Davies and S. Encel (eds.), *Australian Society, a Sociological Introduction*, second ed., Cheshire, 1970, p. 80.
10 *Flats – a survey of Multi-Unit Construction in Australia*, Department of Housing, Canberra, 1969, p. 2.
11 Bernard Barrett, *The Inner Suburbs, the Evolution of an Industrial Area*, Melbourne University Press, 1971.
12 Athol Congalton, *Status and Prestige in Australia*, Melbourne, 1969.
13 Regrettably, no census questions are asked on income in Australia, despite pressure from research, professional and community groups.
14 Ronald F. Henderson, Alison Harcourt and R. J. A. Harper, *People in Poverty, a Melbourne Survey*, Cheshire, for the Institute of Applied Economic and Social Research, University of Melbourne, 1970, pp. 3–5.
15 I am grateful to Professor R. Henderson, Dr C. A. Price and the Academy of Social Sciences of Australia for making available unpublished cross-tabulations of the Survey of Living Conditions in Melbourne, which are used both in this chapter and chapter 10.
16 G. Halliday, 'Poverty and the large family in Sydney', unpublished Ph.D. thesis, Australian National University, 1971.
17 *Report of the Melbourne and Metropolitan Board of Works*, 1964.
18 *Report of Fourth University Committee on Education*, 1972.
19 T. Roper, 'Statistics show the west is losing', *The Review*, 1 July 1972.
20 T. Roper, *The Myth of Equality*, Education Department, National Union of Australian University Students, Heinemann Educational Australia, 1971, p. 34.
21 Otis Dudley Duncan and Beverley Duncan, 'Residential distribution and occupational stratification', *American Journal of Sociology, 60*, March 1955, p. 493.
22 B. Harris, 'Quantitative models of urban development: their role in metropolitan policy making', in H. Perloff and L. Wingo Jr. (eds.), *Issues in Urban Economics*, Baltimore, 1968, pp. 363–412.
23 James M. Beshers, *Urban Social Structure*, Free Press, New York, 1969, Ch. 3.
24 J. Allingham, 'Occupational and social mobility in Australia', Ph.D. dissertation in Demography, Australian National University, 1967.

9

The social structure of large cities

R. J. STIMSON

The social structure of large cities has been analysed from a number of viewpoints. Geographers have displayed particular concern with investigating areal patterns of social differentiation within residential areas and in developing models of urban spatial structure and growth. Sociologists have been concerned more with analysing the nature of behaviour within neighbourhoods and in studying processes which give rise to social stratification in urban society. The analysis of social structure of society and the spatial ramifications of the interaction of socially differentiated population sub-groups within urban areas has been enhanced by the development of techniques such as ecological correlation and residential segregation indices, the recognition of processes of ecological competition and succession, and the formulation of theories of urban structure such as the concentric zone, sector and multiple nuclei models, all of which have resulted from the synthesis of concepts and methods developed by urban geographers, sociologists and economists.

In this chapter initial brief mention is made of the development of a methodology for analysing and describing the nature of urban social structure. Reference is made to studies that have been made of the social structure of Australia's larger cities. The major part of the chapter, however, is concerned with outlining the results of a study of the factorial ecology of Adelaide in which the dimensions underlying the social structure of its residential areas are described and their spatial patterns analysed.

A methodology for studying urban social structure

Probably the greatest advance in synthesizing the approaches of the geographer and sociologist in studying the nature of urban social structure came in the early 1950s with the development of the Shevky–Bell social area typology.[1] As originally developed by Shevky and Bell and their associates, social area analysis provided a systematic classificatory schema for analysing residential areas in cities. Its purpose may be seen as specifying the nature and effects of structural changes in modern urban–industrial society. It was hypothesized that social differentiation in residential areas could be viewed from the basis of three broad trends in urban society, which relate to three constructs that could be described in terms of a limited range of measures derived from readily available census enumeration district data. Briefly, these three trends and constructs may be described in terms of: (1) changes in the distribution of skills, and subsequently the arrangement of occupations based on function, which give a socio-economic status (social rank) construct; (2) changes in the way of living involving the movement of women into urban occupations, and the diversification of family patterns which give a familism (urbanization) construct; and (3) changing composition of the population through the redistribution in space of ethnic and religious groups, due to both internal and international migration, which gives an ethnicity (segregation) construct.

Shevky and Bell maintained that these three constructs could be identified and described by means of selected indices taken from census tract data relating to characteristics of populations and households. The use of the census tract as an areal unit of analysis and as a data source for selecting indices describing the constructs meant that the social area typology for enquiring into the changing structure of urban industrial society was made synonymous with the study of social differentiation in residential areas of cities.

While there has been considerable criticism of the conceptual basis and methodology of the classic social area typology, empirical applications of the Shevky–Bell schema, particularly when modified to permit the identification of social dimensions derived from multivariate analysis of a wide-ranging battery of population and dwelling characteristics of residential areas of a city, have led to general validation of the hypothesis that the three indices, derived from the constructs of socio-economic status, familism and ethnicity, are necessary to describe the social differentiation that occurs in an urban ecological system.

The ready availability of computer facilities since the mid-1950s has meant that researchers have tended to employ techniques such as principal components and factor analysis to identify the nature of dimensions of urban social structure. Where a large battery of variables relating to the occupational, educational and income levels of the workforce, the sex, age structure and fertility rates and ethnic background of populations, and nature of tenancy and dwelling characteristics of residential areas are analysed, it has become common to refer to such studies as factorial ecologies of cities.

It has been typical for dimensions relating to the Shevky–Bell social area constructs to be identified. Invariably between four and ten factors (or components) or urban social structure, explaining about three-quarters of the total variance, are extracted from the data inter-correlation matrix for identification. It has become the rule to compute component scores for residential areas for each of the identified dimensions of social structure, and to analyse the spatial distribution of these scores, often with the intention of testing for the presence of a zonal or sectoral structure of the social dimensions.

The development of social area analysis and factorial ecology studies of urban social structure have thus provided a common framework by which cities may have their social structures compared and by which the stability of the social structure of a particular city over time may be determined. Obviously the selection of variables in the data-mix will greatly influence the nature and the dimensions of the urban social structure identified, but it has become apparent that there is a high degree of stability between cities in their social structures which may be adequately described in terms of the social area constructs of socio-economic status, familism and ethnicity. However, these dimensions need not necessarily be independent of each other. Furthermore, the factor ecological approach enables the identification of constructs additional to those hypothesized by Shevky and Bell.

The social structure of Australian cities

Over the past decade there have been published the results of a number of independent studies by individual researchers enquiring into various aspects of the social structure of Australia's larger cities. These studies fall into a number of categories.

First, there are those concerned with analysing the spatial patterns of a city's residential structure, of which Johnston's paper on zonal and sectoral patterns in Melbourne's structure is an example.[2]

Second, there are studies in which the processes of evolution of and spatial change in specific types of residential areas, such as high status suburbs, are discussed.[3]

Third, there are studies in which the patterns of distribution and segregation of particular population sub-groups in a city, such as migrant groups, are analysed.[4]

Fourth, there have been a limited number of attempts to derive a social ranking of suburbs of a city via the reputational approach, whereby a sample of residents are asked to rate suburbs according to their perception of the relative social prestige of those suburbs.[5]

Finally there have been a number of attempts to use the social area typology or factorial ecology approach to investigate the dimensions of social structure in a city and describe the spatial expression of those dimensions over the residential areas of a city.

It is unfortunate that analysis of the urban social structure of Australian cities who have pursued the last-mentioned approach have used different area bases, different sets of data variables and different methods of data analysis. Thus, it is difficult to draw comparisons between such studies, and even more difficult to do anything more than offer tentative conclusions about the stability of underlying dimensions of social structure of residential areas in Australia's larger cities.

While it is possible to make the general statement that Australian cities have much in common with those of the United States, they have experienced rapid expansion in the post-1947 era, this growth being due in large part to a programme of massive immigration from European countries as well as the United Kingdom. The expansion has been in the form of low density housing suburban development, with actual population decline characterizing many inner city areas. Only in very recent years, and only in Sydney and Melbourne, has there been a significant degree of redevelopment of a medium to high density nature in the near city-centre localities.

As has been found to be the case in North American and Scandinavian cities, Australian cities tend to have underlying dimensions that are readily described in terms of, and which relate to population differences in, socio-economic status, family characteristics and ethnicity. Socio-economic status and familism are usually independent of each other, but in some cases ethnicity was related to low socio-economic status dimensions. As to be expected from the variety of migrant sources from which new settlers have come, it was not uncommon to have identified a number of dimensions which relate to rather specific migrant groups. In addition, some cities, depending on the nature of variables used in the analysis, displayed specific dimensions relating to growth and density of development. However, no attempt has yet been made to establish what dimensions, hypothesized in terms of the social area constructs or combinations of them, are essentially stable within the structure of Australian urban society and which are specific factors of social differentiation unique for a city and related to its peculiar circumstances of urban development or specific types of population sub-groups, especially ethnic concentrations.

The factorial ecology of Adelaide

The data

In this study of the factorial ecology of Adelaide 1966 census data for collectors districts were used, but these units were aggregated to form an areal base of aggregated collectors districts (A.C.D.).

Aggregation was effected so as to form units which approximated suburb boundaries and which had populations as close as possible to 5,000. The area studied covered the elongated metropolitan area of Adelaide, plus some urban areas to the south and east. It stretched from Elizabeth Field in the north to Port Noarlunga in the south, and from the coastal suburbs along St Vincent's Gulf in the west up the scarp of the Mt Lofty ranges into the Crafers-Bridgewater area in the hills to the east. The 111 variables used to analyse the social structure of these A.C.D.s are listed in Table 9.1. They were chosen to give a wide-ranging cover of socio-economic status, demographic, ethnic and household characteristics of Adelaide's population and the dwellings in which they reside. Variables 1 to 50 are surrogate measures of socio-economic status, variables 51 to 75 refer to familism and household characteristics, and variables 76 to 111 are measures of the ethnic and religious characteristics of the population.

TABLE 9.1. *Rotated seven-factor solution (varimax criterion) for Adelaide A.C.D.s 1966*

| Variables | \multicolumn{8}{c}{Factor loadings} |
	I	II	III	IV	V	VI	VII	h^2
1 % MWF employers	91							89
2 % FWF employers	74							62
3 % MWF self-employed	58			46				74
4 % MWF employees	−87							88
5 % FWF employees	−41		−51					49
6 % MWF helpers								05
7 % FWF helpers	33							15
8 % MWF unemployed		68	31					73
9 % M non-WF pensioners					77			75
10 % M non-WF retired or indep. means	63				49			67
11 % MWFI primary production				39				32
12 % MWFI mining and quarrying	36				−35			42
13 % MWFI manufacturing	−84							82
14 % FWFI manufacturing	−84							85
15 % MWFI electricity, gas, water				30				35
16 % MWFI building and construction				39	−61			72
17 % MWFI transport and storage	−51					31		52
18 % MWFI communications			−33			−57		57
19 % MWFI finance and property	87							87
20 % FWFI finance and property	52		−32			−36		68
21 % MWFI commerce	77					33		85
22 % FWFI commerce								10
23 % MWFI public authority, defence							−75	65
24 % MWFI prof. and business services	90							86
25 % FWFI prof. and business services	72							66
26 % MWFI amusements, hotels, personal services	46	70						82
27 % FWFI amusements, hotels, personal services		69						59
28 % MWFO professional, technical	90							90
29 % FWFO professional, technical	76							68
30 % MWFO administrative, executive, managerial	91							92

TABLE 9.1 (*contd.*)

Variables	Factor loadings							
	I	II	III	IV	V	VI	VII	h^2
31 % FWFO administrative, executive, managerial	73							68
32 % MWFO clerical	59		−31	−31	30	−32		83
33 % FWFO clerical	38	−43				−36	41	76
34 % MWFO sales	80					−34		84
35 % FWFO sales	−39				−39	−35		66
36 % MWFO craftsmen, production, process workers, labourers	−92							96
37 % FWFO craftsmen, production, process workers, labourers	−85					32		87
38 % MWFO service, sport, recreation		78						63
39 % FWFO service, sport, recreation	−41	53						55
40 % MWFO armed services							−77	65
41 % MWF with tertiary educ. quals.	92							94
42 % MWF with sub-tertiary (incl. trade) educ. quals.		−35		−33	−66			85
43 % MWF with no educ. quals.	−50				38			56
44 % private dwellings owner-occupied	42	−51					56	80
45 % private dwellings tenanted		75			40			84
46 % private dwellings govt. tenanted	−54			−34			−54	79
47 % private dwellings with T.V. set	−31	−56		−41	−34			77
48 % private dwellings with no car		65			60			93
49 % private dwellings with one car		−45			−61			73
50 % private dwellings with 2 or more cars	61	−53						78
51 Male/female ratio	−54				−35			46
52 % population 0–14 years	−31	−42			−70			87
53 % population 15–19 years			−62		32		−41	77
54 % population 20–29 years			47	39	−43			58
55 % population 30–39 years			31		−77			76
56 % population 40–49 years			−71	−30				71
57 % population 50–59 years			−43		−78			91
58 % population 60 years and over	38	38			72			84
59 % popn. aged 15 and over never married		55	−38		49		−36	86
60 % popn. aged 15 and over non-single widowed	37	46			69			86
61 % popn. aged 15 and over non-single divorced or separated		86			35			92
62 Dependency ratio		−41	32		−67			84
63 Fertility ratio	−30	−38	49		−64			90
64 % male popn. in the workforce				31	+50			45
65 % female popn. in the workforce		68	−30					62

TABLE 9.1 (*contd.*)

Variables	I	II	III	IV	V	VI	VII	h^2
66 % workforce females	39	60						60
67 % female popn. aged 15 and over non-single in home duties		−50						33
68 % popn. aged 15 and over pensioners		36			82			86
69 % change in population 1961–6			36					22
70 % private dwellings built 1961–6			49		−65			75
71 % private dwellings flats	37	52			39			61
72 % dwellings non-private		79						73
73 % private dwellings shared				37	56			62
74 Rooms per private dwelling		−82						74
75 Persons per dwelling	−43				−64		−33	79
76 % popn. born in Australia	45		−72		37			89
77 % Australian born popn. born outside South Australia		33	42				−39	51
78 % popn. born overseas	−45		72		−37			89
79 % popn. born in Continental Europe	−34			79		36		95
80 % popn. born in U.K. and Ireland			68	−45	−41			92
81 % popn. born in Netherlands					−68			56
82 % popn. born in Germany					−64	42		69
83 % popn. born in Austria					−40	45		51
84 % popn. born in Hungary		33		51				49
85 % popn. born in Czechoslovakia						48		37
86 % popn. born in Poland	−36					70		73
87 % popn. born in the Baltic countries			−53	31				51
88 % popn. born in the U.S.S.R.	−32		−31			73		77
89 % popn. born in Yugoslavia	−39			35		64		79
90 % popn. born in Italy				80				69
91 % popn. born in Greece		35		49	44			67
92 % popn. born in Malta		43						39
93 % popn. born elsewhere in Europe				39	30			31
94 % popn. born in New Zealand	78							69
95 % popn. born in U.S.A. or Canada	58							50
96 % popn. born in Asia		41				36		42
97 % popn. aliens				81				85
98 % o'seas-born popn. aliens				80				77
99 % o'seas-born popn. resident 0–5 years			81					84
100 % o'seas-born popn. resident 6–12 years				49			−36	51
101 % o'seas-born popn. resident 13–19 years			−85					83
102 % o'seas-born popn. resident over 19 years	54		−35		64			86

TABLE 9.1 (*contd.*)

Variables	Factor loadings							
	I	II	III	IV	V	VI	VII	h^2
103 % population Baptist					31			31
104 % population Catholic	−38			63				66
105 % population Church of England	38		40	−70				89
106 % population Methodist		−35	−57			−32		66
107 % population Presbyterian				−54				48
108 % population Greek Orthodox		33		51	44			70
109 % population Lutheran					−57			53
110 % population Hebrew	61							46
111 % population with no religion			39				−33	41
Percentage of total variance	24.21	18.95	7.69	6.17	3.94	3.14	2.64	

Key

MWF	male workforce
FWF	female workforce
M non-WF	males not in the workforce
MWFI	male workforce in industry group
FWFI	female workforce in industry group
MWFO	male workforce in occupation group
FWFO	female workforce in occupation group

Data analysis

Data analysis involved the use of factor analysis of the inter-correlation matrix between the variables. A principal axis solution and varimax rotation criterion were employed, and standardized factor scores for areas were calculated using rotated factor loadings of variables on the factors identified.

There has been considerable debate over the best method to obtain an initial and derived solution in principal components and factor analysis, and on deciding the number of factors on which to rotate. Needless to say this decision is subjective, and for this study a varimax rotation solution for the first seven factors was decided on, this being taken on the basis that one would be hard put to meaningfully describe dimensions of social structure pertaining to additional factors, that any additional factor did not account for more than 3.0 per cent of the total variance, and that with such a large number of variables it was better than expected that the factors used for rotation accounted for almost two-thirds of the total variance. In accordance with a practice suggested by some writers that one should rotate one factor more than the required solution to overcome the effect of residual variance adhering to the last rotated factor, only the first six factors are interpreted and described.

Dimensions of urban social structure

Analysis of the factor loadings of variables on the first six factors leads to the identification of the following dimensions of urban social structure for Adelaide:

 I Socio-economic status (24.2% variance)
 II Household composition (18.9% variance)
 III Recent and U.K. migrant settlers (7.7% variance)
 IV High ethnicity (6.2% variance)
 V Familism (3.9% variance)
 VI Eastern European migrants (3.0% variance)

These dimensions relate to the three social area constructs of socio-economic status, familism and ethnicity, which has been the case in many similar studies of the factorial ecology where a large battery of census variables have been used,[6] and which is to be expected in view of the fact that variables were selected as surrogate measures for these constructs. Factor I identifies a socio-economic status dimension and accounts for the quite high figure of almost 25 per cent of the total variance. Factor II is associated with household characteristics, plus some occupational and ethnic characteristics that may well relate to the 'zone in transition' area of a city, while factor V identifies a familism dimension rather than a more general household characteristics dimension. Factors III, IV and VI relate predominantly to various ethnic characteristics of Adelaide's social structure, factor IV being a general ethnicity dimension, factor III relating to a more specific dimension identifying rapidly growing fringe areas characterized by high concentrations of British migrants, and factor VI being more specifically a dimension related to eastern European migrants.

The detailed composition of these factors, plus the spatial character of the dimensions of urban social structure they identify, may be obtained from a closer analysis of the factor loadings in Table 9.1 and the distribution of standardized factor scores for A.C.D.S.

I Socio-economic status. Variables with the highest positive loadings on this factor include employers; those in the finance and property and professional and business service industries; persons in professional, technical, administrative, executive and managerial occupations; males in the workforce with tertiary educational qualifications; dwellings with two or more cars; and persons who were born in New Zealand, Canada or the U.S.A., those who are pre-1947 migrants, or who are Jewish. Conversely, variables indicative of low socio-economic status have the highest negative loadings on this factor, such as employees, persons in crafts, production and labouring occupations, and males without educational qualifications. It is notable that few variables relating to family status and household composition were strongly associated with this dimension, whereas some of the migrant groups from European countries displayed a degree of negative association.

There is a distinct concentration of high socio-economic status suburbs in the eastern and south-eastern sectors of the city, stretching up to the foothills and over the scarp of the Mt Lofty ranges, plus some of the coastal suburbs south of Glenelg, a few of the old-established inner-city suburbs such as Unley Park and North Adelaide-Walkerville, and some of the former market garden areas along the Torrens River, such as Lockleys. The top rating suburbs on this scale were Tusmore, St Georges, Beaumont, Kensington Gardens, Springfield, Myrtle Bank, Walkerville, Toorak Gardens, Belair and Kingswood.

In contrast, suburbs with the lowest socio-economic status are located almost exclusively in the industrial suburbs in the western and north-western sector of the city stretching from Bowden to Port Adelaide, and the northern suburbs including the satellite city of Elizabeth. Many of the lower status areas were developed by the Housing Trust. In addition, their incidence is closely associated with both old and newer suburban industrial areas.

II Household composition. Variables with high factor loadings on this dimension mainly relate to characteristics of family structure and dwellings. Those with the highest positive loadings include unemployed males, those in the amusement, hotel and personal service industries, the proportion of the population above 15 years that is unmarried, divorced and separated adults, the proportion of the workforce that is female, the proportion of dwellings that are flats, that are tenanted and that are non-private, and dwellings with no car. The proportion of married women in home duties, the number of rooms per private dwelling, owner-occupied dwellings, dwellings without a T.V. set, and dependency and fertility ratios had the highest negative loadings.

It is evident that this factor, which accounts for almost one-fifth of the total variance, identifies what is typically called a zone-in-transition type of dimension that is characterized by low familism, unmarried members of the workforce, higher than average unemployment rates, flats and non-private dwellings, and low rates of car ownership relative to elsewhere in the city. There is also some relationship of Greek- and Maltese-born migrants with this dimension.

The pattern of factor scores shown is one where areas with the highest scores were in the old-established inner city and City-Port Adelaide north-western sector, such as St Peters, Unley, Thebarton, Goodwood, Parkside, Norwood, Adelaide City and Glenelg. In contrast, suburbs with the lowest scores were predominantly the newer fringe suburbs in Elizabeth,

Salisbury and Tea Tree Gully to the north and north-east, Eden Hills and Blackwood in the hills suburbs, and the southern fringe areas around Christies Beach. The pattern is one of a distinct gradation of scores from high positive in the inner suburbs to low negative in the fringe areas. This is confirmed by the significant negative correlation ($r = -0.51$) between factor scores for suburbs and road distance from the C.B.D.

III Recent and U.K.-born migrant settlers. The dimension identified by factor III clearly relates to areas with high concentrations of British migrants and recently arrived overseas settlers. These areas also have relatively high proportions of youthful age groups, especially 0–5 and 20–29 years, a high fertility ratio, and a high proportion of dwellings built during the previous five years. The factor loadings indicate that there was marked negative association with this dimension of the Australian-born, migrants who were pre-1954 arrivals, per cent population aged 15–19 and 40–49 years, and the proportion of female workforce that were employees.

The pattern of factor scores clearly shows how the rapidly growing suburbs on the northern, north-eastern and southern fringes of the city had highest scores on this dimension. Over half the population of the Elizabeth and Salisbury districts, in particular, are British migrants. In contrast, the inner suburbs, the eastern and south-eastern and hills suburbs, and most coastal areas, had relatively low scores. Not suprisingly this pattern of zonal variation gave a correlation of $r = +0.62$ between the factor scores of suburbs and distance from the C.B.D.

IV High ethnicity. Factor IV emerges as one identifying an ethnicity dimension. Areas with high scores tended to have high proportions of European migrants, especially from Italy, Greece, Yugoslavia and Hungary, and a high proportion of aliens in general. In addition some religious variables, such as Catholics and Greek Orthodox, had high positive loadings on this factor. Not one of the variables relating to socio-economic status characteristics of suburbs had a loading that exceeded ± 0.50. The situation is similar with regard to familism and household characteristics of suburbs.

Those suburbs with highest ethnicity were located almost exclusively in the inner city suburbs and the north-western sector of the city, plus some suburbs such as Athelstone and Paradise along the Torrens valley east of the C.B.D. Adelaide City, Thebarton, Torrensville, Bowden, Hindmarsh, Norwood, Parkside and Hectorville had highest ethnicity. Basically Greek migrants tended to be concentrated mostly in these areas, plus Port Adelaide, whereas Italian migrants, as well as having high concentration in the inner city suburbs, have become concentrated in the suburbs stretching along the Torrens River, such as Marden, Felixstow,

Klemzig, Cambelltown, Newton and Athelstone to the east and Underdale, Flinders Park and Fulham Gardens to the west, these all being areas where market gardening was an important activity until recent years.

The rapidly growing fringe areas to the north, north-east and south, plus the coastal and eastern, south-eastern and hills suburbs, all had low scores on this dimension.

In general there is a strong sectoral pattern associated with areas of high ethnicity, in addition to the central zone of high ethnicity.

V Familism. A relatively large number of variables had high loadings on this factor, which accounts for only 4.4 per cent of the total variance. It may be described as a general familism dimension. Areas with high positive scores on this factor tend to have an ageing population, relatively high proportions of pensioners, retired persons, unmarried adults, divorced and separated persons, and a high proportion of shared dwellings and flats. In contrast, the youthful age groups, fertility and dependency ratios, and proportion of dwellings built in the previous five years were the variables with most marked negative factor loadings.

In many respects this factor identifies a dimension that is similar to that identified by factor II, but from a close analysis of factor loadings of variables, factor V probably is more specifically one associated with areas of low familism.

From the pattern of factor scores, a roughly zonal arrangement in the metropolitan area is evident, there being a marked negative correlation ($r = -0.62$) between factor scores of suburbs and distance from the C.B.D.

Areas with lowest familism were Adelaide City, Tusmore, Toorak Gardens, Glenelg, Unley Park, Malvern, North Adelaide and Goodwood. These, plus other suburbs with high scores, are exclusively located in the inner suburbs, the eastern sector, and around Port Adelaide and Glenelg. Not surprisingly, high familism suburbs are in the fringe areas to the north and north-east, the southern suburbs stretching to Christies Beach, and the hills suburbs of Eden Hills, Bellevue Heights and Blackwood. In particular, the Elizabeth, Salisbury, Para Hills and Tea Tree Gully areas had highest familism.

VI Eastern European migrants. The final factor for which a dimension of social structure has been identified relates to European migrants, predominantly from Poland, the U.S.S.R., Yugoslavia and Austria in particular, and to a lesser extent from Germany and Czechoslovakia, these being migrants from eastern and central Europe.

The pattern of distribution of suburb scores on this dimension is one contrasting central and northern suburbs, which have positive scores, with the suburbs south of the city, which have low or negative scores.

Adelaide City, Thebarton, Hindmarsh, Bowden, Croydon Park, Unley, Parkside and Norwood in the inner city area, and Rosewater, Ottoway, Semaphore, Port Adelaide, Athol Park and Wingfield in the north-western sector had the highest scores. The coastal suburbs, eastern, south-eastern and foothills areas, and some of the outer north-eastern and southern fringe suburbs had the lowest scores on this dimension.

The independence of dimensions

The degree to which there is interdependence between dimensions derived from factor analysis using an orthogonal solution, such as the varimax rotation, has received considerable attention in the literature on the factorial ecological approach to the study of urban social structure, especially in a recent paper by Johnston,[7] in which he has demonstrated that there are theoretical grounds on which socio-economic status and ethnicity dimensions in particular are interrelated.

As a crude test of the degree to which dimensions of urban social structure identified in the manner employed in this study are interrelated, the Goodman test of interdependence was used. From the results given in Table 9.2 it is evident that there was significant interdependence between many of the factors at the 0.01 level, and between most factors at the 0.05 level.

TABLE 9.2. *Test of independence of dimension of urban social structure in Adelaide*

Factor	Z score					
I Socio-economic status	—					
II Household composition	0.94	—				
III Recent and U.K. migrant settlers	5.20^a	3.13^a	—			
IV High ethnicity	2.81^a	6.03^a	0.26	—		
V Familism	3.94^a	5.72^a	6.11^a	2.40	—	
VI Eastern European migrants	5.06^a	4.72^a	0.75	6.71^a	2.21	—
	I	II	III	IV	V	VI

^{a} Significant at 0.01 level.

In particular, there was a considerable degree of interdependence between factor I (socio-economic status) and factor III (recent and U.K. migrants), factor IV (high ethnicity), factor V (familism) and factor VI (eastern European migrants). Not surprisingly there was a highly significant degree of interdependence between factors II and V. Most of the three factors relating to an ethnicity-type dimension are interrelated with the household composition and familism dimensions.

Thus, there appears to be lack of independence of dimensions identified from one another, an occurrence which is not peculiar to Adelaide.[8]

A typology of residential areas

Having described the nature of the dimensions of urban social structure and the spatial patterns of residential area factor scores on each dimension, it is possible to develop a typology, or classification, of suburbs on the basis of their standardized factor scores on the dimensions discussed above. For this purpose one of many available hierarchical polythetic classificatory strategies has been employed. The utility of these procedures for classificatory purposes in urban geography has been discussed elsewhere by the author.[9] The methodology was also employed by Jones in his study of the social areas of Melbourne to classify surburbs.

Briefly, areas are fused, or combined, on the basis of their degree of similarity as measured by a set of common variables, so that at any point in the progressive fusion of individual or already grouped areas into new groups there is greater within-group similarity of member areas on the variables used for classificatory purposes than there exists between groups.[10] As with most classification techniques the level at which one decides to cease breaking down large fused groups of areas into smaller groups is subjective.[11] In this case, Adelaide suburbs have been classified into twelve categories following an initial breakdown of the city into four broad groups.

Four broad residential categories. Initially it is possible to distinguish between suburbs in *group 276* which are broadly the outer suburbs to the east, north and south and south-west of the city, characterized by low ethnicity and medium to high ethnicity, and suburbs in *group 275* that are characterized by high ethnicity, low familism and generally low socio-economic status, located in the inner city and the north-western sector, plus the southern industrial suburbs.

Within group 276, two clearly different categories of suburbs exist. First, those belonging to *group 271* are the high socio-economic status suburbs to the east and south-east of the city and in the hills and bayside areas. Second, *group 273* suburbs are the rapidly growing areas on the northern, north-eastern and southern fringes of the city, with low or medium socio-economic status, high familism and extremely high scores on the recent and U.K. migrant settlers dimension.

The broad group 275 is split into two distinctive sub-categories. *Group 272* are the inner city 'zone-in-transition' suburbs with high ethnicity, low familism, high scores on factor II (household composition) and low to middle socio-economic status. *Group 269* suburbs are basically located in the industrial sector that stretches from Bowden to Port Adelaide, plus the industrial suburbs of the north around Wingfield and Kilburn and of the south around Edwardstown and Clovelly Park. They are low socio-economic status areas, have lower scores on factors II and III, but have higher rates of familism than group 272 suburbs.

Refining the classification. (i) Within *group 272*, the inner city suburbs, two categories have been distinguished. Both have high ethnicity, and low socio-economic status, high scores on the household composition dimension, and low familism. *Group 265* (3 members) forms the area bounded by the City of Adelaide local government area. *Group 264* (12 members) are adjacent old suburbs to the east, south and west where working class villages developed soon after the intial settlement of Adelaide. *Group 264* suburbs are characterized by lower scores on factors II, I and V than *group 265* suburbs.

(ii) Within *group 274* three subdivisions have been derived. *Group 243* (5 members) are the sparsely settled areas in the vicinity of Port Adelaide around Ottoway and Wingfield. They have extremely high scores on factor VI (eastern European migrants), and are of very low socio-economic status, which differentiates the group from *group 269*. The other two groups, *group 267* (21 members) and *group 266* (20 members), both have low socio-economic status and relatively low scores on factor III (recent and U.K. migrants), but are differentiated by the higher degree of ethnicity and higher scores on the household composition and familism (i.e. low) dimensions possessed by *group 267*.

(iii) Within *group 271*, it is possible to separate out *group 263* (20 members), which is differentiated from the remaining suburbs by virtue of the high scores its suburbs possess on the household composition component while maintaining above average socio-economic status. Similarly, members of this group tended to have lower familism, which is not surprising as they are located mainly in either the inner southern suburbs or the old coastal areas around Glenelg and Grange. Of the remaining suburbs within the broad higher status subdivision of Adelaide, *group 237* (7 members) and *group 262* (22 members) are differentiated on the basis of the former's extremely high scores on the socio-economic status dimension, low familism and extremely low scores on the recent U.K. migrants dimension. Overall both these groups possess low scores on all those dimensions relating to the ethnicity characteristics of their populations. *Group 262* suburbs, being located predominantly in the rapidly developing foothills and hills suburbs and the south-western coastal sector, have medium to high familism as well as being of high socio-economic status.

(iv) Within *group 273* four categories are differentiated in what are basically the northern and southern fringe areas of Adelaide. *Group 257* (9 members) suburbs are all located in the Elizabeth and Para Hills areas.

They are characterized by extremely high scores on the recent and U.K. migrants dimension and very low socio-economic status, and high familism and low scores on factor II. *Group 225* (4 members) suburbs are located in relatively recently developed former market garden areas along the Torrens River at Fulham Gardens and in the Newton-Paradise area, and, while having below average socio-economic status, they are characterized by higher ethnicity scores than other sub-categories within the broad *group 273*, this being a result mainly of the relatively large numbers of Italian migrants that live in these suburbs. In addition, *group 225* suburbs have high familism and low scores on factor II. The remaining two categories, group 255 (9 members) and group 250 (7 members), are located in the Salisbury, Para Vista and Tea Tree Gully areas on the northern and north-eastern fringe of Adelaide, and the Reynella-Christies Beach area in the southern fringe. They are both below average in socio-economic status, especially *group 255* which has higher scores on factor VI (eastern European migrants) than *group 250*. *Group 250* are higher familism suburbs than are *group 255* suburbs.

Conclusion

Urban populations are residentially differentiated in terms of many and diverse characteristics. The factor ecological method of analysing the dimensions of social structure that underly that population and the study of the variations that occur in the spatial patterns of those dimensions has become standard practice in recent years. In this study of Adelaide it has been shown that residential areas are socially differentiated basically in terms of the Shevky-Bell social area constructs relating to socio-economic status, family status and ethnic status. The six dimensions identified, following factor analysis of a large number of census variables relating to population and dwelling characteristics of aggregated collectors' districts, displayed quite marked variations in their areal expression, ranging from a broad sectoral pattern for the socio-economic status dimensions to a marked zonal pattern for the household characteristics dimension. In general the findings confirm those reported in studies of other Australian cities, despite the many differences in data and methodologies employed.

The identification of the dimensions of urban structure of residential areas of cities and the development of a typology of residential areas from the factor scores possessed by residential areas on those dimensions represent a means whereby urban areas may be residentially stratified. This provides a suitable basis for the study of other aspects of the social geography of cities, especially some of the dynamic characteristics of urban populations, such as residential mobility.

NOTES

1 E. Shevky and W. Bell, *Social Area Analysis: Theory, Illustrative Application and Computational Procedures*, Stanford, 1955.

2 R. J. Johnston, 'Zonal and sectoral patterns in Melbourne's residential structure', *Land Econ.*, *45*, 1969, pp. 463–7.

3 R. J. Johnston, 'The location of high status residential areas', *Geogr. Ann.*, *48*B, 1966, pp. 23–35.

4 R. J. Stimson, 'Patterns of European immigrant settlement in Melbourne, 1947–1961', *Tijd. voor Econ. en Soc. Geogr.*, *61*, 1970, pp. 114–26.

5 A. A. Congalton, 'Status ranking of Sydney suburbs', *Studies in Sociology*, no. 1, 1961, University of N.S.W.

6 R. A. Murdie, *Factorial Ecology of Metropolitan Toronto, 1957–1961*, Chicago, 1969, Department of Geography Research Paper no. 116.

7 R. J. Johnston, 'Some limitations of factorial ecologies and social area analysis', *Econ. Geogr.*, *47*, 1971, Supplement, pp. 314–23.

8 J. Forrest, 'Factorial ecology of Dunedin, New Zealand', 43rd A.N.Z.A.A.S. Congress, Section 21, Brisbane, 1971; F. L. Jones, *Dimensions of Urban Social Structure: the Social Areas of Melbourne*, Canberra, 1969.

9 R. J. Stimson, 'Hierarchical classificatory methods: an application to Melbourne population data', *Aust. Geogr. St.*, *8*, 1970, pp. 149–72.

10 In this study a Euclidean metric and flexible sorting strategy with $\beta = -0.25$ was employed. No weighting was given the six variables used as the basis for classification, these being standardized factor scores of A.C.D.s on the six factors described earlier.

11 The problem of subjectivity in classificatory strategies is discussed by R. J. Johnston, 'Choice in classification: the subjectivity of objective methods', *Annals, Assoc. Amer. Geogr.*, *58*, 1968, 575–89. In this study a programme GROUPER, available at the Division of Computing Research, C.S.I.R.O., Canberra, was used. Its attributes are discussed in G. N. Lance, P. W. Milne and W. T. Williams, 'Mixed data classificatory programs: III diagnostic systems', *Aust. Computer Jour.*, *1*, 1968, 178–81. The programme produces comparison of variable means and contributions for similarity for each variable between groups into which A.C.D.s are assigned using a fusion programme, MULTCLASS, discussed in N. G. Lance and W. T. Williams, 'A general theory of classificatory sorting strategies: 1. hierarchical systems', *Computer Jour.*, *9*, 1967, 373–80.

10

Social ecology of immigrant settlement in Australian cities

I. H. BURNLEY

Comparatively little research, numbering only some seven published papers, has been undertaken on any facet of immigrant settlement in Australian cities in the post-war era, and no definitive study has as yet been published. Yet immigration has played a paramount role in the post-war urbanization process in Australia and has become with its ethnic diversity a major factor in residential, ecological and even social class differentiation within the major cities. The largest immigrant communities which have developed in Sydney, Melbourne and Adelaide are of a size which can support a host of ethnic institutions, voluntary associations, shops and services, as well as the maintenance of cultural patterns and folkways of old world societies. It will be shown, however, that with certain exceptions, the ghetto model of immigrant settlement and adjustment is not readily applicable to the Australian post-war situation. However, many of the ecological processes described by Park, Burgess, Frazier, Wirth and others in the American metropolis in the early decades of the twentieth century[1] are identifiable in the contemporary Australian metropolis.

Migrant numbers

The pattern of immigration to Australia post-war has been very different from that of pre-war days, when the migration rate to Australia was not only much smaller but British immigrants were predominant in the ratio 10:1.[2] Post-war, not only was immigration increased so that it was directly responsible for 0.8 per cent of population being added to the Australian total per annum, but the non-British Isles-born population increased to 61 per cent of the total net migration of 2,039,000 between 1 July 1947 and 30 June 1970.[3] Although the British Isles contributed 874,000 net migrants between these dates, southern Europe contributed almost 527,000, of whom 277,000 were Italians, 170,500 Greeks and 58,600 Maltese. Other large groups were 109,500 Netherlands born, 83,000 Germans, 107,600 born in Yugoslavia and 81,000 from Poland.

By the 1966 census, large groupings from these countries of birth had formed in the three southern State capitals of Sydney, Melbourne and Adelaide in particular, as well as Perth and Wollongong. In 1966, there were over 92,000 Italian-born in Melbourne and 53,500 in metropolitan

Sydney, while by 1972 it was estimated that there were over 100,000 persons of Italian birth in Melbourne. It is estimated that by 1971 there were 70,000 Greeks born overseas in Melbourne and 50,000 in metropolitan Sydney.

It is difficult to calculate the number of children born in Australia to Greek and Italian or other immigrant parents and particularly so for any geographical unit below the national level. However, estimates have been made in order to assess the actual size of the first and second generations together in the main cities. On the basis that the peak *Italian* migrations of persons especially between the ages of 16 and 40 took place in the 1950s, so that most marrying in Australia and starting families had begun to do so by 1971, it is estimated there were an additional 25,000 second generation Italians in Melbourne by that date. Thus there were probably almost 130,000 in the Italian community in Melbourne in 1971 and perhaps 70,000 in Sydney. On the other hand, the peak Greek migration to Australia took place between 1961 and 1966 so that fewer children would have been born to Greeks in Australia by 1971, when it is estimated that there were over 80,000 first and second generation Greeks in Melbourne and over 60,000 in Sydney. The second generation children born to British, Dutch and Germans in Australia in the post-war era would have constituted smaller proportions of their respective communities, because family migration under the various assisted passage schemes meant that *relatively* fewer children would have been born in Australia.

Social origins of immigrant groups

The social origins of the large immigrant minorities in the Australian metropolis in the post-war period have varied considerably between birthplace groups. Thus when one considers the patterns of ecological and social adjustment of migrants in Australian urban society, what at first may appear to be an ethnic characteristic may in fact be one of the relatively few forms of adjustment possible to migrants with limited educational and occupational attributes. This is partly bound up with migration forms, discussed at greater length below, and is further illustrated in the next chapter.

On the basis of a survey of announcements of immigrants' intentions to naturalize in Sydney, Melbourne and Adelaide for the period 1952–5 inclusive,[4] and a field survey, it is estimated that over 75 per cent of the Dutch and Germans were born in cities or large towns, whereas over 80 per cent of the Greek- and Italian-born and over 70 per cent of persons from Yugoslavia were estimated to have been born in small towns or rural villages. These were all post-war arrivals. Thus with most southern Europeans, urbanization has taken place along with transoceanic migration, so that two adjustments were required in Australia: that of folk/peasant community members in an urban industrial milieu and that of the cultural integration of diverse ethnic groups into Australian society.

Educational background may provide an important clue as to the residential, occupational and social adjustment of migrants in the Australian metropolis. In the 1966 census, information on education by birthplace was available for the first time, and unpublished tabulations were available for each section of each State. In metropolitan Melbourne 3.4 and 3.8 per cent of Italian and Greek males over 20 years of age had no schooling and for Maltese males the figure was 8.5 per cent, compared with 0.3 per cent of Australian-born men. For women, percentages over 20 with no schooling were higher, those Italian-, Greek- and Maltese-born being 6.0, 7.4 and 10.6 per cent respectively, while Yugoslav- and Polish-born proportions were 3.2 and 3.1 per cent, compared with only 0.3 per cent of the Australian-born. Percentages of both males and females from southern Europe with no schooling in the upper age groups were even higher: over 11 per cent of Greek males aged 55–69 had had no schooling compared with almost 18 per cent of those over 75, while with Italians, almost 10 per cent of males over 50 had had no schooling. Among the Maltese, over 20 per cent of males over 45 had not attended school. Female proportions who never attended school over 40 were high for all three groups and also for the Yugoslav-born.

German- and British Isles-born as well as Polish males had proportions of adult men with university degrees not too greatly at variance with the Australian-born (5.6 per cent), whereas the equivalent southern European proportion was under 0.2 per cent. Similarly the percentages of north-western Europeans and Poles with other tertiary education and matriculation or its equivalent were very much higher than those of the southern Europeans. Among the Poles, however, it is likely that there was an important difference between Jewish and non-Jewish migrants in this respect. The implications from these figures for the integration of immigrants are that a considerable proportion of older southern Europeans, especially women, would have an inadequate command of their own national languages and their facility in acquisition of English and in social adaptation generally would be impeded. Second, their vocational skills and occupational opportunities in urban Australia would be exceedingly limited, as indicated in a study by C. A. Price which discussed occupational skills of various groups on arrival, and in a survey by Zubrzycki on the structural assimilation of migrants in Australia.[5]

Residential distribution of migrants in the Australian urban system

Examination of the residential adjustment of the eight largest immigrant groups in metropolitan Sydney and Melbourne brings some understanding of the problems and processes involved in the integration of culturally dissimilar populations. Turning to Tables 10.1 and 10.2, it is clearly evident that distinctive areal distributions of the major birthplace groups have evolved in the 1947–66 period.

The distribution of persons born in the British Isles was relatively similar in both cities, with some concentrations in certain outer industrial and high status suburbs, but, on the whole, not markedly at variance with that of the total population. The Dutch were much more decentralized than the total population, favouring rural–urban fringe suburbs – both industrial and higher status sectors – while Poles favoured middle distance suburbs of both mixed and high status and also outer industrial suburbs of relatively low socio-economic status.[6] Greeks were strongly centralized, and also concentrated in a few areas within the central suburbs and some middle distance suburbs. Italians too were concentrated within inner suburbs, but less so than the Greeks, and were also found in groups within some middle distance suburbs, some outer industrial suburban localities and certain rural–urban fringe areas. A striking feature among Maltese settlers was their major concentration in outer industrial suburbs and market garden areas, with secondary groupings in the inner metropolitan areas.

Despite tendencies to concentration, none of these immigrant groups was confined to any one quarter or sector of Sydney or Melbourne. Paradoxically, the largest single immigrant group proportion of the population at the collector's district level[7] was found in the local government area of Elizabeth in north Adelaide, where *British Isles*-born constituted over 65 per cent of four collectors' district populations, rather than among southern European migrants who are commonly assumed to group themselves greatly. Even in the areas of densest minority group settlement, those of Greeks and Italians in central Sydney and Melbourne, Maltese in Fairfield (west Sydney) and Yugoslav-born at Cringila (Port Kembla, Wollongong), the immigrant groups individually did not exceed 40 per cent of the total population in any collector's district. If children born to migrants are included by estimation, it is possible that persons of Greek and Italian origin together constituted up to 70 per cent of the population of several collectors' districts in Fitzroy and Collingwood (Melbourne) and northern Marrickville and Petersham (Sydney). Each of the collectors' districts in question corresponded to two to four street blocks in area. It should be noted, however, that although considerable overlap occurred in Greek and Italian settlement areas, in C.D.s where either group constituted over 20 per cent of the total population the other minority group's presence was relatively slight. Further, in the main settlements, numbers of British-Australians were still present in the C.D. population, although in parts of Carlton (Melbourne) and Richmond (central Melbourne), Norwood (Adelaide) and Redfern and Petersham (Sydney) individual street blocks

TABLE 10.1. *Percentage distribution of major birthplace groups in metropolitan Sydney 1966*

Residential area	British Isles	Germany	Netherlands	Poland	Yugoslavia	Greece	Italy	Malta	Total population
Inner metropolitan	5.39	7.59	4.02	7.11	15.81	29.71	7.63	18.02	6.51
Older residential inner suburbs	10.67	11.99	5.36	12.30	17.80	33.60	29.99	15.04	11.76
Middle distance suburbs	41.98	35.22	27.44	45.82	33.33	30.39	33.03	23.01	41.38
Outer industrial suburbs	10.44	21.14	20.64	21.31	18.15	2.19	13.84	39.07	10.90
Other residential and rural–urban fringe suburbs	31.52	24.06	42.54	13.46	14.91	4.11	15.51	4.86	29.45
Total metropolitan	100.00	100.00	100.00	100.00	100.00	100.00	100.00	100.00	100.00

Source: Census of the Commonwealth of Australia, 30 June 1966.

TABLE 10.2. *Percentage distribution of major birthplace groups in metropolitan Melbourne 1966*

Residential area	British Isles	Germany	Netherlands	Poland	Yugoslavia	Greece	Italy	Malta	Total population
Inner metropolitan	3.46	3.17	2.05	4.24	9.90	11.25	14.11	11.38	4.89
Older residential inner suburbs	4.31	3.78	1.88	3.26	10.47	32.34	16.86	11.38	7.10
Middle distance suburbs	41.26	41.35	22.33	62.61	45.50	43.27	42.55	21.31	46.38
Outer industrial suburbs	11.51	20.81	10.98	18.52	21.63	6.02	10.87	48.18	10.40
Other residential and rural–urban fringe suburbs	39.46	30.89	62.76	11.37	12.50	7.12	15.61	7.74	31.23
Total metropolitan	100.00	100.00	100.00	100.00	100.00	100.00	100.00	100.00	100.00

Source: Census of the Commonwealth of Australia, 30 June 1966.

(of 100–300 people) were dominated by Greeks or Italians at the focal points of settlement.

Because of the age structure of inner city areas containing numerous post-war immigrants and an ageing British-Australian population with few children, settlement of Greek and Italian families resulted in a disproportionate number of first and second generation migrant children in schools. Thus in Melbourne in June 1971, of 16,895 children enrolled in 33 primary schools in the inner suburbs, 9,204 were from non-English homes (54 per cent), according to an unpublished survey. In the largest primary school, Hawksburn, 738 out of 1,074 (69 per cent) were from non-English homes. Almost 18 per cent came from homes in which no English whatsoever was spoken.[8] In another large primary school in Lee Street, Carlton, 60 per cent of the students were from non-British-Australian families and 35 per cent were from homes in which no English at all was spoken. As the Greek and Italian school children were growing older, the children of new immigrant groups had by 1971 made their presence felt in primary schools, for Turkish, Serbo-Croatian, Macedonian and Arabic had become significant minority-group languages in households of children in school. At the high school level, in Richmond, Fitzroy and Brunswick, children from non-British-Australian families constituted over 60 per cent of the high school enrolment. Children of recent migrants from south-eastern Europe and the Middle East will enter the secondary schools in the mid-1970s. Similar trends have become apparent in Petersham, Marrickville, Newtown and Annandale in central Sydney.

As well as having distinctive areal distributions, the major immigrant groups have varied in degree of residential concentration. Table 10.3 presents residential concentration scores using the Index of Dissimilarity developed by O. D. Duncan, S. Lieberson and others.[9]

TABLE 10.3. *Residential concentration scores for major immigrant groups, Sydney and Melbourne 1966*

	Sydney		Melbourne	
	By L.G.A.	By C.D.	By L.G.A.	By C.D.
British Isles	8	17	12	21
Germany	25	35	17	33
Netherlands	29	42	34	46
Poland	34	48	36	49
Yugoslavia	31	50	33	49
Greece	53	63	50	59
Italy	32	45	38	50
Malta	49	60	52	64

Source: Census of the Commonwealth of Australia, 30 June 1966.

The indices, calculated for both local government areas and collectors' districts, are ranked on a continuum 0–100, in which zero equals no concentration and 100 maximum concentration or complete segregation. The concentration score is the percentage of a given birthplace group that would have to redistribute itself by local government areas or collectors' districts to have the same percentage distribution as the total population. On this measure Greeks and Maltese were the most residentially concentrated in Sydney and Melbourne, while British and Germans were the least concentrated. The relatively high Greek and Maltese scores reflect in part recency of arrival but also the fact that Greek and Maltese settlement has remained concentrated in relatively few areas with few secondary concentrations and less dispersion from the main areas. The intermediate Netherlands score reflects some concentration in higher status outer suburbs, but not on anything like the scale which has occurred with Greeks, Italians and Maltese, more essentially in inner suburbs.

The association between immigrant distributional patterns and ecological factors is recorded in Tables 10.4–8. In the first table, Spearman's Co-efficient of Rank Correlation was used to correlate immigrant distributions and average rent levels for private houses by L.G.A., rent levels being a fair indicator of house and land values and indirectly of socio-economic status of areas within Sydney. Thus, average private home rents in 1966 ranged from lows of $6 and $7 in the inner Sydney and Leichhardt L.G.A.s to intermediate levels of $8–9 in the surrounding L.G.A.s, and in the outer western L.G.A.s, Fairfield, Blacktown and Holroyd, and higher values of $12–13 in most North Shore L.G.A.s, with peaks of $14 in eastern Woollahra and $18 in the northern Kuringai L.G.A.

It can be seen from Table 10.4 that the percentages of southern European birthplaces in the population were strongly negatively correlated with rank order average rents, while lesser negative correlations occurred with the Polish- and German-born. The British Isles- and Netherlands-born were

TABLE 10.4. *Rank order correlation between immigrant group distributions and average rent levels for private houses by local government areas, Sydney 1966*

United Kingdom and Ireland	+0.40	Yugoslavia	−0.56
Germany	−0.31	Italy	−0.52
Netherlands	+0.45	Greece	0.60
Poland	−0.34	Malta	−0.67

Sources: Birthplace data by L.G.A., 1966 census; unpublished tabulations of average rent by L.G.A., 1966.
Note. Spearman's Co-efficient of Rank Correlation was the measure used.

TABLE 10.5. *Rank order correlations between birthplace proportions of the population and males with university and other tertiary education, by collectors' districts, 1966*

	Sydney	Melbourne
British Isles	+0.29	+0.23
Germany	−0.07	+0.06
Netherlands	+0.10	+0.08
Poland	−0.15	+0.03
Yugoslavia	−0.37	−0.32
Greece	−0.28	−0.35
Italy	−0.36	−0.45
Malta	−0.46	−0.44

Source : Census of the Commonwealth of Australia, 30 June 1966.

TABLE 10.6. *Rank order correlations between birthplace proportions of the population and males in managerial and professional occupations 1966*

	Sydney	Melbourne
British Isles	+0.30	+0.23
Germany	−0.10	+0.04
Netherlands	+0.10	+0.09
Poland	−0.17	−0.01
Yugoslavia	−0.41	−0.41
Greece	−0.31	−0.46
Italy	−0.38	−0.51
Malta	−0.49	−0.52

Source : Census of the Commonwealth of Australia, 30 June 1966.

TABLE 10.7. *Rank order correlations between birthplace proportions of the population and males as craftsmen, production process workers and labourers, by collectors' districts, 1966*

	Sydney	Melbourne
British Isles	−0.22	−0.09
Germany	+0.07	+0.09
Netherlands	+0.01	+0.10
Poland	+0.15	+0.01
Yugoslavia	+0.29	+0.33
Greece	+0.11	+0.26
Italy	+0.32	+0.44
Malta	+0.43	+0.46

Source : Census of the Commonwealth of Australia, 30 June 1966.

TABLE 10.8. *Rank order correlations between birthplace proportions of the population and ratio of children 0–14 as percentage of females aged 16–45, by collectors' districts, 1966*

	Sydney	Melbourne
British Isles	−0.27	+0.05
Germany	−0.10	−0.07
Netherlands	+0.17	+0.29
Poland	−0.12	−0.34
Yugoslavia	−0.14	−0.23
Greece	−0.38	−0.40
Italy	−0.16	−0.18
Malta	+0.09	+0.09

Source: Census of the Commonwealth of Australia, 30 June 1966.
Note. Spearman's Co-efficient of Rank Correlation was the measure used.

positively correlated, both groups preferring intermediate or high rent residential areas.

Ecological correlations of the distributions of immigrant groups with selected socio-economic characteristics, shown in the next tables, partly conformed with expectations but the degree of association was less than expected. It was shown above how the southern Europeans, Yugoslav-born and Polish-born entered Australia predominantly as unskilled workers, a fact confirmed by analysis of the occupational structures of the major birthplace groups in Sydney and Melbourne presented below.

It will be noted that the distributions of Greek, Italian, Maltese and Yugoslav-born were negatively correlated with university and other tertiary educated males in both Sydney and Melbourne, all four groups tending to avoid areas where the tertiary educated were found in high proportions. The negative correlations between these immigrant groups and proportions of males in managerial and professional occupations were slightly higher, while the British Isles-born were weakly positively correlated with higher status and educated areas. There was no significant correlation between these variables and Netherlands- or German-born distributions, despite positive correlations at the local government area level between high rent areas and the distribution of the Netherlands-born. The British Isles-born distribution was positively correlated with C.D.s of higher educational and occupational status although the relationship was relatively weak.

Negative correlations of low value existed between the distribution of British Isles-born and male occupational proportions in craftsmen, production process workers and labourers (blue collar workers), while positive correlations of medium value existed between the distributions of Italians and Maltese in particular and males in these manual occupations. The relatively weak relationship in the case of the Greeks was surprising, considering the high percentage of Greeks in manual and particularly unskilled occupations. Minor negative correlations of possibly little significance existed between southern Europeans (Greeks and Italians) and proportions of children to the number of females of child-bearing age (e.g. high familism). These negative values, particularly those of the Greeks, in part reflect settlement in inner city areas with relatively few host society families and an ageing Australian-born population.

TABLE 10.9. *Indexes of dissimilarity between managerial and unskilled workers within immigrant groups, and between unskilled members of immigrant groups and the Australian-born population in Sydney, by collectors' districts, 1966*

Birthplace	Between managerial and unskilled members within groups (males)	Between unskilled members (males) of immigrant groups and the Australian-born unskilled male population
Australia	38	—
British Isles	33	18
Germany	47	27
Netherlands	49	30
Poland	49	34
Yugoslavia	48	44
Greece	51	54
Italy	45	44
Malta	48	59

Source: Unpublished cross-tabulations, birthplace by occupational level by collectors' districts, developed from 1966 census data.

The absence of very strong negative or positive correlations between the various group distributions probably reflects the fact that non-quantifiable factors (at least with existing census data), such as social needs and cultural values, influence the settlement patterns of particular groups. The relations shown, of course, do not reflect causal relationships but simply indicate some tendencies for groups to be distributed in residential areas with certain socio-economic characteristics.

One problem has been to ascertain whether ethnic concentrations reflect social class factors, or whether groups segregate themselves even within relatively homogeneous socio-economic areas within the Australian metropolis. To explore this problem, cross-tabulations were developed in which occupations were reclassified into a nine category system based on degree of skill, developed by Lancaster Jones, Leonard Broom and George Zubrzycki at the Australian National University. Thus, skilled tradesmen were separated out from unskilled manual workers and tabulations made of occupations for the eight major immigrant groups and the Australian-born by collectors' districts for each group. The results of a preliminary run for metropolitan Sydney are presented in Table 10.9.

Not only were managerial and unskilled manual male workers within each immigrant group quite strongly dissimilar in spatial distributions within Sydney, but the unskilled members of the southern European groups were spatially separated in considerable degree from unskilled Australian-born workers. The British-, German- and Netherlands-born unskilled workers were less dissimilar in their distributions to Australian-born unskilled. Thus, although social origins and occupational status of immigrants affect their location in the residential stratification system, and also their pattern of residential segregation, some groups are clearly segregated within one occupational class (the least skilled) from the Australian-born in that class, suggesting that socio-cultural and other factors affect residential segregation of immigrant groups.

Chain migration, social origins and settlement evolution

The southern European communities in Sydney, Melbourne and Adelaide began to grow as early as 1900, by the process of chain migration which has been defined as a movement of people from particular villages or regions to a new country from which immigrants assist relatives to migrate.[10] Through time, numbers of persons from particular localities, who are linked through kinship ties, evolve settlements in the new country. Such persons have been referred to in the United States as 'urban villagers'.[11] Lancaster Jones has described chain migration and settlement formation among southern Italians in Carlton, Melbourne,[12] while in New Zealand, recent studies have described ethnic concentrations in which village or region of origin were significant factors in separate settlement formation or neighbourhood groupings.[13]

By using a sample of naturalization papers taken out between 1900 and 1947, it is evident that in central Sydney, a pre-war Darlington concentration of Italians originated in the Valtellina, Lombardy, while those south of the central business district, in King Street, Newtown and in Surry Hills, came from the island of Salina off the Sicilian coast. The nucleus of the main present-day Italian concentration in metropolitan Sydney, between Parramatta Road, Balmain and Hill Streets, Leichhardt, began to form before World War I with immigrants from the Lipari Islands, Sicily and Vicenza and Udine in north Italy. In the rural–urban fringe areas of Penrith, Fairfield and Holroyd, settlers from Sicily and Reggio Calabria became fruit growers and market gardeners.

The location of these early concentrations influenced the place of settlement of the much greater number of post-war Italian migrants. Additional nucleations developed of migrants from Lipari in outer suburban Sutherland, in Clissold and Palace Streets, in inner suburban Ashfield, and in King Street, Newtown, south of the old Italian area in Leichhardt. Other concentrations of migrants from Panarea (Sicily) and Adrano in Catania Province (Sicily) formed in Botany, while a strong grouping of migrants from Spadafora and Comiso, Sicily, formed in Church and Prospect Streets, Leichhardt. Other clusters of migrants from Martone (Reggio Calabria) formed in Eastwood.

In Melbourne in the post-war era, concentrations from Ragusa and Solarino (Sicily) developed in Brunswick, especially in Evans and Eveline Streets, along with migrants from Licodia Eubea, Catania (Sicily). In West Brunswick, concentrations from Vizzini, Catania (Sicily) and San Marco in Lamis, Foggia (south Italy) formed in Shamrock, Waxman and Barkly Streets. Concentrations from San Marco in Lamis also formed in Gertrude Street, Fitzroy and in Holden and Barkly Streets (Fitzroy). Migrants from Ferruzzano were grouped in Ascot Vale and families from Rizziconi, Reggio Calabria, in Pine Street, Cobram. However, perhaps the strongest chain migration-produced settlement was that of persons from Viggiano, Potenza (Basilicata), documented by Lancaster Jones[14] in the inner suburb of Carlton.

In Adelaide, the strongest chain migration of Italians in the post-war period has been of migrants from Molfetta (Bari), who grouped strongly in Gillies and Marke Streets near the central business district but who also formed lesser concentrations in Marylands and Solomontown. Another strong chain migration was that from Taurianova, Casilonia and Caulonia, Reggio Calabria, migrants from which formed concentrations in Vernon Street, Norwood and in Fulham, Lockleys and Torrensville. Migrants from Molochio and Varopodio (Reggio Calabria) also formed small neighbourhoods in Seaton Park and in Payneham.

As with the Italians in Sydney, the location of the small early Greek concentrations influenced the location of many of the far greater number of Greek migrants who came to Sydney in the post-war period. Greek settlement before 1947 was concentrated south of the C.B.D. in Sydney L.G.A., where migrants from Castellorizo and Kythera were grouped in George Street (Redfern) and King Street (Newtown), while other nucleations of settlers from Cephalonia, Arcadia, Ithaca, Samos and Smyrna settled in these areas and in Darlinghurst. Post-war, these chain migrations continued while persons from Levkas formed a subconcentration in Redfern[15] and new migrations from Crete, the Peleponnesos and Macedonia contributed to the growth of concentrations in Redfern, Newtown and Erskineville in Sydney L.G.A. and in adjacent Enmore in Marrickville

L.G.A. Other groupings of migrants from Castellorizo developed in Randwick, Maroubra and Coogee, the latter two being eastern suburbs. A chain migration of Greek migrants and their relatives from Port Said, Egypt, developed in Matraville, particularly in Murrabin Avenue and Perry Street. Although most chain migrations led to the formation of settlement nucleations in the inner suburbs, some small groupings of Greeks did form in some middle distance and outer suburbs.

In Melbourne, the strong migration from the Florina district (Macedonia) resulted in substantial concentrations of migrants from Polipotamos and Atrapas in Docker and Tanner Streets (Richmond) and in Langridge Street (Collingwood). A grouping from Epirus developed in Gelenlyon Street (East Brunswick), while Greeks from Ithaca grouped in Drummond and Barry Streets (Carlton). A further grouping of familes from Luandaficia (Macedonia) formed in Newry, Percy and Condell Streets, Fitzroy, also within inner Melbourne, while another group from Vevi, Florina (Macedonia) formed in Sydney Road and Bell Streets, Coburg.

Perhaps more than Greeks and Italians the Yugoslav-born who came as chain migrants grouped themselves in terms of region, rather than village or town of origin (birth), partly because of the different folk communities in the different regions of Yugoslavia – Serbs, Croats, Slovenes, Macedonians. With the exception of concentrations in Fairfield (west of Sydney), Keilor and Altona (Melbourne's western industrial suburbs) and Cringila (Wollongong), where the Yugoslav-born constituted almost 30 per cent of the population in one collector's district in each locality, Yugoslavs spread their settlement quite widely through low-rent and low-cost housing in the inner city and outer industrial areas.

In Sydney, migrants from Dalmatia, and especially from Bijevcino Selo, settled in small clusters of Croatians in Darlinghurst, although a group of Slovenes from small towns near Zagreb settled in Darlinghurst Road, in the inner city. Migrants from Smederevo (Serbs) settled in Harris Street in the outer Sydney suburb of Warriewood, while Croatians from Podgorica settled in Cabramatta. Groups of Slovenes grouped in small clusters in Marrickville, an inner suburb, while a major grouping of families from Dalmatia formed in outer western suburban Fairfield.

In Melbourne, Croats settled in Preston, especially in Gilbert Road, while migrants from Hercegovina grouped in small clusters in Richmond. Slovenes from Ljubljana and its hinterland settled in Gibdon and Adam Streets (Richmond), while migrants from the Blato area settled in Gore Street, Fitzroy, an inner Melbourne suburb. In the outer western industrial suburb of Sunshine, a group of Slovenes formed a concentration in Suspension Street. However, in Sydney, Melbourne and Wollongong, the densest nucleations of Yugoslav-born consisted mainly of Croatians. Not all the Yugoslav-born regional settlement aggregations resulted from chain migration; many former displaced person refugees gravitated together through time after earlier settlement in other areas, while many others did not group themselves in terms of town, region, folk community or ethnic group of origin at all, but simply settled in areas of low-cost housing.

The chain migration phenomenon has not been restricted to southern Europeans of peasant origin: there are some instances of chain migration of British Isles-born, from Sheffield to a Wollongong suburb, for example, and also from Manchester to Elizabeth in Adelaide, although these migrations were on a small scale and did not extend beyond close relatives and friends. There were some small Dutch chain migrations: from Zaandam to Maroubra (Sydney) and Red Hill (Melbourne), and particularly from Tilburg and also Eindhoven in the province of Noord Brabant to Campbelltown, an outer south-western Sydney suburb, and to Frankston, Aspendale, Moonee Ponds and Seaford in Melbourne.

However, most British and Dutch migrants were from urban, industrial backgrounds, and were officially assisted to migrate and hence were not dependent on assistance from relatives in emigrating. Even among the southern Europeans, over two-thirds of whom were not *officially* assisted to migrate (and thus were dependent on relatives or close friends for nomination, sponsorship and often the financing of the migration), there was considerable mixing of migrants from different source regions in some areas. Moreover, the regional or village groupings mentioned may be the result of networks based on family connections rather than regional associations per se.

Occupations of immigrant minorities

The residential patterns described above become more comprehensible when the occupations of migrants after a period of time in Australia are considered. It has already been noted that in contrast to migrants from north-west Europe, a large proportion of southern Europeans have been unskilled on arrival. In 1966 in Sydney, 43.5 per cent of Greeks were in unskilled manual work, compared with 33 per cent of Italians and 35.8 per cent of Maltese. By comparison only 17.1 and 13.2 per cent of British Isles- and German-born were unskilled workers, while the comparable figure for the Australian-born was only 15.3 per cent. Proportional differences were similar in Melbourne. The percentages of southern Europeans in professional, managerial or clerical employment were very low, while with the exception of clerical work, proportions of north-west Europeans in white collar occupations were similar to those of the Australian-born. Proportions of north-west Europeans in skilled trades were significantly higher than among the Australian-born.

As with residential concentration, then, north-west European groups were the least occupationally dissimilar from the Australian-born population and the east Europeans (Poles) were moderately dissimilar, while the southern Europeans were more markedly dissimilar. With major concentrations in unskilled work, often segregated in particular industries and factories, e.g. the Greeks in the motor assembly industry, especially in South Melbourne, the southern Europeans had less economic choice available in place of residence within the urban social system. Hence working class neighbourhoods in older, cheaper housing areas towards the city centres and in some industrial outer suburbs became more and more southern European in character.

Migrants and housing

The occupational status of migrants has a direct bearing on the type and quality of housing they occupy. It is thus true that Greeks have settled in poorer areas of terrace and semi-detached houses in Sydney and in old semi-detached villas and bungalows in Richmond, Collingwood and Prahan in Melbourne. In Sydney, Italians have tended to occupy old but not necessarily poor homes in Leichhardt and Drummoyne, while in Melbourne they have settled predominantly in terraces in Carlton, but in detached homes in Brunswick, Preston and Coburg. The neighbourhoods are not ghettos or tenements, however, but are areas of predominantly *privately* owned dwelling units.

The incidence of private ownership became in fact higher for southern Europeans than the Australian-born population in Sydney. In 1966, for example, whereas 69.9 per cent of Australian-born household heads in Sydney owned or were buying their own homes (of those living in private dwellings), 82 per cent of Italian and 73 and 76 per cent of Greek and Maltese household heads were owners and buyers.[16] In Melbourne, Italian, Greek and Maltese home ownership was 82.3, 73 and 70 per cent respectively, compared with 74.5 per cent for the Australian-born heads of households. North-west Europeans did not appear to favour home ownership as much as southern Europeans. There is some evidence among the Greeks, Italians and Maltese, however, that concealed beneath the high owning and buying percentages is the fact that a considerable number of relatives beyond the nuclear family were in the household of the nuclear family head, so that for many home ownership was not a reality.

From the Survey of Living Conditions in Melbourne, 1966, conducted by the Institute of Applied Economics, University of Melbourne, there was evidence that some migrants, unskilled and consequently on low incomes, may have rashly committed themselves to private ownership of old homes needing repair and to repaying mortgages at high interest rates, creating financial stress for themselves. Despite the high degree of private ownership reported for Greeks and Italians in Melbourne the number of those living in rooms and sharing facilities, rather than in flats, was much higher than average. Over 26 per cent of Greek households were accommodated in rooms compared with 2 per cent of the Australian-born population of Melbourne in 1966.[17] Almost 33 per cent were sharing bathroom, lavatory or kitchen compared with only 3.4 per cent of the Australian-born. These were mostly recent arrivals.

The quality of housing was ranked on a scale from 'very good' through 'comfortable' and 'just adequate' to 'poor' and 'very poor' housing. Over 31 per cent of Greek-occupied dwellings in Melbourne in 1966 were ranked as poor or very poor in quality compared with 13 per cent of homes occupied by the Australian-born. Only 11 per cent of Greek dwellings were assessed as being comfortable or of very good condition compared with nearly 40 per cent of Australian-born. Over 21 per cent of Maltese dwellings were described as being poor and very poor in quality. Italian housing quality was on the whole not significantly poorer than that of the Australian-born, however. To an extent Greeks and Italians may have contributed to overcrowding, for over 31 per cent of Greek and 22 per cent of Italian households consisted of extended families compared with only 9 per cent of the Australian-born. Some of these occupied rooms only. Economic factors contributed to this overcrowding: in 1966 over 40 per cent of Greek and 32 per cent of Italian income unit heads were earning under $39 compared to 9 per cent of the Australian-born.[18] Migrants came together in order to pool incomes, but a considerable proportion of extended family households included aged, non-working relatives.

Despite financial stresses through the mortgage repayments at high interest rates necessary on old properties mentioned above, property ownership is a form of mobility for unskilled and under-educated migrants lacking other securities in a new country.[19] As Price and Stimson[20] have noted for Sydney and Melbourne, and Glazer and Moynihan for New York,[21] in areas of migrant private ownership much improvement to run-down residential suburbs has been made by persons with pride in home possession.

Conclusion

It has been shown how southern European communities are, in general, more residentially and occupationally concentrated in Australia's large cities than those from north-west Europe, and thus less assimilated. However, assimilation is not essential if it means the complete merging of minority groups and cultures into Australia's urban host society. In reality, the maintenance of cultural distinctiveness and social control in many migrant areas may prevent conflict within an individual and provide him with an anchorage within a possibly anomic industrial or post-industrial society. His eventual *integration*, whereby he becomes a good citizen and yet retains some of his heritage, may in fact be facilitated.

It has been shown how many elements are involved in ethnic settlement formation–socio–economic factors including income and level of skill of migrants and migration patterns, along with cultural preferences and differences perhaps in residential choice and desirability. It is the socio-economic factors, however, that should be of concern to policy makers in the fields of urban planning and immigration policy planning.

First, in the immigration policy area, the allowing of massive migration (prior to the 1971–2 economic recession in Australia) of groups with limited education and little or no skills has brought an ethnic dimension into the pattern of residential and occupational (and thus social) stratification developing in Australia's metropolitan industrial society. Thus in Melbourne in 1966, almost 50 per cent of the unskilled labour force were migrants and 27 per cent were persons born in southern Europe. Further, most of the unskilled from southern Europe have had very limited choice in standard and location of residential accommodation within the cities, and housing difficulties have often been accentuated, not only by low income and high mortgage debts, but also by debts to relatives from the necessity of borrowing to be able to financially afford migration and resettlement itself. This could be ameliorated by the extension of the assisted passage scheme to include the great majority of close relatives of persons already in Australia from southern Europe wishing to migrate to Australia, thereby avoiding the often severe economic burdens experienced soon after arrival and in the first few years of settlement. It is not suggested that the overall volume of immigration be significantly increased: in fact there should be gradual movement to a system whereby migrants from many source areas, irrespective of ethnic group or colour, could be selected on a points basis in which a certain number of marks (based on level of skill, education, youthfulness etc.) has to be scored before entry is allowed, unless the migrant is a close relative or dependent of a person who migrated earlier.

Second, in the urban planning area, great care should be exercised in the handling of redevelopment projects and urban renewal, where old houses are to be removed and their inmates rehoused either in massive high-rise blocks or in public housing near the urban periphery. By 1972, there were several ethnic neighbourhoods in which street blocks were earmarked for redevelopment and from which migrants were unhappy about having to move. One answer to this problem may be for public authorities to construct medium density townhouses and allow migrant (and other) families to rent or purchase these with low interest rates, so as to allow ethnic groupings to be preserved for as long as individuals need or desire. Another may be to make building materials available for modest fees and/or with subsidization for individual initiative in house renovation or reconstruction, providing adequate building standards are maintained.

Finally, Australian society itself should examine the consequences of a

36 pp.

migration system whereby some less fortunate settlers are forced for economic reasons to congregate, not in ghettos certainly but nevertheless in semi-segregated areas characterized by poorer housing, relative poverty, inadequate school facilities and teaching. Schools in such areas have large numbers of children with language problems, and substantial districts have problems of occupational and social inequality, including inequality of opportunity compounded by ethnicity. What is emerging is a plural society with considerable and noteworthy diversity and it is likely that the main southern European and Jewish concentrations, along with some Dutch and Polish groupings, will survive for some decades to come. But Australians should not be indifferent to the consequences of ethno-cultural and social inequality reinforced by social class differentiation within the urban social system.

NOTES

1 E. W. Burgess, 'The growth of the city: an introduction to a research project', *Publication of the American Sociological Society*, 1924, pp. 85–97; Louis Wirth, 'Human ecology', in *Community Life and Social Policy*, University of Chicago Press, 1956; R. E. Park, *Human Communities*, Free Press, New York, 1952.
2 C. A. Price (ed.), *Australian Immigration: a Bibliography and Digest*, no. 2, A.N.U. Press, 1970, p. A3.
3 Ibid. p. A83.
4 A survey was undertaken of all migrant announcements of intention to naturalize published normally in the public notices section of the daily newspapers in Sydney, Melbourne and Adelaide during the four years when it was obligatory or at least customary to announce one's intention to naturalize. A field survey was undertaken with case study interviews of migrants from the main source areas in Sydney, Melbourne and Adelaide.
5 C. A. Price, 'International migration – Australia and New Zealand, 1947–1968', International Union for the Scientific Study of Population General Conference, September 1969, 9.1.12; J. Zubrzycki, 'Some aspects of structural assimilation of immigrants in Australia', *International Migration*, *11*, no. 3, 1968, pp. 102–11.
6 I. H. Burnley, 'European immigration settlement patterns in metropolitan Sydney, 1947–1966', *Australian Geographical Studies*, *10*, April 1972, pp. 61–78.
7 Collectors' districts, equal in population to approximately a quarter of the American census tract, are approximately 800–1,000 persons in numerical size and are the smallest geographical unit for which data are available.
8 Unpublished survey of inner suburban schools in Melbourne, by R. G. Jennings and others, 1971. Calculations are from tabulations presented and submissions made to the board of enquiry on conditions in schools.
9 S. Lieberson, *Ethnic Patterns in American Cities*, Free Press, New York, 1963.
10 C. A. Price, *Southern Europeans in Australia*, Oxford University Press, 1963.
11 H. J. Gans, *The Urban Villagers*, Free Press, New York, 1962.
12 F. Lancaster Jones, 'The Italian population of Carlton', unpublished Ph.D. thesis, Australian National University, 1962.
13 I. H. Burnley, 'The Greeks', in K. Thomson and A. D. Trlin (eds.), *Immigrants in New Zealand*, Massey University, 1970, pp. 100–24; A. D. Trlin, 'The Yugoslavs', in K. Thomson and A. D. Trlin (eds.), *Immigrants in New Zealand*.
14 F. Lancaster Jones, 'Ethnic concentration and assimilation: an Australian case study', *Social Forces*, *45*, 1967, p. 3.

15 A. Jakubowicz, 'Changing patterns of community organisation', unpublished Honours thesis, University of Sydney, 1969.
16 Unpublished census cross-tabulations, Census of the Commonwealth of Australia, 1966.
17 Unpublished tabulations, 'Survey of Living Conditions in Melbourne, 1966'.
18 Income units in the 'Survey of Living Conditions in Melbourne' were defined as (i) a single person aged 15 years or more, no longer engaged in full-time education or (ii) a married couple and their dependent children, or (iii) any parent (widowed, divorced or separated) and his/her dependent children.
19 Constance Cronin, 'The Sicilian family in Sicily and Australia', Ph.D. thesis in Anthropology, University of Chicago, 1967; M. E. Spiro, 'The acculturation of American ethnic groups', *American Anthropologist*, 57, 1955.
20 C. A. Price, 'Immigrants', in A. F. Davies and S. Encel (eds.), *Australian Society, a Sociological Introduction*, second. ed. Cheshire, 1970, pp. 181–99; R. T. Stimson, 'Distributional aspects of immigrant settlement in Melbourne, 1947–1961, a quantitative analysis', 18th A.N.Z.A.A.S. Congress, Section P, Christchurch, New Zealand, 1968.
21 N. Glazer and O. Moynihan, *Beyond the Melting Pot*, Massachusetts Institute of Technology, 1963.

11

The social and demographic impact of international immigrants on Melbourne: a study of various differentials

H. WARE

Australians have long combined an apparently insatiable curiosity concerning immigrants with an intense reluctance to study themselves.[1] This dual standard has resulted in the lack of any well-defined yardstick against which to measure whether and how the immigrants differ from the native-born. The failure or success of assimilation has been discussed at length without any sustained attempt to define the norm: Australian behaviour patterns and attitudes themselves. This chapter endeavours to begin to redress the balance by discussing the characteristics and ideals of the whole population, immigrant and native-born.

The Melbourne survey

All the data in this chapter are drawn from 2,652 interviews carried out in Melbourne in August–December 1971 as a part of the Australian Family Formation Project of the Demography Department of the Australian National University. The sample, designed by the Bureau of Census and Statistics, was a three-stage areally stratified cluster sample with probability of selection of first and second stage units proportional to size. No clustering was employed at the tertiary stage of selection and the sample was entirely self-weighting. The probability of selection of any address was slightly less than 0.01. In each of the 5,398 dwellings selected, interviews were attempted with all once-married women who were under 60 years of age and still living with their husbands. The total percentage of eligible accessible respondents who refused the full interview was 12.8; but information on twenty-three basic characteristics (including three relating to birth control practice) was obtained for all refusals. The interview lasted for two hours on average, covering a wide range of topics including the basic socio-economic background; the life cycle of the family; women's employment; family planning practice, with special emphasis on the use of the pill; attitudes towards population growth, immigration, family size and abortion; and a series of psycho-social indices.

The major nativity divisions

The Australian-born still predominate amongst the wives of Melbourne: 62 per cent of the women interviewed were Australian-born, 19 per cent were immigrants from southern Europe,[2] 15 per cent immigrants from other regions of Europe and the remaining 4 per cent were non-European by birth, although only 1 per cent were non-European by race.

Much of the analysis which follows is based on four-way cross-tabulations in which three components, nativity, education and religion, are constant and only the fourth component varies. For this purpose the sample is divided into three major nativity groupings: the Australian-born, the southern European-born, and the remainder. The rationale behind this tripartite division is that, as more detailed analysis demonstrates, within these three groups differences in behaviour and attitudes are governed by educational experience and religious affiliation rather than by individual country of birth.

Amongst the immigrants, the southern European-born stand out as a distinct group comprising half of all immigrants. They are distinct in religious affiliation (89 per cent of the Orthodox and 37 per cent of the Catholics in the sample are southern European born – only 5 per cent of these migrants belong to neither of these religious groups); in educational experience (93 per cent of those with less than seven years of formal education are southern European-born) and in lack of communication with the mass of the community (94 per cent of those who had to be interviewed in a language other than English were southern European-born). The remaining immigrants are predominantly from northern and eastern Europe; almost half have migrated from Britain.

The low level of immigration associated with the pre-war depression is reflected in the fact that in almost nine-tenths of cases both of the Australian-born wives' parents were also born in Australia; and even of the tenth with overseas-born parents the great majority are of British stock. Some 57 per cent of the native-born in Melbourne have always lived there, 9 per cent come from Sydney and a further 10 per cent from cities with populations of 50,000 or more. The rural component of the Australian-born is very small; only 9 per cent of these wives came from rural properties or townships.

Characteristics of the immigrants

Half of the southern European-born wives were the daughters of peasant farmers or rural labourers; the corresponding proportion amongst both the native-born and the remaining immigrants was only one in twenty. Amongst the less well educated of the Greek- and Yugoslav-born (i.e. those with less than eight years of formal education) the proportion of wives of peasant origin reaches three-quarters. The southern European-born Catholics (71 per cent of whom are from Italy) were much more urbanized than the Orthodox Greek- and Yugoslav-born; at the age of 13, 34 per cent of the Catholics in contrast to 65 per cent of the Orthodox were living on farms or in villages of less than 1,000 inhabitants.

Many of the southern European immigrants are primarily rural–urban migrants and only secondarily international migrants. Having decided to move from the countryside, they chose the urban centre which they felt had most to offer in terms of employment and other opportunities. They chose to come to Melbourne or Sydney rather than to Australia.

Certainly the southern European immigrants in Melbourne have been disproportionately drawn from the rural areas of southern Europe. At the 1961 census, 44 per cent of the Greek population lived in centres with less than 2,000 inhabitants, yet 66 per cent of the wives who have come from Greece came from centres of less than 1,000 inhabitants. In Italy in 1961, 47 per cent lived in centres of 20,000 or more residents yet in our sample only 37 per cent of wives from Italy came from centres with 10,000 or more residents.[3]

The fathers of the southern European immigrants were strikingly low in occupational skills and status. Noticeably lacking in the immigrant stream from this region are the daughters of white collar workers, or even of skilled craftsmen. Only 4 per cent of the southern European-born wives were the daughters of white collar workers, in contrast to 23 per cent of the Australian-born and 26 per cent of the remaining immigrants. Equally, only 13 per cent of the southern European-born were the daughters of skilled craftsmen, as compared with 28 per cent of the Australian-born and 23 per cent of other immigrants. The southern European immigrants do not represent a full cross-section of the nations from which they come, but are drawn very largely from the reserves of the underprivileged, especially the rural underprivileged. In contrast the northern European-born immigrants are more representative of the whole social spectrum of their countries of origin.

The southern European-born immigrants form a very disadvantaged group in Melbourne. Many of their subsequent deprivations are related to their original lack of education. With little education they find it difficult to learn English and this further handicaps them in the search for employment, with the result that they are most likely to find themselves in underpaid, unskilled jobs with very little prospect of anything better in future. Some 74 per cent of the southern European-born wives in contrast with 2 per cent of the Australian-born and 4 per cent of the remaining immigrants have had less than seven years of full-time formal education. Most educationally deprived of all are the Greek-born wives, 87 per cent of whom fall below the seven year minimum.

The non southern European-born immigrant wives were actually better educated than the Australian-born, 32 per cent of them having had twelve or more years of formal education in contrast with only 20 per cent of the native-born. Some University education has been received by 4 per cent of the native-born wives, by 0.6 per cent of the southern European-born and by 6 per cent of the remaining immigrants. In the discussion of attitudes and behaviour below, it should be remembered that these massive educational differentials do much to explain why it is that in nearly all measures of modernity or liberalism the non southern European-born immigrants lead the way followed by the Australian-born and then, at a considerable distance, by the southern European-born.

The educational prospects for the children of the southern European migrants are far from bright. The proportion of mothers who cannot speak more than a smattering of English rises from 67 per cent amongst those from Italy, to 70 per cent amongst those from Yugoslavia, to a startling 84 per cent amongst those from Greece. The children move in an enclosed world where English is not spoken at home, where shopping can be done in one's own language and where the schools are overburdened with the sheer proportion of immigrants needing to learn English before they can learn anything else.[4] Although the parents have little contact with the schools, which frighten them, they are far from undervaluing the importance and benefits of prolonged education. Whereas only 33 per cent of the Australian-born would definitely wish their sons to attend university full-time, 43 per cent of the southern European-born immigrants and 41 per cent of other immigrants would do so. In the case of a daughter, the equivalent percentages are 24, 32 and 35. Some 64 per cent of those from Greece would wish to have a university education for their sons, a tribute to education which is all the more remarkable considering the extreme lack of education of the present generation.

As the overwhelming majority of attitudinal and behavioural measures within the survey show, the one important religious differential in Australian society as a whole is that between Catholics and those who are not Catholics. In many cases the Orthodox are apparently a disparate group but this effect generally disappears once education is controlled. Some 22 per cent of the native-born and 23 per cent of the non southern European-born immigrants are Catholics, in contrast with 55 per cent of the southern European-born immigrants. The Australian-born Catholics are the most active church members: 56 per cent of them attend Church at least once a week in contrast to 30 per cent of the southern European-born Catholics and 42 per cent of the other Catholic immigrants. The members of the other religious groups are much less active. Only 8 per cent of the Orthodox attend services once a week, and only 11 per cent of Australian-born Protestants do so. That Catholicism has such a marked effect upon attitudes and behaviour is to some extent the result of the fact that its adherents are more actively involved with their Church than the often merely nominal members of other denominations.

Satisfaction and length of residence in Australia

Most of the immigrants are relatively recent arrivals.

However, there is a very marked difference between the period of residence of the southern European-born immigrants and the remainder. Whereas 30 per cent of the northern European-born immigrants had lived in Australia for twenty years or more, only 7 per cent of the southern European-born had done so.

One reason why the southern European immigrants are much further removed from Australian behaviour patterns and attitudes than other immigrants is simply that they have on average a less prolonged experience of living in Australia.

An indirect measure of the satisfaction of immigrants together with a more general measure of appreciation of Melbourne is provided by the answers to a question as to where the respondents would choose to live. On the whole, the degree of contentment is high; two-thirds of wives would choose to live at their present address, one-sixth would choose to live elsewhere in Melbourne, one-seventh elsewhere in Australia, and less than one in twenty-five would choose to live abroad. Satisfaction with present accommodation is almost as high amongst immigrants as amongst the native-born, except amongst the more highly educated immigrants who are more likely to feel that their accommodation and the area in which they are living does not match up to their expectations. (Amongst the native-born the more highly educated are not only more dissatisfied, they are also markedly more mobile.) Generally, the longer international immigrants have been living in Australia, the more likely they are to be satisfied with their housing, with the southern European immigrants being considerably more satisfied than those from northern Europe.

In terms of wanting to return home, the proportion wishing to live abroad rises with education in each immigrant group but never rises above one in eight. The most satisfied are the Greek and Yugoslav immigrants, only one in sixteen of whom would wish to return home; the least satisfied are the immigrants from Catholic southern Europe, predominantly from Italy, one in ten of whom would like to return home. The immigrants from northern Europe contain the highest proportion of those who would wish to move on and sample a new country, rather than wishing to return home, a reflection of their higher education and higher mobility.

Melbourne is appreciated because it provides a livelihood and because it has become home rather than because of civic pride in Melbourne itself, or pleasure in the facilities which the city affords. Some 34 per cent of the sample named the availability of employment as Melbourne's best feature, 19 per cent said that they liked Melbourne because this was the city where they grew up or the only place they knew in Australia, and a further 18 per cent said that the best thing was that they had relatives or friends living close by. Most migrants chose Melbourne as their destination because of the employment opportunities it offered: this was the most important feature for 60 per cent of southern European immigrants, for 52 per cent of all international immigrants and for 34 per cent of all internal migrants, as compared to only 19 per cent of those who had been born in Melbourne. Naturally those who had been born locally stressed the familiarity of the town and access to friends and relatives to a greater extent than the migrants; more than half simply said that the best things about Melbourne were its familiarity and the ties it provided. Still, one in eight of the international immigrants and one in five of the internal migrants thought that the best thing about Melbourne was family or friendly ties. It is interesting that a question designed to measure the persistence of the idealization of rural life in one of the most urbanized countries of the world did bring out a marked nativity differential. Whilst more than two-thirds of the native-born (nearly 60 per cent of whom have always lived in Melbourne) believe that 'life in the country is more pleasant than life in the city', only half of the southern European immigrants would accept this dictum. Nostalgia for the countryside is strongest amongst those who have never faced up to rural discomforts for more than a brief holiday; the daughters of the peasant farmers of southern Europe are much less entranced by the rural idyll.

Satisfaction with life in Melbourne is considerable; one in five respondents could not name one disadvantage of living in Melbourne, and more than half could not name two. Although the level of satisfaction may have been exaggerated by the inarticulateness of some of the less well educated, who are disproportionately represented amongst the complaintless, it is nevertheless impressive that so many respondents were so contented as to have no complaints which immediately sprang to mind. Once education is controlled for, there are no marked nativity differentials in dissatisfaction with Melbourne. The chief complaint against the city allows of little direct amelioration: 28 per cent of all the wives consider that the climate is the greatest discomfort to be borne in Melbourne. The remaining evils cited however are all man-made: 14 per cent of wives are most disturbed by pollution as exemplified by the state of the Yarra and the beaches, and a further 8 per cent are concerned with overcrowding within the city, especially with relation to transport problems. In contrast to these environmental hazards of the city, its expensiveness is complained of by only 7 per cent of wives. Southern European immigrants are somewhat less worried about environmental issues and somewhat more concerned with the expensiveness of the city, where both wages and prices were higher than they were accustomed to, and with the extent of crime within the city. The latter concern is in part a reflection of the greater visibility of crime in the poorer areas where these migrants are obliged to live, and also, possibly, of a certain insecurity.

The socio-economic background

Immigrants have different attitudes and behaviour patterns from the native-born not merely because they were born into a different culture but also because their experience here and now in Australia is very different from that of the native-born. In occupation, in income and in housing, the immigrants, and more especially the southern European-born immigrants, are in a disadvantaged position compared to the native-born.

The husbands of the native-born respondents have the best jobs: 14 per cent were in professional occupations, 13 per cent in managerial, 19 per cent in other white collar occupations, 30 per cent were foremen or skilled craftsmen and 24 per cent were semi-skilled or unskilled labourers. In striking contrast only 0.4 per cent of the husbands of southern European-born respondents were professionals, 0.6 per cent managers, 2 per cent in other white collar occupations, 21 per cent were foremen or skilled crafts-men, but 76 per cent were semi-skilled or unskilled labourers.

The occupational differential between the husbands of the native-born and the husbands of the southern European-born is mirrored by an equally sharp income differential. Some 32 per cent of the husbands of the southern European-born earn less than $3,000 a year – 69 per cent earn less than $4,000: the comparable proportions for the husbands of the native-born are 5 per cent and 28 per cent; and for the husbands of the northern European-born they are 3 per cent and 20 per cent. The proportions earning $8,000 a year or more in these groups are 3 per cent, 20 per cent and 15 per cent. The median income of the husbands of the southern European-born is approximately $3,300 a year, that of the husbands of the northern European-born $5,400 a year, and that of the husbands of the native-born $5,600.

In any discussion of the differences between the attitudes and behaviour of the southern European-born and the native-born or the other immi-grants, it should always be remembered that, whereas 10 per cent of the husbands of the native-born and 11 per cent of the husbands of the northern European-born are unskilled or semi-skilled workers earning less than $4,000 a year, 62 per cent of the husbands of the southern European-born fit into this category. Thus, one of the major reasons for the differences in behaviour and attitudes between the southern European-born and the remainder of the community is simply that, whereas only a tenth of the remainder of the community are poor and without prospects, almost two-thirds of the southern European-born suffer this fate.

Almost half of the wives in the sample were working wives. There are considerable differentials in levels of workforce participation by nativity, education and religion. Those least likely to be employed were the less well educated amongst the native-born Catholics; 34 per cent of those with less than thirteen years' education were employed. Those most likely to be working, and to be working full-time, were the southern European immigrants, irrespective of religion or education: 50 per cent of this group were employed and five-sixths of them full-time.

There are two quite distinct groups of working wives within the sample: those who work largely for interest and those who work because they have to. If their husbands' earnings after tax were raised to the level of their current joint income, 35 per cent of the working wives would gladly stay home, 45 per cent would continue to work because of the interest provided by their work, and a further 18 per cent would continue to work partly for interest but also for money to buy extras for the family. Amongst the Australian-born, those who work for interest predominate and the better educated the wife the more likely she is to be employed. This trend applies to Catholics and non-Catholics alike amongst the native-born, but, within each educational group, Catholics are less likely to work outside the home than non-Catholics. Many of the southern European-born wives come from areas where wives traditionally help with the poorer farms, but the ideal is that women should concentrate upon domesticity and not need to work outside the home. Three-quarters of this group believe that wives should only work when forced to do so by poverty. The group which most disapproves of the employment of married women is thus the group with the highest proportion of working wives. That this is the effect of poverty overcoming disinclination can be seen from the fact that two-thirds of the southern European wives who do work would gladly stay home if their husbands' wages were raised to the level of their joint income.

Currently the opportunities for employment available to the immigrant wives from southern Europe are very far from being equal to those available to the native-born. Ninety-four per cent of all southern European working wives are blue collar workers, employed in factories or as domestics or in other less pleasant service industries, but only 41 per cent of the native-born workers are similarly employed. Certainly these immigrants are handicapped by their lack of education, but, even at the same educational level, the Mediterranean immigrants are more likely to be found working in factories than their native-born peers. Of the 510 southern European migrants in the sample only four held professional or managerial positions, while a further eleven held white collar jobs of any kind.

A quarter of both native-born and immigrants are freehold owner-occupiers, but there are more native-born than immigrants currently buying their homes on mortgages (53 to 45 per cent). The longer the immigrants have lived in Australia the more likely they are to own their homes and the less likely they are to live in rented accommodation. This relationship between length of residence and home ownership is considerably more marked amongst the southern European-born than amongst the immigrants from northern Europe. After living in Australia for at least fifteen years 53 per cent of the southern European-born and 32 per cent of the northern European-born own their homes outright, whilst the proportions still living in rented accommodation are 13 and 15 per cent. Of those who have lived in Australia for less than six years 4 per cent of southern Europeans and 1 per cent of northern Europeans own their homes and 49 and 67 per cent live in rented accommodation. The eagerness of the southern Europeans to gain the security of owning their homes is reflected in the extent to which they take out mortgages earlier and pay them off sooner than the northern Europeans. Within the first five years in Australia, 43 per cent of southern European immigrants but only 29 per cent of northern European immigrants have given up paying rent and taken out a mortgage on a home of their own.

The survival of the extended family amongst the southern European-born even in Australia is reflected in the proportion living in shared accommodation, almost invariably with relatives. A third of the southern European-born who have lived in Australia for less than six years live in shared accommodation; only one in fourteen of the northern European-born do so. Only one in thirty of the Australian-born live in shared accommodation. There has never been an urban tradition in Australia, as there long was in Britain, that newly married couples could live with their parents until becoming established.

The longer the immigrants have lived in Australia the higher their socio-economic status is likely to be and the more likely they are to be satisfied with their position and confident of their ability to weather financial reverses. To a limited extent this trend results from the fact that the earlier arrivals were somewhat better qualified in education and occupational skills than the more recent immigrants. However, to a far greater extent it reflects the fact that conditions do improve over time; immigrants do succeed in learning the language, in securing better jobs and in buying their homes.

There is a surprisingly close fit between the level of income and the level of financial satisfaction amongst the Melbourne wives. Not only were those with very low incomes much more likely to be dissatisfied, but also those with high incomes were more likely to be satisfied. The proportion of those who were 'very dissatisfied' about the financial situation of their families fell from 26 per cent of those whose husbands earned less than $3,000 a year to 3 per cent of those whose husbands earned $13,000 dollars a year or more; whilst the proportion who were 'very satisfied' rose from 2 per cent to 51 per cent. In Melbourne, perceived poverty is much less of a relative concept than one might anticipate.

The overall level of financial satisfaction is high; less than a third of wives were not satisfied with the financial situation of their families. Yet 66 per cent of the most recently arrived southern European immigrants were dissatisfied in contrast to only 26 per cent of those resident for twenty years or longer, or 23 per cent of the native-born. A more sensitive measure of the insecurity of the newly arrived immigrants was the proportion who believed that they could not survive three months of unemployment without exhausting their savings and running into debt: this rose from 31 per cent of the longest established southern European-born to 78 per cent of those who had lived in Australia for less than six years. A major factor in the greater security of the long-established immigrants was the higher proportion owning their homes (54 to 4 per cent). A similar, though less dramatic, increase in security with prolonged residence was felt by the northern European-born.

However long their period of residence in Australia, the southern Europeans never feel as secure as the native-born, but the northern European immigrants achieve the Australian-born level of financial security after ten years in Australia. The continued feeling of financial insecurity amongst the southern European-born reflects a real income differential.

Building a family

The various nativity, religious and educational groups within Australian society have markedly different attitudes and practices in relation to family building. There are differences in family size ideals, in actual family size, in levels of usage of contraception and in the methods of contraception used, which excellently demonstrate the extent to which Australia is a plural society even within the confines of one city.

One interesting measure of family size ideals, because of its relevance to the attainment of zero population growth, and the strong differences to be found, is the proportion who consider that the two child family is unacceptably small. The two child family is most acceptable to Australian and northern European-born wives of Protestant or no religious persuasion. These groups make up almost two-thirds of the community and only 16 per cent of them reject the two child family. Within this group, British and other northern and eastern European immigrants are most in favour of small families in accordance with the generally lower family sizes that have prevailed in their countries of origin as compared with Australia.

In contrast, the very small family is least acceptable to Australian-born Catholics, who have shared in the pronatalist traditions of the long-established Catholic Church and society in Australia, both of which were predominantly Irish in origin. Australian-born Catholics constituted one-seventh of the sample, and more than a third of them find the two child family too small.

The middle ground is largely occupied by those born in southern Europe; there is some overlap with other groups, the most educated southern Europeans being closer to the small family attitudes of the native-born and northern European-born non-Catholic groups and the least educated, southern European-born Catholics evidencing attitudes similar to the native-born Catholics. Of the southern European immigrants, 30 per cent find the two child family unacceptable.

The ideological nature of the religious division amongst the native-born is substantiated by the reactions of the various sub-groups. Whereas rejection of the two child family declines with more prolonged education amongst the native-born non-Catholics, it actually increases with education amongst the native-born Catholics. Amongst immigrant Catholics, however, greater education does lead to less rejection of the very small family. Thus, the native-born Catholic population is unique in its attitudes, with education reinforcing its pronatalism in contrast to all other groups including immigrant Catholics. These attitudes are reflected in the fertility differentials within the country, where in 1954, Catholic fertility was estimated to be between one-fifth and one-quarter higher than non-Catholic fertility and where the proportion of Catholics with five or more children was substantially above that of non-Catholics in all age groups.[5]

If the actual reproductive performance of the various religious groups within the sample is examined, it can be seen that Catholics have the highest fertility, and the Orthodox the lowest, with the Protestants and those of no religion occupying the middle ground. When the main nativity groups amongst the Catholics are examined separately it can be seen that Australian Catholics have markedly higher fertility than Catholic immigrants. Thus at age 35 or older, when the major part of child-bearing has been completed, 35 per cent of Australian-born Catholics, 19 per cent of southern European-born Catholics and 23 per cent of other immigrant Catholics have families of five or more children (the average numbers of children for these three groups at this age are 3.7, 3.1 and 3.5). Contrary to the popular stereotype, southern European immigrants are no more likely to have large families than the native-born (of southern European immigrants aged 35 or older 16 per cent had five or more children – the comparable proportion amongst the native-born is 15 per cent).

Amongst the women aged 45 or older, who have almost invariably completed their child-bearing, there are marked differentials in the proportion of women who have small families of no more than two children. The better educated are more likely to have such small families: 56 per cent of those with ten or more years of formal schooling have no more than two children, as compared with 48 per cent of those with seven to nine years, or 30 per cent of those with less than seven years of education. The one marked occupational difference in fertility is that between the semi-skilled and unskilled workers and the rest; when past child-bearing 39 per cent of the former but 53 per cent of the latter have less than three children.

The difference between the proportions of craftsmen and foremen and of white collar workers with such small families is surprisingly small (52 to 55 per cent). In terms of income, the dividing point at which small families of no more than two children begin to represent a majority of all families is approximately $5,000 a year. It is regrettable that large families and small incomes should still go together.

Approval of family planning is almost universal in Melbourne: only 7 per cent of wives disapprove of the practice whilst 86 per cent accept it without reservations and the remaining 7 per cent accept with qualifications. Immigrants are disproportionately represented amongst those who disapprove. Of Australian-born Catholics, only 3 per cent disapprove of all forms of family planning; amongst non-southern European immigrant Catholics, 12 per cent disapprove; but, amongst southern European-born Catholics, 31 per cent disapprove. The disapproval of the southern European-born Catholics is as much the result of lack of education and a general distrust of interfering with nature as of specific religious objections. Some 17 per cent of the southern European-born Orthodox, whose Church has no doctrinal objection to family planning, also disapprove of the practice.

As would be expected, levels of usage reflect levels of approval. The proportion of wives who have never used any form of birth control rises from 11 per cent of the native-born, to 13 per cent of the non-southern European immigrants, to 18 per cent of the southern European-born. Within each nativity group, there is a marked religious differential; 9 per cent of Australian-born non-Catholics have never used birth control as opposed to 19 per cent of Australian-born Catholics; 11 per cent of non-southern European non-Catholics as opposed to 17 per cent of non-southern European Catholics have never used birth control. Most marked of all is the religious differential between the Catholic immigrants from southern Europe who are least likely of all groups to have used birth control (26 per cent have never done so) and the Orthodox immigrants from the same area who are the most likely of all to have used birth control (only 7 per cent have never done so). The contrast between the reported levels of family planning of the southern European-born Catholics and of the Orthodox and between the rates of approval and practice of contraception reported by the Orthodox highlights the difficulties of communication even where bilingual interviewers are employed. Undoubtedly, when the Orthodox wives who had co-operated in contraceptive measures said that they disapproved 'of married couples doing *something* to plan families', they thought exclusively of the use of contraceptives, despite the wording of the question. Many of the Greek wives who said that they had never done anything to avoid pregnancy, suddenly realized what was being discussed when asked whether their husbands used withdrawal, and then revealed that they had considered the practice to be so universal that they had not appreciated that it could be one of the anti-natal practices being investigated. The Greek interviewers were much more at ease with the contraceptive questions than the Italian interviewers.[6] In part the difference between the two groups of interviewers and the rates of contraceptive use reported by the Greek and Italian born wives are reflections of the same genuine cultural difference in approach to sexual matters.

An examination of the relationship between period of residence in Australia and levels of contraceptive usage amongst the southern European-born shows that contraception has been practised by 85 per cent of those who have lived in Australia for ten years or less, in contrast to only 79 per cent of those who have lived here for a longer period. This is very largely a reflection of the fact that there is a direct relationship between length of residence in Australia and age. The southern European-born immigrants who have lived longer in Australia are older and therefore less likely to have used contraception in any case. However, this finding would also suggest that the high levels of contraceptive use within the host society have little effect upon immigrants. The more intimate the behaviour, and the more closely it is related to deeply held beliefs, the less likely it is to be influenced by the behaviour of the majority encompassing the minority.

Given that at least three-quarters of all the major nativity, educational and religious groups have used some form of contraception, the really important differentials are in the methods of contraception used rather than in overall usage rates. The real difference between the daughter of a Sicilian peasant and the daughter of an Australian bank manager is not that one practises contraception and the other does not, but that, whereas the former co-operates in withdrawal, the latter takes the pill. Some 57 per cent of less educated southern European-born Catholics have used withdrawal as opposed to 21 per cent of better educated Australian-born non-Catholics; in the case of the pill the respective proportions are 5 per cent and 70 per cent. Despite the Catholic Church's emphasis upon the use of rhythm, it is only amongst the tertiary educated Australian and northern European-born Catholics that the proportion who have ever used rhythm rises above half.

Use of any form of contraceptive is rare amongst the southern European immigrants. The most commonly used methods (artificial) amongst them, the pill and the condom, have only been used by 12 and 7 per cent respectively in contrast to 49 and 28 per cent of the remainder of the community. However, it would be wrong to assume that because the southern European-born immigrants restrict themselves largely to the use of withdrawal, followed at some distance by rhythm and abstinence, the use of such 'ineffective' methods must necessarily lead to large families. The effectiveness of a contraceptive method, unless it be sterilization, depends as much upon the motivation of those using it as upon its clinical effectiveness. There are only two methods of contraception whose consistent use can be shown to have had a marked effect upon the fertility of the women who have completed their fertility in Melbourne. The first of these is rhythm; women who have used rhythm have had larger families than average, in part because rhythm is the method often chosen by those who want large families, and in part because rhythm is a difficult method to use. The second is withdrawal; women who have co-operated in withdrawal have smaller families than the average. At the age of 35 or older, 56 per cent of the Orthodox, who rely almost entirely upon withdrawal, have two children or less. In contrast, at the same age, the Protestants and those of no religious affiliations, who rely largely upon contraceptives, have only 48 per cent with less than three children. The Orthodox have an ardent desire for advanced education for their children, which they can ill afford; as an aid to achieving this end they limit the size of their families using a 'crude' birth control method with remarkable success. Much more could be done to help those who have already done so much to help themselves by modifying the education system to take into account the needs of the children of these immigrants.

Conclusion

Twenty years ago Australia had a native-born proletariat of British ancestry. The greatest change brought about by the massive influx of immigrants from southern Europe during the past two decades has been the part-substitution of a foreign-born proletariat of Mediterranean stock. For the native-born it was relatively easy to pass out of the proletariat; the boundaries were fluid and at some points indistinguishable, and educational or financial success provided an easy exit. For the southern European-born immigrants and their children the barriers are much less yielding. They are cut off from the rest of the people by language and cultural differences in a way that the native-born proletariat never were. They start with a much greater disadvantage than merely being at the base of the ladder as the native-born proletariat were. Because of the vast difference between the education and occupational skills of southern European-born and even the most disadvantaged of the native-born the bottom rung of the ladder has effectively been removed.

There are three major factors which serve to reinforce the division between the southern European immigrants and the remainder of Australian society both in status and in attitudes and behaviour. The first is the lack of out-marriage: only 5 per cent of southern European-born wives and 9 per cent of husbands are married to non southern European-born spouses. The second is the level of residential segregation: although only 19 per cent of the sample were southern European-born, there were areas within the sample such as Brunswick-Northcote and Collingwood-Fitzroy where nearly 60 per cent of respondents were southern European-born, whilst in Richmond the proportion reached 82 per cent. The third factor is the extent to which immigrants keep in touch with their origins and fail to make contact with the new world which surrounds them: 23 per cent of southern European-born wives have parents and 52 per cent siblings who live in Melbourne whom they visit regularly. There is nothing inherently wrong with the maintenance of family ties, with marriage within nativity groups, nor even with residential segregation. Unfortunately, however, within the context of Australian society and the creation of a segregated proletariat, all of these factors serve to separate further the southern European immigrants from the remainder of Australian society.

More than a hundred years after their first arrival, the poverty and cultural distinctiveness of the original Irish immigrants is still reflected in the fact that on every socio-economic measure the native-born Catholics are less advantageously placed than the native-born non-Catholics. If the children of the southern European-born immigrants are not to inherit an even more disadvantageous position in perpetuity, the first priority should be to provide specialized educational facilities to give them the opportunity to attain the standards reached by the children of the native-born. It would also appear to be good policy to actively encourage the immigration of more tertiary educated and skilled southern Europeans to partially redress the balance and to provide leaders for these immigrant communities.

NOTES

1 Cf. H. Ware (ed.), *Fertility and Family Formation: Australasian Bibliography and Essays*, Canberra, 1972.
2 Southern Europe as defined here includes Spain, Portugal, Malta, Italy, Greece, Yugoslavia, Albania, Cyprus and Turkey.
3 United Nations, *Demographic Yearbook, 1970*, New York, 1971. For Italy see Table 6, 'Population in localities of 100,000 and more and 20,000 and more inhabitants', p. 498. For Greece see Table 6, 'Population by sex, age and urban/rural residence', p. 330.
4 Cf. Brotherhood of St Laurence, *Two Worlds, School and the Migrant Family: a look at the attitudes of eighty migrant children and their parents*, Melbourne, 1971.
5 L. H. Day, 'Family size and fertility', in A. F. Davies and S. Encel (eds.), *Australian Society; a Sociological Introduction*, Melbourne, 1965, pp. 156–67; L. H. Day, 'Natality and ethnocentrism: some relations suggested by an analysis of Catholic–Protestant differentials', *Population Studies*, *12*, March 1968, pp. 36–50.
6 The Greek speaking interviewers were of a very high standard and were exceptionally skilled in putting respondents at their ease in discussing 'personal' matters (witness the fact that only 3% of Greek wives failed to report their frequency of sexual intercourse). In contrast, it proved extremely difficult to recruit Italian speaking interviewers who were not themselves somewhat frightened by the questions, with the result that 21% of Italian wives did not report their sexual frequency.

PART III

The impact and consequences of
urbanization: the role of planning

12

Planning the metropolitan areas

P. HARRISON

From the beginning of this century the Australian State governments have been concerned to establish some form of urban administration for the capital cities. Intermittent efforts were made towards the creation of governments to assume overall responsibility for the functions of the patchwork of municipal councils, the variety of State departments and special purpose authorities which between them exercised public responsibility for metropolitan development. The idea of a 'greater metropolitan' council was adopted by the Queensland government by the Greater Brisbane Act of 1924 which eliminated twenty-two municipalities and established the Brisbane City Council as the largest local government body in Australia. With almost 40 per cent of the State population and a Lord Mayor elected at large the Brisbane Council assumed some of the characteristics of a state within a state. Relationships with the central government have never been easy. The other State governments came to regard metropolitan planning as a means by which many of the purposes of a metropolitan government could be fulfilled without requiring them to relinquish their authority to elected bodies which could in some respects become political rivals.

Action towards establishing town planning legislation was stimulated by the Commonwealth government's enquiry into post-war housing needs. The report of the Commonwealth Housing Commission (1944) formed the basis for the Commonwealth and State Housing Agreement Act 1945 by which Commonwealth funds became available for the States' public housing programmes. The Act required that each State should ensure that adequate legislation existed to enable it at all times to control throughout the State (a) rental housing projects, (b) slum clearance, and (c) town planning.

Sydney

The first of the metropolitan plans was prepared for Sydney by the Cumberland County Council, a special purpose second-tier authority elected and paid for by the constituent councils of the metropolitan region. The legislation, modelled on the then current English planning legislation, provided for the preparation of statutory planning schemes 'regulating and controlling the use of land' by means of maps and ordinances, but reserved to the Minister for Local Government the authority to amend, suspend or reject the whole or any part of a planning scheme.

The Cumberland County Plan was submitted to the Minister in July 1948 within the stipulated three year period, but the government of New South Wales hesitated a further three years before the planning scheme was promulgated. The principal features of the plan were:

1. The zoning of land for urban purposes to provide for an increase in population from 1.8 to 2.4 million up to 1972, the continuous urban area delimited by a permanent green belt zone with a general prohibition against building on sites less than five acres in area.
2. A general prohibition of new buildings on lands designated for public open space and county roads.
3. The zoning of land for manufacturing industry in the middle and outer suburbs as well as the confirmation of predominantly industrialized localities in the inner areas. This was a conscious attempt to provide employment in suburban locations having regard to the prospective residential location of factory workers. Suburban dispersal of manufacturing plants would have occurred in any case but would have otherwise been hampered by the lack of available sites.
4. As a corollary to 3 above, many of the older inner areas of terrace housing regarded by realtors as future commercial and industrial areas were zoned as living areas which protected them from further industrial penetration and encouraged their rehabilitation and renewal. Although some of these localities were labelled as due for 're-housing within twenty-five years' spontaneous rehabilitation by owner-occupants (mostly European migrants) of what was then predominantly rental housing has left very few areas which today could be regarded as deserving of renewal. The N.S.W. Housing Commission had cleared 74 acres (32 ha) of dilapidated housing and built some 3,800 dwellings in rehousing schemes to June 1970.

These were the weightiest influences on the patterns of post-war urban growth although the Cumberland Plan had wider aspirations. Sixteen suburban centres were zoned as district centres with the intention that they would assume more important roles as central places and relieve the central city of some of the increased activity arising from population growth.

Detailed land use planning by the thirty-nine local councils within 1,750 square miles (4,530 sq. km.) of the County of Cumberland was not pursued with much enthusiasm, most of them preferring to exercise the wide discretionary powers over development applications conferred on them by the Cumberland County Planning Scheme Ordinance. Australian governments are generally reluctant to impede development, and local governments are no exception. Unless it can be shown that a development proposal is positively harmful (and not always then) development proposals are usually regarded with favour.

The green belt zoning had effectively restrained the continuing proliferation of subdivisions which the Cumberland County Council regarded as among the major problems which the planning scheme should try to correct. The difficulty of providing network services at public cost to the extensive fringe areas of widely scattered housing was clearly shown by the lag in the provision of piped sewerage. About 530,000 of the metropolitan population of 1.83 million in 1951 lived in areas without main sewers while the sewered areas included some 13,000 vacant building lots. Over the ten years to 1961 when the population increased to 2.14 million and the green belt remained more or less intact, the Metropolitan Water Sewerage and Drainage Board was able to extend water and sewers to 150,000 extra lots; vacant sewered lots were reduced to 8,000, but the backlog increased; more than 600,000 of the metropolitan population lived in areas awaiting main sewerage.

Although the urban zones within the green belt had the capacity for a population of 2.4 million, by 1958 the broad acres of land available for subdivision were exhausted. The New South Wales Housing Commission was seeking tracts of low cost land for its metropolitan programme. The claims by the Housing Commission were reinforced by pressures from private developers who had acquired interests in areas of green belt land in the expectation of a retraction of its boundaries, and local councils had scant sympathy for the restraints it imposed on the growth of their municipalities. In December 1959 a new Minister for Local Government exercised his prerogative to 'suspend' the greater part of the green belt to allow its conversion to urban zoning, demonstrating that he, not the Cumberland County Council, was the final authority.

The move aroused unexpectedly hostile reactions in the press. The County Council took advantage of the Minister's embarrassment to obtain agreement that the areas released should become available for development only after detailed planning schemes for each of the areas had been prepared, making proper provision for schools, parks, through routes and other public purposes. The Council also successfully pressed for the financial responsibility for water and sewer reticulation and a share of the cost of trunk connections to become the responsibility of the developers.

These radical policy changes in development administration were without precedent in Australia but have been adopted, not without hesitation and in varying degrees, in each of the State capitals. The New South

Wales government was, nevertheless, uneasy about the influence and behaviour of the Cumberland County Council. The Council publicized its aims and intentions and, when the occasion demanded, its disagreement with the Minister. The Council was abolished in 1963 and its responsibilities for metropolitan planning were taken over by a new body, the New South Wales State Planning Authority, which according to the Act under which it is constituted, is 'subject in all respects to the direction and control of the Minister'.

The Authority in 1968 produced the *Sydney Region Outline Plan*. The new plan proposes that only 1.75 million of the additional population should be accommodated in suburban 'corridor' extensions of metropolitan Sydney within the County of Cumberland; it assumes that half a million population can be diverted to decentralized locations in other parts of New South Wales and a further half million to Gosford and Wyong beyond the metropolitan area on the coast north of Sydney.

The Outline Plan Report emphasizes the public costs involved in meeting the needs of the expanded metropolis; $1,850m for water and sewerage alone, almost three times the recorded value of the capital assets of the Metropolitan Water Sewerage and Drainage Board in 1967.

The expected increase in value of the rural lands to be converted to urban use was estimated at $3,000m; the government believed it to be 'not unreasonable that part of the increment in value which arises primarily from the expenditure of public and private funds on essential services should be made available to meet the cost of such services'. The Land Development Contribution Act of 1970 provides for the collection of 30 per cent of the increase in value of land arising from urban zoning calculated from a base date of August 1969 and applies to all non-urban land in the Sydney region. The State Planning Authority announced in May 1972 that $3 from the land development fund would be loaned to municipalities in the growth areas on generous terms.

The most significant move towards ensuring the fulfilment of the Outline Plan is the State Planning Authority's role in promoting the development of Campbelltown-Camden, at the end of the south-western growth corridor, where the Authority has acquired some 10,000 acres (40 sq. km.) for a town centre, industrial areas and estates for the Housing Commission.

The recovery of 'betterment' under the Land Development Contribution Act and the development programme in Campbelltown-Camden are positive steps beyond the conventional statutory planning processes for 'regulating and controlling the use of land'. No other planning authority in Australia has moved so far but, as noted later, public authority participation in metropolitan development has been an important element in the growth of Adelaide.

Melbourne

Rather than create a new special-purpose authority for metropolitan planning the Victorian government made the Melbourne and Metropolitan Board of Works responsible for the preparation of a master plan for Melbourne. The Board of Works is a long-established water supply and sewerage authority, a second-tier government body of fifty-two members elected by the aldermen of the constituent councils. Unlike Sydney's Cumberland County Council the possibility of its abolition is more than remote.

The local councils of metropolitan Melbourne were empowered under the Town and Country Planning Act 1955 to prepare planning schemes controlling land use under the general supervision of a Town and Country Planning Board responsible to the Minister for Local Government. Both the councils and the Planning Board urged the preparation of a metropolitan plan; the 1944 Act was amended accordingly.

The Board of Works completed the Melbourne Metropolitan Scheme in 1954. Although not adopted as a statutory scheme it was made effective as a means of controlling land use by an Interim Development Order promulgated in 1955. With revisions and amendments the planning scheme was finally adopted as a statutory plan in 1968. The planning area of 688 square miles (1,780 sq. km.) was not as extensive as the County of Cumberland, most of it lying within a 15 mile (24 km.) radius of the central city. The original scheme of 1954 provided for urban zoning of 266 square miles (690 sq. km.), calculated as sufficient for population growth from 1.4 million to 2.5 million within 30 to 50 years. There was no intention of restricting the outward spread of the suburbs, nor the diversion of growth to satellite towns, as such ideas were considered to be beyond the scope of the Board's responsibilities. As in Sydney there were proposals for the planned dispersal of employment to improve the relative distribution of population and jobs and in particular the growth of five existing centres to relieve the central city of some of the demands generated by the increase in population. The suburban centres have missed out entirely as alternative locations for central city activities: the 'regional' shopping centres established in the 1960s have each been located on sites remote from the centres nominated in the 1954 plan. The suburban dispersal of manufacturing has, as in Sydney, been facilitated by the prescription of industrial zones, but employment in the inner areas has continued to increase while the suburbs have spread at a greater rate than could have been foreseen in 1954. As well as the underestimation of the growth of the metropolitan population, which reached 2.5 million in 1972, there was an unexpected movement of residents from the inner areas, a movement which land use zoning was powerless to counter. By 1967, when the population was 2.1 million, urban zoning had been extended to 320 square miles (830 sq. km.), reaching beyond the boundaries of metropolitan planning area. The Board of Works reported in *The Future of Growth of Melbourne* (1967) that a population of 5 million should be allowed for by the end of the century.

The latest planning proposals are embodied in the Board of Works publication, *Planning Policies for the Melbourne Metropolitan Region* (1971). The most important changes proposed are for the enlargement of the metropolitan planning area to embrace 1,942 square miles (5,030 sq. km.) and the designation of future urban growth corridors along each of the eight major radial railways. The Planning Policies report stresses for the first time the importance of the 'green wedges' between the radial corridors and the problems of retaining their landscape qualities and recreational potential.

As in Sydney the urban zoning has proved effective in controlling the proliferation of premature subdivision and widely scattered housing around the urban fringe. Between 1955 and 1958, before land owners realized the seriousness of the planning intentions, 428 applications for subdivisions in the non-urban areas totalling 11,500 acres (46.5 sq. km.) were refused by the Board of Works. But urban zoning has been progressively extended without any of the drama attaching to the release of Sydney's green belt. The Board of Works has not achieved the same degree of control over the detailed planning of the areas converted from rural to urban uses but has been successful in using its planning powers to require subdividers of land to meet the costs of water (in 1962) and sewerage reticulation (1970) and to contribute to the cost of the headworks.

The influence of planning

There is little to suggest that planning has made any significant difference to the patterns of urban growth and change over the post-war period. The spread of low-density suburbs has followed the suburban rail services which were electrified in the 1920s far ahead of any real (as distinct from speculative) demands for suburban land and the process of suburban spread has been encouraged by rail fare concessions for commuters. The most important difference is the measure of control which has been brought to bear on the rural-to-urban conversion process and the restraint on the premature subdivision of rural land.

Despite the early ideas for subcentralized employment embodied in the metropolitan plans the central and inner areas still account for the greater part of employment with continuing emphasis on jobs in tertiary activities. The inner areas served by a close web of public transport, railways, bus routes and (in Melbourne) tramways, occupy little more than 10 per cent of the total urban area but contain more than half of the total employment; in Melbourne 64 per cent, in Sydney 54 per cent. The extent of the zoning for commercial and industrial purposes in these inner areas is such that the administration of land use controls does not offer any restraint to the continuing build-up of employment.

The residential zones of the inner areas have allowed the replacement of houses with blocks of flats and the flat building boom since the early 1960s was expected to produce significant increases of population in these areas, but there has been a steady decline. The replacement of older houses by commercial premises and the reduction in the average size of households occupying both the old dwellings and the new flats have resulted in a loss of population in the inner areas.

Neither has the flat boom apparently had much influence on the demand for the suburban house-and-garden. Although flat completions in Sydney and Melbourne have formed an increasing proportion of the annual output of dwellings, it appears that flats are only a partial substitute for houses. Most of the demand for flats appears to have arisen as a result of increasing affluence which enables single persons, childless couples and unrelated groups, who would in less prosperous times be sharing accommodation, to rent or buy a flat.

Although development control exercised by planning has not had much tangible influence on the distribution of population and employment, it has been at least partly successful in sorting out incompatible land uses and reserving lands designated for open spaces and highway routes pending public acquisition. Significant tracts of land for recreational open spaces have been saved and acquired at less cost than would otherwise have been the case. In Sydney most of the routes for about one hundred miles of urban expressways have been acquired although only sixteen miles had been built in 1970; in Melbourne about thirty miles have been completed.

Transportation

Four of every five Australian households own one or more cars. The number of registered motor vehicles has increased from less than 2 million in 1955 to 5 million in 1970. The ratio of vehicles per thousand of the population has increased over the same period from 248 to 394 per thousand.

The transportation studies undertaken for each of the State capitals (except Sydney where a study is due for completion in 1973) recommend plans with the greatest emphasis on new highways. The Melbourne study of 1964 recommended 307 miles of freeways and 103 miles of new arterial routes. The total estimated cost of the transportation proposals, including an underground railway loop in the central area (currently under construction), was $2,616m to 1985. The current $1,000m programme for building Sydney's expressway system over thirty years follows and extends the proposals incorporated in the Cumberland Plan of 1951.

Commonwealth government has since 1923 made conditional grants to the States for roadworks. The amount of the contribution has been progressively increased but the programmes have been criticized as being inequitable in the distribution of funds between the States and in strongly favouring rural developmental and country roads to the neglect of urban roads. The current five year programme, set out in the Commonwealth Aid Roads Act 1969, for the first time makes specific provision for expenditure on 'urban arterial roads', which while subject to matching funds from the States, clearly improves the prospects for the ambitious proposals of the metropolitan transportation studies.

The increasing use of the motor car has led to a marked fall-off in the use of public transport which has not been offset by the increase in the metropolitan populations. The use of public transport in the five mainland capitals has fallen from 327 trips per head each year in 1954, when the five capitals had a total population of 5 million, to 163 trips per head in 1969, when the total population had increased by 50 per cent to 7.5 million. The heaviest losses have occurred in the off-peak and weekend services while peak-hour demands have remained much the same or have reached even higher levels. Rising costs have not been met by substantial fare increases nor have they been effectively reduced by the pruning of services. Estimated deficits on public transport services in the five mainland capitals for the year 1970-1 totalled $53.5m (about $7.50 per head of population), an increase of almost 50 per cent over the losses incurred two years before in 1968-9.

The journey to work

Surveys conducted by the Bureau of Census and Statistics in 1970 showed that most of the journeys to work in the mainland capitals were made in private cars. Work journeys to the central areas make more use of public transport. In Sydney 87 per cent of peak-hour travellers to the central city in 1966 used public transport, the electric train services carrying 81,000– 55 per cent of the total peak-hour arrivals. In Melbourne, where a more generous road system is less constrained by topography, public transport to the city centre in 1965 accounted for 68 per cent of work journeys, 32 per cent of the workers using private cars, as compared with 13 per cent in Sydney. Electric train services carried 41 per cent of the total, rather less than in Sydney.

Despite the operating losses incurred by the suburban railways the metropolitan planning authorities base the planned suburban expansion of both Sydney and Melbourne on the rail routes which form the 'transport spines' of their corridors of urban growth. With eight radial routes the expansion of Melbourne is not impeded and the railway service should become more effective with the completion of the central underground loop. The Sydney Region Outline Plan, more constrained by topography, proposes a wider dispersal of growth: two rail-based corridors within the

County of Cumberland and additional growth directed northwards beyond the metropolitan area into Gosford and Wyong, which are already becoming long-distance commuter suburbs.

Brisbane, Adelaide and Perth are each approaching their first million of population half a century later than Sydney and Melbourne, at a time when investment in suburban railways does not have the prospects of competing profitably with other forms of transport and the cities themselves are not of a size at which road congestion is a serious deterrent to the use of the private car. Each has prepared metropolitan planning schemes and completed transportation studies. Each has adopted widely differing policy attitudes to planning and the prospects of growth.

Brisbane

The Greater Brisbane Council took over the responsibilities of twenty-two local councils with an area of 375 square miles and a population of 240,000 in 1925. It assumed control of a range of urban services wider than those of any other single urban authority in Australia. Power, water supply, sewerage, traffic and public transport, usually the responsibility of State departments or special purpose authorities in other cities, became part of the Council's responsibilities. The State retained responsibility for rail services, ports and harbours, main roads and public housing; the Council itself remained ultimately responsible to the Minister for Local Government.

The Council has prepared surveys and plans and exercised some measure of control over land use since 1935 but until 1965 the attempts to establish a statutory planning scheme were unsuccessful. The difficulties have been attributed to State governments which were other than sympathetic to the city government. A new State government in 1958 referred the planning proposals, first submitted to the Minister for Local Government in 1952, to a specially constituted Greater Brisbane Town Planning Committee and passed the City of Brisbane (Town Plan) Act in 1959. The planning scheme prepared under the supervision of the Committee was completed and exhibited in 1962 and was still in the process of revision when American consultants were commissioned by the Minister for Main Roads, acting in conjunction with the Council, to prepare a transportation study. The study recommendations submitted in 1965 were for a major road system of 80 miles of freeways, 16 miles of expressways and 300 miles of new or improved arterial roads at a cost of $340m. Because these proposals differed from those appearing on the planning scheme and neither the State government nor the Council were prepared to assume responsibility for any major road programme, all proposals for new roads were removed from the scheme before it was finally gazetted as a statutory plan in 1965. Responsibility for building the improved road system became an area of lively controversy between the Council and the Queensland government, ending in a compromise. A revised plan exhibited in 1969 protects some of the road routes adopted by the State as the first stage of a revised highway plan; other arterial routes are the responsibility of the Council. The current plan, promulgated in 1971, is more limited in its scope than most but, like other statutory land use plans, is subject to variation and amendment. Lomg-term intentions for urban expansion are not indicated; land use changes, including the conversion of rural lands to urban use, are negotiated rather than prescribed. Since 1965, when the enabling legislation provided for the Council to make agreements with developers and subdividers to meet the cost of water supply and sewerage services, the Council has been accused of the 'improper and arbitrary use of power'. A commission of enquiry appointed in 1966 found that 'No one has been guilty in a criminal sense' but was strongly critical of the Lord Mayor and others concerned with development administration. The Lord Mayor has been reported as claiming: 'We are doing a magnificent job of planning in Brisbane – on a day to day basis.'

The most recent amendment to the City of Brisbane Town Planning Act requires that future revisions of the town plan shall include a statement of intentions of goals and policies, but the machinery of development administration and zoning amendments is such that policies can be eroded in practice more readily than in most metropolitan planning arrangements.

The urban areas of Brisbane already extend beyond the boundaries of the 375 square miles under the City Council's control. A public transport study of south-east Queensland carried out for the Minister of Transport by the consultants who undertook the Brisbane transportation study shows the close functional relationship of the contiguous urban areas and projects a metropolitan population of 1.7 million by the year 2000, more than double the 1971 figure of 866,000. The 'anticipated land use pattern' of the Brisbane region used for the purpose of public transport study, adopts the existing suburban rail routes as the main basis for the location of the areas of urban expansion. Although the suburban rail services carried only 24 per cent of the 113 million public transport journeys in 1970–1, it was the only element in public transport which had increased its loadings in the previous ten years. The consultants recommended the electrification and general improvement of the system to form a north–south spine with branch lines, about 100 miles (160 km.) in all. While noting that electric rail service revenues in Sydney and Melbourne covered no more than one-third of outgoings, the improved rail system co-ordinated with bus services under the control of a 'Brisbane Regional Transportation Authority' was considered to be the least costly means of providing public transport services for the extended urban areas.

The absence of long-term land use proposals for directing suburban expansion and the current practice of exercising development control by negotiation have been criticized as totally inadequate. A submission to the Queensland government in 1968 by five professional institutes urged an enquiry into the setting up of a State planning authority and the introduction of town and regional planning legislation. No enquiry has been instituted but expectations have been aroused by the passage of the State and Regional Planning and Development, Public Works Organisation and Environmental Control Act 1971. The Act invests the State Co-ordinator General with remarkably wide powers over the plans and developments of all public authorities including local governments, and provides for the planning of 'State Development Areas'. The full scope and possibilities of the Act are not yet clear, but the indications are that the State intends to assume a more positive role in metropolitan planning. The vague expectations of the metropolitan co-ordination which would be possible under a more comprehensive metropolitan government have not been fulfilled: the interests of the State government are proving to be too strong to be surrendered to a political rival. It is unlikely, however, that political or administrative changes will impose new directions or restraints on the trends of metropolitan growth.

Adelaide

Although Adelaide was the last of the metropolitan areas to adopt statutory planning, control of suburban sprawl has been exercised by the requirement that new subdivisions in the metropolitan area were allowed to proceed only if they could be economically served with water and sewerage by the State Department of Engineering and Water Supply. This virtually eliminated the premature subdivision of land and ensured that metropolitan expansion had some measure of order; Adelaide is the only metropolitan area without a serious backlog in the provision of main sewerage.

The South Australian government has been more active in urban development than the government of any other State. Adelaide is the only mainland capital which has managed to accommodate rapid growth without marked inflation of land prices. With limited natural resources in South Australia the government has been active over three decades in the promotion of manufacturing industry. The provision of cheap and fully serviced land and, where needed, rental premises for industrial plants was the lesser part of the total programme. The major effort was made in the area of public housing through the operations of the South Australian Housing Trust, a semi-independent government instrumentality. The housing of needy, although not neglected, was incidental to the main purpose of providing adequate middle-range housing at low cost for the industrial workforce.

Throughout the post-war period the Trust has built more than a third of the new houses in South Australia and penetrated heavily into the lower end of the private housing market. All the Trust's land requirements were purchased by negotiation (powers of compulsory acquisition were not used) and its most spectacular achievement is Elizabeth, a well-equipped community of 60,000, 17 miles (27 km.) north of the centre of Adelaide. Although the Trust's programme has been achieved by a squeeze on other State expenditures, including schools and hospitals in the early post-war years, the result has been that the prices of housing and land have not increased to the same extent as in other cities in spite of a metropolitan growth rate as high as 4.6 per cent per annum in the period 1961–6 when the population reached 730,000. It is claimed for Adelaide (with some justification) that living costs are lower, industrial relations easier and housing problems minimal as compared with the other mainland capitals of Australia.

This singular state of affairs was achieved without a statutory metropolitan land use plan but not without planning and co-ordination by the Housing Trust and the other instrumentalities concerned with urban development. The important distinction from the other States has been a continuing commitment by the State government in both policy and practice to a programme of development in which the government itself maintained the initiative and was the principal participant.

The creation of a State Planning Authority and the adoption of a Metropolitan Development Plan in 1967 were nevertheless considered necessary to provide formal channels of co-ordination between the government authorities and the local municipalities, control private developments, acquire open spaces and generally express in the form of a plan the policies and intentions for growth.

The *Report on the Metropolitan Area of Adelaide*, prepared by a select committee appointed by the government in 1955, was submitted in 1962. Doubts about the impediments that the plan might impose on both private and public enterprise delayed its acceptance until the passage of the Planning and Development Act 1966–7, which constituted the State Planning Authority under the control and direction of the Minister for Local Government. The plan provides for growth to 1991 with provision for a metropolitan population of almost 1.4 million, most of the urban expansion being in six 'metropolitan districts' (including the town of Elizabeth) extending north and south on the Adelaide Plain between the Mount Lofty ranges and the coast.

In 1965, before the adoption of the Metropolitan Development Plan, the government commissioned American consultants to prepare a metropolitan transportation study which was presented in 1968. The *Metropolitan Adelaide Transportation Study* proposed a massive programme of roadworks, $280m for 60 miles (97 km.) of freeways and $344m for expressways and arterial roads. Public transport improvements were proposed in a $105m programme which included an underground rail link in the central city, designed to overcome the disadvantages of the stub-ended city rail terminus.

Car ownership in Adelaide is above the average of the State capitals and the use of public transport, at 102 passenger journeys per head in 1969, is the lowest; but the exhibition of the transport proposals aroused widespread public controversy. Unlike Brisbane, where the principal concern was confined to how the cost of roads should be shared between the Brisbane Council and the Queensland government, the agitation in Adelaide centres around the destructive effect the new freeways will have on the environment. Particular concern has been expressed for the encroachment on the central city's park belt, the renowned feature of Light's original plan of 1937, where the road proposals stop short and avoid showing how the traffic should be handled.

Government initiative in metropolitan development is being maintained through the work of the South Australian Housing Trust, which is currently preparing for action in developing a southern counterpart to the new town of Elizabeth at Noarlunga 20 miles (32 km.) south of Adelaide. A new city centre and satellite community of 150,000 people is being planned as an essentially public enterprise.

More recently the South Australian government declared its intention to establish a major new town at Murray Bridge, 50 miles (80 km.) east of Adelaide. In speaking to the Murray New Town (Land Acquisition) Bill in March 1972 the Premier observed that the consequences of the growth of Adelaide had been 'brought home to South Australians when the implications of the Metropolitan Adelaide Transportation Study became apparent . . . people were not willing to accept the effect on their environment . . .' The Premier went on to say that the measure was regarded 'as only one of the steps necessary towards achieving a more even distribution of population throughout the State'.

Perth

The Metropolitan Region Planning Authority was set up in 1959 under the Metropolitan Region Town Planning Scheme Act to implement an advisory plan for the metropolitan region prepared in 1955 by the office of the State Commissioner for Town Planning. The statutory plan adopted in 1963 embraced a region of 2,080 square miles (5,390 sq. km.) and outlined the areas for staged urban expansion from a population of half a million to 1.4 million.

The constitution of the Authority was designed to ensure that the major public agencies and local government would be directly represented and that six 'Special Purpose Committees' would include representative organizations, public and private, concerned with urban development and management. In its first annual report the Authority made its role clear;

(a) Major regional planning decisions must reflect State government policies and be endorsed and supported by the government.

(b) State government instrumentalities and other public authorities must participate effectively in regional planning decisions.

(c) A wide range of specialist professional skills must be applied in support of decision-making.

(d) The complete process of regional planning goes beyond the statutory jurisdiction of the Metropolitan Region Planning Authority in administering the region scheme: there must be a focus of organized co-ordination which embraces all the agencies whose development works are needed for urban growth.

Smaller in size than their counterparts in New South Wales and Victoria, the authorities participating in the Metropolitan Region Planning Authority have been more successful in achieving working relationships in planning and development by the public sector. The private sector has, however, proved to be more recalcitrant and the orderly process of urbanization has been seriously impeded by land speculation.

A committee of enquiry (the McCarrey Committee) reported in *Land Taxation and Land Prices in Western Australia* (1968) that land prices had been increasing at rates from 15 to 22 per cent per annum and a speculative boom was witholding land from the market. Against a background of accelerated economic growth arising from the exploitation of rich mineral resources in Western Australia the Committee suggested that a contributing cause was the Metropolitan Region Planning Scheme which had, since interim development controls were imposed in 1956, restrained premature subdivision but at the same time 'made clear the probable path of future development' providing, as one realtor put it, 'a punter's guide to successful speculation in real estate'.

The land market in the Perth metropolitan region exhibited many of the characteristics of the land boom of the pre-depression years, with the formation of syndicates for the purchase of rural lands extending beyond the zoned urban areas and press advertisements promising investors profits of two or three hundred per cent within five years. Local government taxes, although levied on the site values, are too low to constitute a deterrent to these activities.

The McCarrey Committee made a number of recommendations including the imposition of a surcharge on the State land tax on unimproved lands, public participation in the provision of subdivided land for bona fide builders, the recovery of a betterment levy, and annual reassessment of unimproved land for tax purposes. A surcharge on the State land tax has since been imposed which increases the tax to a maximum of 5 per cent annually on the owners of unimproved urban land with aggregate values of $100,000 or more, but this is refunded if the land is developed within four years. In 1969 the Metropolitan Region Planning Authority reported that the boom in land prices appeared to be levelling out. The surcharge tax, agreements reached with some land developers, the entry of the State-owned Rural and Industrial Bank into the land development business and the tempering of the extreme optimism of the minerals market contributed to the dampening effect.

The purchase by speculators of rural lands well beyond the areas planned for urban expansion to the 1.4 million mark, acquired with the intention of seeking zoning changes, influenced the Authority to produce a longer term plan to indicate the ultimate extent of the urban areas within the region. *The Corridor Plan for Perth* was adopted by the Authority in 1970 and published in 1971. It proposes that expansion beyond the 195 square miles (505 sq. km.) of urban zoning already planned should be in four corridors; two extending north and south along the coast and two inland, each reaching to the boundaries of the metropolitan planning area; and five sub-regional centres, including the port town of Fremantle, were proposed to attract retail and office activities with the aim of reducing work journeys and curtailing the growth of further office employment in the city centre.

Concurrently with the formulation of the Corridor Plan a twenty year regional transport study was prepared which, after examination of alternatives, adopted the 'dispersal solution' of the Corridor Plan as the most appropriate distribution of land use. The recommendations of the *Perth Regional Transport Study 1970* are based on a 'balance between the use of public transport and the private car as a vital factor in the solution of the transport problems of the city centre'. The study recommends a $346m road programme including 28 miles (45 km.) of freeways and 56 miles (90 km.) of expressways; public transport improvements will require $52m over the twenty year programme. Forty-four miles (71 km.) of suburban railways were proposed to be converted to busways as part of a system of exclusive bus routes with the possibility of the replacement of buses by rapid transit if necessary at some future time. Current indications are that the government intends that the suburban railway system should be electrified rather than replaced by buses, although the train services carry only a small proportion of public transport journeys.

A second *Report on the Corridor Plan for Perth* was published by the Metropolitan Region Planning Authority in July 1972 and the proposal is currently being considered by a royal commission of the parliament. Indications are that the principles of corridor growth and sub-regional centres will be recommended but some reservation short of unqualified endorsement seems likely.

The prospects

All State governments are committed to the principle of planning and in theory the metropolitan plans are expressions of public policy. In practice there is a reluctance to impede private investment and an inadequacy of funds for public investment which generally inhibits the public sector from assuming an initiating role. The plans for Sydney and Melbourne have been drastically amended to meet the demands of growth; in Brisbane changing the metropolitan plan is a matter of regular negotiation.

The controls and restraints imposed on metropolitan development by statutory land use controls have been of limited influence on post-war urban growth. Some success has been achieved in bringing a measure of order to the spreading suburbs, most notably in the conscription of private capital to share the costs of converting rural land to urban use. Zoning provisions have sorted out incompatible land uses and have helped to maintain the amenity of residential areas but the broad course of growth and change within the existing urban areas has not been impeded.

The most significant examples of orderly urbanization have been achieved by public authorities acquiring land and assuming an initiating role. The work of the South Australian Housing Trust at Elizabeth, the project for a similar but larger enterprise at Noarlunga and the proposed new town at Murray Bridge, designed to relieve metropolitan Adelaide of some of the demands and consequences of growth, are government enterprises far beyond the scope of the usual statutory processes of land use planning and control. Statutory planning has the important but limited function of establishing a framework which prescribes the nature of the permitted development but does not promote it except in a negative way by imposing restraints in other areas. Restraints can be sustained only if the needs can be met by the offer of opportunities in other directions. In South Australia the government has assumed this entrepreneurial role, but with the exception of the New South Wales State Planning Authority's project at Campbelltown, the other State governments have not assumed any initiatives.

Metropolitan growth is still applauded by most State governments as tangible evidence of progress, but increasing popular concern about the environment and the 'quality of life' in metropolitan centres has evoked a political response at the Federal level. Although the Commonwealth Housing Commission report of 1944 held promise of Commonwealth assistance to the State governments in town planning and urban development it became clear after the Liberal–Country Party Coalition came to office in 1949 that Commonwealth assistance would not be extended beyond the agreement already made for funding State public housing programmes.

Since 1965 the Australian Labor Party opposition has been pressing a range of urban issues to such good effect that the government has belatedly been persuaded to indicate its willingness to become involved in what it has traditionally insisted is a State responsibility. In November 1972, a few weeks before the Federal elections, a National Urban and Regional Development Authority was set up.

The Prime Minister spoke of the Commonwealth and States working together in 'the development of a small number of carefully selected centres' and 'sub-metropolitan centres that offer the greatest potential for rapid development'. But the National Urban and Regional Development Authority has been criticized by Labor Party spokesmen as a body without muscle and the Labor Party promises to create a Ministry of Urban Affairs.

Meanwhile, the State governments of New South Wales and Victoria have not been slow to stake their claims and assume the initiative by dusting off some long dormant ideas for public action. The New South Wales government has announced the choice of the towns of Bathurst and Orange for a new 'corridor city' centred about 150 miles (240 km.) west of Sydney and has discussed a large-scale land acquisition and development programme, which would require finance of $60m to $150m over fifteen years, to counter the rising costs of home sites in Sydney's spreading suburbs.

The Victorian government has revived a neglected programme for decentralized 'regional capitals', but without actually nominating a choice of centres. The government of Western Australia has pointed to the Pilbara, a rapidly expanding mining region, as an appropriate place for a new industrial city. Alone among the States, South Australia had already established clear lines of action for the ordering of urban growth in Adelaide and beyond.

Both government and opposition parties have, for the first time in Australian political history, made the problems of the cities an election issue. Both promise to assist the States in improving their rail systems but the Labor Party proposes more direct participation in urban development, including the acquisition of land for private and public housing and finance to overcome the backlog in sewerage services. At Albury-Wodonga, lying across the New South Wales and Victorian State borders, the Labour Party claims that the Commonwealth has the constitutional jurisdiction to establish 'another inland city the size of Canberra' and proposes to take the initiative in the urban expansion of Townsville in northern Queensland. In Sydney it proposes to use a large tract of Commonwealth land at Holsworthy for a new metropolitan district of 200,000 population, making land available at low cost 'to break the back of the inflation of Sydney's housing land prices'.

The election campaign has made it clear that the problems of urban growth are established as national issues and are likely to remain a permanent concern of Commonwealth governments. Given that a unity of purpose can be achieved, the extent to which Commonwealth and State intervention can influence the distribution of population to slow the growth of the existing metropolitan areas is not likely to be dramatic. Diversion of funds to promote new growth centres at the expense of public investment in such things as roads, public transport and other services in the existing metropolitan electorates, where four of every five householders are home owners (and car owners), will not make for political popularity. The continued concentration of growth in the large cities is not likely to be modified; any change will require unswerving political commitment over a generation or more.

REFERENCES

Commonwealth Ministry of Post-war Reconstruction, *Commonwealth Housing Commission Final Report*, 1944.
Cumberland County Council, *The Planning Scheme for the County of Cumberland New South Wales*, Sydney, 1948.
De Leuw, Cather *et al.*, *Metropolitan Adelaide Transportation Study*, 1968.
Melbourne and Metropolitan Board of Works, *Melbourne Metropolitan Planning Scheme 1954*, vol. I: *Surveys and Analysis*, vol. II: *Report*.
  The Future Growth of Melbourne, 1967.
  Planning Policies for the Melbourne Metropolitan Region, 1971.
New South Wales State Planning Authority, *Sydney Region Growth and Change; Prelude to a Plan*, 1967.
  Sydney Region Outline Plan, 1968.
Perth Metropolitan Region Planning Authority, *The Corridor Plan for Perth*, 1971.
  Report on the Corridor Plan for Perth, 1972.
Perth Regional Transport Study Steering Committee, *Perth Regional Transport Study 1970*.
South Australia Town Planning Committee, *Report on the Metropolitan Area of Adelaide*, Government of South Australia, 1962.
[South Australia] State Planning Authority, *Planning News* no. 8, December 1971.
G. Stephenson and J. A. Hepburn, *Plan for the Metropolitan Region Perth and Fremantle*, 1955.
Wilbur Smith *et al.*, *Melbourne Transportation Study*, vol. I: *Survey*, vol. III: *The Transportation Plan*, 1969.
  Brisbane Transportation Study, vol. I, 1965.
  South-East Queensland – Brisbane Region Public Transport Study, 1970.

13
Urban renewal

E. VANDERMARK

In a little more than a decade the skyline in each of Australia's six State capital cities has undergone a metamorphosis, a vivid illustration of the monumental proportions of urban renewal.

The processes of urban renewal and its reverse, urban decay, are complex, with many interrelated factors playing a part. As a result they are inadequately understood. It may well be that different factors determine the outcome in different cities or at different times in the same city. In Australia the decisions that determine urban renewal have been largely made in the private sector of the economy. The market in recent years has been operating under the impact of changes in the traditional factors that guided supply and demand, and of new forces. Two of the traditional variables that influence the property market and have undergone drastic change are the rapid increase in city population (Australia's urban explosion) and the unprecedented rise in personal incomes since the end of World War II. Obsolescence of buildings is another traditional factor behind urban renewal, but its pace has been accelerated by recent technological innovations, one of the new variables. The new financial resources available for urban redevelopment, and government involvement in urban renewal, are other facets of forces in the market that have been introduced in recent years.

Rising population in a city is normally accompanied by a relative and absolute increase in the value of sites at the centre, a consequence of the rising demand for centrally located premises. Redevelopment of such sites, usually at higher density, is necessary to meet the demand. In order to pay the higher price of sites higher rentals or sales prices are needed.

Increasing personal income will result in increasing consumption of housing, whether in the form of better quality, more room space per person or bigger allotments. As the demand for housing services increases over the whole range of the income scale, a 'filtering' process will begin to operate characterized by new construction at the top and upgrading and/or lower occupancy at the bottom of the housing ladder. At the same time it may become profitable to redevelop properties in areas suffering from a low level of resource use.

Obsolescence of buildings will sooner or later lead to redevelopment, the economic life span of buildings being determined by factors such as quality of the structure; residential, commercial or other use of the building; whether it is privately or publicly owned and the demand for the site for other purposes. Private residential property may not be redeveloped for sentimental reasons, even though profitable in economic terms. For business premises, however, the cycle of construction–depreciation–renewal is largely determined by the property market. As actual or projected demand for floorspace or accommodation in a particular area increases even sound and substantial structures may become obsolete. The impact of this 'economic' ageing has been particularly noticeable in the central business districts (C.B.D.s) which experienced a sudden increase in demand for office accommodation.

The so-called 'technological' force behind urban renewal has led to changes in land use, in construction techniques and in the requirements of occupants. One instance is new construction techniques and engineering skills making it economic to construct much taller buildings. Changes in demand for different uses of urban space have led to the demolition of buildings to make way for freeways and parking structures. This is a result of the increasing use of the private motor car. New standards of convenience demanded by 'consumers' of buildings lead to accelerated obsolescence. At present complete airconditioning has become a normal requirement in quality office accommodation, making many perfectly sound office buildings without such modern conveniences 'substandard'. This change in requirements has had profound repercussions on urban renewal.

In spite of powerful forces working towards renewal there remain in many modern metropolises areas described in various euphemisms as resistant to progress, as having a deteriorated physical environment, as suffering from suboptimal resource use, or, in plain language, as slums. The reasons for the problem of chronically depressed areas are complicated and have not been adequately explained. The failure of the private market, due to the peculiar nature of the property market, is considered a major factor by many economists. But superimposed on this factor are other influences, such as low income, low community morale, inadequate business and civic leadership. These and other influences create a psychological and physical environment unfavourable to urban renewal.

Several writers, such as Harry W. Richardson,[1] claim that the peculiarities of the property market make government involvement crucial to urban renewal. The line of argument is that slums tend to result from the interplay of imperfections and external interferences in that market. Government involvement, in the form of assembling land and selling it to private developers, makes it possible to internalize 'externalities' in the market due to 'neighbourhood effects'.

The meaning of this technical concept 'externalities' may be best explained by giving two examples of its impact. Firstly, the market value of a particular property is strongly influenced by the quality of adjoining properties and by the 'status' of the neighbourhood in which it is located. Redevelopment of a single property in a rundown area will be unprofitable, as the value of the improvements will be depressed by the low values in the neighbourhood. The same interdependence of property values will lead to undermaintenance of property. An owner obtains the highest return from his property if it is undermaintained while others in the area remain well maintained. The second aspect of market externalities is the influence on property values of non-compatible land uses. The value of residential sites is usually lowered by proximity to industrial activities. Property values may drop not only as a result of manufacturing encroaching on residential areas, but also from increasing sensitivity to noise, smell and fumes. These economic 'spillovers' may well generate a vicious circle, in which no further investment in property in the area or on a site leads to reduction in maintenance in nearby property, to be followed by further reductions till even essential maintenance and repairs are stopped.

The case for government involvement in urban renewal to counter 'the neighbourhood effects' in the property market rests further on the scale of the operation, which may require many acres of land, and the problems in assembling large enough tracts. This may be beyond the resources of private enterprise. Without powers of compulsory acquisition, to be used as a last resort against unreasonable owners, projects that could benefit a whole neighbourhood may have to be shelved because of one obdurate owner. Urban renewal by public authorities can also take into consideration social benefits and other non-monetary consequences which cannot be incorporated in feasibility studies based on private costs and benefits.

One of the most important public inputs in urban renewal should be statutory planning schemes. The 'planning solution' to areas that have suffered progressive deterioration of the environment would involve a selected combination of redevelopment, rehabilitation and conservation of existing buildings. Considerable outlay may also be required on the urban infrastructure in the form of new road works, new reticulation networks and other utility services as well as open space and landscaping, creating a new urban environment. Urban renewal perceived from a planning perspective is based on two principles: that the problem of redevelopment is essentially a problem of updating an *environment*, rather than one of single sites and buildings, and that modernizing and changing an environment requires a mixture of public works, new buildings and the preservation and restoration of selected existing buildings. The planning principles and the economic arguments seem to support each other in pointing to a government policy toward urban renewal.

In spite of the enormous public expenditure on urban renewal, especially in the United States, little research has been done on the effectiveness of government attempts to counter the process of urban environmental degradation in certain areas. In the United States the Federal government has been an active partner in urban renewal since 1949. The scope of the involvement can be gauged from the sums that have been granted to help local government authorities to finance renewal projects. Under the 1949 National Housing Act the Federal government was authorized to spend $1,000m in loans and $500m in grants over a five year period. This was increased by a series of amendments so that by 1968 the limit to *grants* was $6,150m, most of which had been allocated.

One of the first evaluations of the urban renewal programme was by Rothenberg[2] who, in 1967, attempted to provide an analytic framework on the basis of benefit–cost analysis. His analysis of slum formation and its persistence leads to the conclusion that 'important neighbourhood externalities' help generate slums and help prevent their removal by purely private means.[3] Yet his study does not lead to a clear indication that on the whole the programme has been beneficial, but to the admission that satisfactory measurement will be difficult.

If Rothenberg leaves the question of the benefits from public participation in urban renewal undecided, Richard Muth[4] finds, as the result of his research, 'that many actual and proposed governmental policies will have little effect upon urban decentralisation and housing quality. What effects they have will probably tend to make these problems worse.'[5] Muth concludes, on the basis of analysis of census data, that the location and quality of housing can be explained in terms of household income, transport costs and age of buildings. 'By far the most important determinant of the condition of dwelling units is the income level of their inhabitants.'[6] The thesis on which much enthusiasm for large-scale government-financed slum clearance is based, i.e. that slums cause poverty, is countered by Muth's anti-thesis that poverty causes slums. Muth's recommendation for public intervention in slum clearance is in line with his diagnosis: income subsidies for the poor. Income subsidy is to be preferred to housing subsidy, as it allows the recipients to allocate their income according to their own priorities.

Australia's experience in urban renewal has been unlike the United States', in that the government has virtually played no direct part in urban renewal. A great deal of redevelopment has taken place but almost all in the form of 'spot clearance', the unco-ordinated, piecemeal replacement of individual buildings by private enterprise. Public involvement has been limited to indirect controls through building and siting regulations, covering safety and health measures, setbacks, size of allotments and the imposition of floor space ratios (F.S.R.S) in an attempt to limit the density of building.

The only instance of direct and major public participation in Australian urban renewal is the activity of the State Housing Commissions (s.h.c.) in Victoria and in New South Wales. Large-scale urban renewal based on the principles mentioned above, requiring comprehensive redevelopment schemes, is a very recent phenomenon.

The major emphasis in this chapter will be on the measurement of the magnitude of urban renewal during the period 1965 to 1970. This will be followed by a discussion of the Housing Commissions' role and of the planning schemes dealing with urban renewal, in operation or in preparation.

Magnitude of urban renewal

In the year ending June 1971 the total value of building work done in Australia amounted to $2,674m, of which 64 per cent occurred in the nation's six metropolitan statistical divisions as defined by the 1961 boundaries. These areas, constituting 0.01 per cent of the Australian continent, contained 58 per cent of the population in 1971.

Little if anything is known about the volume and type of building that may be classified as 'renewal', that is building operations on sites with existing buildings. This part of the chapter attempts an estimate of the magnitude of 'urban renewal' but the exercise is faced with two sets of difficulties. In the first place building statistics do not differentiate between development and redevelopment. A way around this problem is to assume that all building in the established parts of the metropolitan areas constitutes renewal. The assumption is arbitrary, as a certain amount of building in these inner areas takes place on sites with no or insignificant previous capital improvements, for instance tennis courts, race courses or land held in reserve. It can be argued, however, that these sites were in 'urban' use and that the 'higher and better uses' to which they are being put constitute urban renewal. A second major difficulty is posed by the question about which part of a metropolitan area should be regarded as fully developed. There is no clearcut answer to this problem as there is no generally valid definition of what constitutes 'vacant' land.

The best we can do is to select in each metropolitan area those inner L.G.A.s about which there is little doubt that virtually all the land has been developed. This is the method adopted by G. J. R. Linge in 1966 in 'Building activity in Australian metropolitan areas: a statistical background',[7] a paper that contains the only published building statistics by L.G.A.s. Calculating building activities in the same areas in 1971 makes it possible to compare absolute and relative levels of building activities in redevelopment areas at two periods in time and to note changes that have taken place during the intervening five year period.

The boundaries of metropolitan statistical divisions were redefined and considerably enlarged from 1966 onwards. Linge's building statistics for

1965–6, however, relate to the 1961 boundaries. As it is important to compare the 1971 and 1966 building figures for identical areas and as it was not possible to adjust 1965–6 building statistics on the basis of the new metropolitan boundaries, the only alternative was to estimate the building activity in 1970–1 within the old boundaries. The biggest impact of this rearrangement was in the Melbourne metropolitan statistical division, considerably enlarged in 1966. The value of work done in 1970–1 in the area as defined by the 1961 Melbourne boundaries was about $60m less than the figure for the 1966 boundaries, a reduction of about 11 per cent, half of which was in one category – houses.

The following L.G.A.s were included in the inner areas of each Metropolitan statistical division.

Sydney: Botany, Leichhardt, Marrickville, Mosman, North Sydney, Randwick, Waverley, Woollahra, South Sydney, Sydney City

Melbourne: Brunswick, Collingwood, Essendon, Fitzroy, Footscray, Melbourne, Port Melbourne, Prahran, Richmond, St Kilda, South Melbourne, Williamstown

Brisbane*   City, North City, South City, Balmoral, East Brisbane

Adelaide: Adelaide, Hindmarsh, Kensington and Norwood, Prospect, St Peters, Thebarton, Walkerville

Perth: Fremantle, East Fremantle, Perth, Subiaco

Hobart: Hobart, Glenorchy, Kingborough, Clarence

In order to put building activity in these areas into some perspective, population figures taken from the 1966 and 1971 censuses are also included.

Population figures show different trends in the metropolitan populations as a whole and the inner L.G.A.s and the cities. Metropolitan population increased by about 840,000 persons or 11.9 per cent, well above the national rate of 9.7 per cent. The inner suburbs on the other hand lost 8,000 persons, a fall of 0.5 per cent, and the Cities lost 15,000 persons, or 4.5 per cent.

The population in the inner L.G.A.s of three of the four largest capitals, except in Sydney, decreased. The Sydney anomaly is due to the considerable increase in population in the eastern suburbs of Randwick, Waverley, Woollahra and Botany. Population in most of the other L.G.A.s fell, paralleling the trends in Melbourne, Brisbane and Adelaide.

These inner L.G.A.s contained 13.8 per cent of national population in 1966 and 12.5 per cent in 1971. Percentages in the cities were 2.8 and 2.4 per cent respectively.

The concentration of national life and activity in these geographically very small areas is emphasized in Table 13.1, which shows that in 1966 21 per cent of all building activity took place in the inner L.G.A.s and 13.0

* Statistical subdivisions of the City of Brisbane.

TABLE 13.1. *Value of work done by state, metropolitan statistical division, inner L.G.A.s and City (per cent of total value Australia)*

	1965–6 (= \$1,493m)				1970–1 (= \$2,674m)			
	State	Metro. stat. div.	Inner L.G.A.s	City	State	Metro. stat. div.	Inner L.G.A.s	City
New South Wales	37.8	26.1	9.5	5.6[a]	38.4	26.9	8.6	4.1[a]
Victoria	27.1	20.5	6.3	3.6	25.3	18.3	5.5	3.1
Queensland	14.2	6.5	1.3	0.9	12.9	5.9	1.6	1.2
South Australia	10.2	5.5	1.5	1.2	7.8	5.4	1.1	0.7
West Australia	8.2	5.8	1.8	1.3	13.0	6.4	2.6	2.2
Tasmania	2.6	0.9	0.9	0.4	2.5	1.2	1.2	0.6
Total	100.0	65.3	21.3	13.0	100.0	64.1	20.6	11.9

[a] Includes South Sydney.

Sources: 1965–6: G. J. R. Linge, 'Building Activity'.
　　　　1970–1: C.B.C.S. unpublished building statistics.

per cent in the Cities, proportions that had declined only slightly by 1971. It is unlikely that such a degree of concentration has been reached in any other modern industrialized state.

There are interesting differences between the States. In three States, New South Wales, Victoria and South Australia, the percentages for the inner L.G.A.s and for the City in 1970–1 are lower than in 1965–6. This development is not surprising and is associated with the 'suburbanization' of industry and other activities in recent years.

There are two main factors behind this process of 'suburbanization': further expansion by firms that have reached optimal production on the original sites and new production methods based on horizontal movement of goods, necessitating much larger sites. As the required broad acres of industrially zoned land are not available in the old-established industrial zones, or only at prohibitively high prices, manufacturers are forced to relocate in outer suburbs. Various smaller firms, supplying specialized goods and services to the major establishments, will follow in the wake of their customers.

This chain of events suggests a certain regular pattern in urban change and growth. In the smaller capitals where land is less intensively used the increasing demand for building sites can be accommodated in the inner suburbs, as illustrated in the figures for Western Australia and Tasmania. In Perth and in Hobart the inner L.G.A.s and the City have claimed a larger share of building activities. In Queensland, however, where Brisbane's inner suburbs and the City itself have increased their shares of building activities, the figures do not seem to fit the pattern that could be expected for a capital of Brisbane's population and age. But Brisbane is characterized by very extensive use of land.

An examination of the type of building carried out in the areas distinguished in each of the capitals will give insight into the kind of development taking place in the metropolis.

Sydney

Table 13.2 shows the absolute value of the major types of building in the Sydney inner L.G.A.s and in the City. The percentage of the total work in the metropolitan statistical division carried out in these areas is also shown.

TABLE 13.2. *Value of work done in inner L.G.A.s and City – Sydney (in $000s and as percentage of metropolitan statistical division total for each category)*

Type of building	1965–6				1970–1			
	Inner L.G.A.s	City	Per cent Metro. stat. div.		Inner L.G.A.s	City[a]	Per cent Metro. stat. div.	
			Inner	City			Inner	City
	$000s	$000s	%	%	$000s	$000s	%	%
Houses	4,315	19	3.7	0.4	8,358	1,129	4.1	0.6
Flats	39,013	6,523	53.8	16.7	53,571	4,970	35.5	3.3
Total dwellings	43,328	6,542	23.0	3.5	61,929	6,099	17.5	1.7
Factories	12,753	5,693	33.1	14.8	14,581	6,983	21.8	10.5
Offices	45,340	43,142	87.8	83.6	87,139	57,399	80.8	53.2
Educational	13,278	5,885	40.9	18.1	13,240	6,838	37.4	19.3
Health	2,529	1,106	29.1	12.6	8,128	2,589	47.8	15.2
Other	29,248	21,400	41.4	30.3	58,195	31,439	42.5	22.9
Grand total	146,476	83,768	37.5	21.5	243,213	111,347	33.9	15.2
Metro. stat. div.	390,416				718,305			

[a] Includes South Sydney but not some parts of the old City transferred to Marrickville, Leichhardt and Woollahra. Provisional figures.

The inner L.G.A.s accounted for a smaller percentage of total building activity in 1970–1 (33.9 per cent) than in 1965–6 (37.5). The main factor is the considerable relative drop in flat building, falling from 53.8 per cent of the metropolitan total in 1965–6 to 35.5 per cent in 1970–1. Offices, the single most important category, more than doubled in the M.S.D. but the inner L.G.A.s' share almost kept up with this rate of growth. This meant that the importance of office building in relation to all building in the inner L.G.A.s has become more pronounced. Whereas in 1965–6 offices constituted 31 per cent of all building in the inner suburbs, the figure had risen to 36 per cent in 1970–1.

The inner L.G.A.s' share of buildings for educational, health and other purposes remained roughly 40 per cent in both years. The grand total of all buildings in these small areas changed only slightly and is still about 53 per cent of all building in the metropolitan statistical division.

Building figures in Table 13.2 should not be used to make comparisons between activities in the City and in the other L.G.A.s, as in 1968 the City not only lost South Sydney but also another 1,300 acres which were transferred to other inner L.G.A.s. Population statistics, however, have been adjusted.

The population in the City decreased by 9,000 persons (a fall of about 13 per cent) but increased in the inner L.G.A.s as a whole by about 4,000 (a rise of less than 1 per cent). The increase is entirely due to population growth in the better class eastern suburbs, which experienced a flat boom and which offset the population drop in the other inner L.G.A.s.

The value of building other than dwelling construction increased from about $103m in 1965–6 to $182m in 1970–1, an increase of 80 per cent. If non-residential building is associated with job opportunities our figures show that overall the journey to work must have become longer in geographic terms except perhaps for those in the higher occupational categories.

Melbourne

The trend in building activities in Melbourne's inner L.G.A.s and City has been quite different (Table 13.3). The inner L.G.A.s account for a larger percentage of flats and offices in 1970–1 than in 1965–6. In 1970–1 44.0 per cent of flats constructed in the metropolitan statistical division were located in the inner L.G.A.s, well above the figure for 1956–6 (40.9 per cent), in spite of the relative drop in flat building in the City. Office construction showed a slight relative decrease over the period – from 93.7 per cent to 88.7 per cent – mainly due to the reduction in the percentage in the City. But the drop is not nearly as pronounced as in Sydney. Building of educational and health premises was more concentrated in the inner L.G.A.s than before. The overall result of these developments was that in 1970–1 each of the two areas accounted for roughly the same proportion of building as in 1965–6.

The population in the inner L.G.A.s decreased by about 12,000 persons in the intercensal period, a fall of 2 per cent. The proportion of total metropolitan population residing in the inner L.G.A.s fell from 23 per cent in 1966 to 20 per cent in 1971. On the other hand non-residential building in the inner L.G.A.s as a proportion of total metropolitan building was about 23 per cent in 1965–6 and in 1970–1. It appears that in Melbourne, as in Sydney, the location of jobs and the location of dwellings are moving further apart.

TABLE 13.3. *Value of work done in inner L.G.A.s and City – Melbourne (in $000s and as percentage of metropolitan statistical division total for each category)*

Type of building	1965–6				1970–1			
	Inner L.G.A.s	City	Per cent Metro. stat. div.		Inner L.G.A.s	City	Per cent Metro. stat. div.	
			Inner	City			Inner	City
	$000s	$000s	%	%	$000s	$000s	%	%
Houses	1,914	99	1.8	0.1	3,014	501	1.6	0.3
Flats	19,191	3,923	40.9	8.4	31,234	4,070	44.0	5.7
Total dwellings	21,105	4,022	13.9	2.6	34,248	4,571	13.5	1.8
Factories	11,602	2,533	24.3	5.3	10,940	2,426	22.8	5.1
Offices	38,550	33,208	93.7	80.7	59,919	48,795	88.7	72.2
Educational	5,734	3,486	28.8	17.5	11,280	8,550	35.2	26.7
Health	3,536	3,383	44.0	42.1	10,220	7,180	52.0	36.6
Other	13,440	6,915	36.1	18.6	21,058	11,235	30.4	16.2
Grand total	93,967	53,547	30.7	17.5	147,665	82,757	30.1	16.9
Metro. stat. div.	306,172				490,543 (old) 553,575 (new)			

Brisbane

In Brisbane, in contrast to Sydney and Melbourne, the overall percentage of building in the City as well as in the other inner L.G.A.s was higher in 1970–1 than in 1965–6 (Table 13.4). The increase is attributable to a continuing concentration of flats, factories and 'other' premises in the inner L.G.A.s. The City itself experienced an increase in the proportion of factories and other premises. Offices, the single most important category, declined slightly in both areas but this was more than compensated by increases in other types of building.

The population in the inner L.G.A.s fell from 86,000 in 1966 to 79,000 in 1971, a drop of 8 per cent. Their share of the total metropolitan population fell from 11 per cent to 9 per cent over the same period. The percentage of non-residential building on the other hand rose from 19 per cent in 1965–6 to 25 per cent in 1970–1, indicating that the trends in job location and residential location are diverging rapidly.

Adelaide

Adelaide experienced a considerable drop in the relative importance of the inner L.G.A.s and the City in building activity (Table 13.5). The suburbanization of office buildings seems to have been the single most important factor behind this decrease. 'Health' also decreased but this category has

TABLE 13.4. *Value of work done in inner L.G.A.s and City – Brisbane (in $000s and as percentage of metropolitan statistical division total for each category*

Type of building	1965–6				1970–1			
	Inner L.G.A.s	City	Per cent Metro. stat. div.		Inner L.G.A.s	City	Per cent Metro. stat. div.	
			Inner	City			Inner	City
	$000s	$000s	%	%	$000s	$000s	%	%
Houses	271	12	0.7	0.0	713	44	1.2	0.1
Flats	1,621	0	18.8	0.0	3,474	46	28.1	0.4
Total dwellings	1,892	12	4.0	0.0	4,187	90	5.8	0.1
Factories	1,135	267	11.1	2.6	3,541	1,328	35.1	13.2
Offices	9,645	9,372	89.8	87.2	15,255	14,810	85.6	83.1
Educational	1,946	935	21.5	10.3	2,917	1,713	20.8	12.2
Health	772	613	49.0	38.9	755	191	20.3	5.1
Other	4,594	2,532	24.4	13.5	17,201	13,528	44.7	35.2
Grand total	19,984	13,731	20.5	14.1	43,856	31,660	28.0	20.2
Metro. stat. div.	97,644				156,675			

TABLE 13.5. *Value of work done in Inner L.G.A.s and City – Adelaide (in $000s and as percentage of metropolitan statistical division total for each category)*

Type of building	1965–6				1970–1			
	Inner L.G.A.s	City	Per cent Metro. stat. div.		Inner L.G.A.s	City	Per cent Metro. stat. div.	
			Inner	City			Inner	City
	$000s	$000s	%	%	$000s	$000s	%	%
Houses	966	79	3.5	0.3	926	18	1.7	0.0
Flats	1,160	334	13.4	3.8	5,275	2,076	21.2	8.3
Total dwellings	2,126	413	5.9	1.1	6,201	2,094	7.7	2.6
Factories	1,608	707	19.9	8.8	1,351	648	21.6	10.4
Offices	6,280	6,118	95.1	92.6	7,582	6,728	79.1	70.2
Educational	2,529	2,027	27.8	22.2	4,235	3,851	35.0	31.8
Health	4,987	4,915	62.1	61.2	691	383	6.8	3.8
Other	5,585	3,756	38.5	25.9	8,652	6,035	33.8	23.5
Grand total	23,115	17,936	28.1	21.8	28,712	19,739	19.8	13.6
Metro. stat. div.	82,341				144,691			

less impact on the overall figures. The spectacular drop can be attributed to the completion of work on a big hospital in 1965–6. The inner L.G.A.s and the City account for a bigger proportion of flats but the category is of small significance in the overall building activities.

The population in the inner L.G.A.s decreased by 6,000 between the two census dates, a loss of 6 per cent in terms of the 1966 population and a drop from 12 per cent of the metropolitan population to 10 per cent. Non-residential building, however, moved in the same direction and fell from 21 per cent in 1966 to 16 per cent in 1971.

Perth

Developments in the Perth metropolitan statistical division (Table 13.6) stand in marked contrast with those in Sydney, Melbourne and Adelaide, but resemble Brisbane's growth. Concentration of building activity in the

TABLE 13.6. *Value of work done in Inner L.G.A.s and City – Perth (in $000s and as percentage of metropolitan statistical division total for each category)*

Type of building	1965–6				1970–1			
	Inner L.G.A.s	City	Per cent Metro. stat. div.		Inner L.G.A.s	City	Per cent Metro. stat. div.	
			Inner	City			Inner	City
	$000s	$000s	%	%	$000s	$000s	%	%
Houses	2,837	2,029	7.6	5.4	4,962	3,596	10.7	7.8
Flats	2,613	1,618	34.2	21.2	4,586	3,721	22.5	18.2
Total dwellings	5,450	3,647	12.1	8.1	9,548	7,317	14.3	11.0
Factories	1,984	578	28.0	8.2	3,139	1,763	29.5	16.5
Offices	5,843	5,507	87.2	82.2	25,172	24,445	89.9	87.3
Educational	2,250	1,517	38.6	26.0	5,885	5,321	38.2	34.5
Health	677	259	21.4	8.2	2,053	976	19.7	9.4
Other	10,186	7,602	56.2	41.9	22,502	18,170	58.2	47.0
Grand total	26,390	19,110	30.7	22.2	68,299	57,992	40.2	34.1
Metro. stat. div.	86,045				169,817			

inner L.G.A.s has risen sharply from an overall share of 30.7 per cent to 40.2 per cent, an increase of 31 per cent, and in the City from 22.2 per cent to 34.1 per cent, an increase of 54 per cent.

The inner L.G.A.s have absorbed a larger share of every type of building except flats, where the 1970–1 percentage is considerably below the 1965–6 figure. Health and education have similar percentage in both years. Figures for the City show a parallel development but with relatively faster growth. A remarkable feature is the heavy concentration of offices, 90 per cent located in the inner L.G.A.s and 87 per cent in the City alone. The increasing importance of the inner L.G.A.s and the City in building is associated with the recent boom in mining in Western Australia. Comparisons between developments in the inner L.G.A.s and the City in the Perth M.S.D. and in the other M.S.D.s should be treated with care as in Perth the geographical boundaries are much larger. Perth City encompasses an area that stretches to the coast. The difference between the percentage of houses in each M.S.D. illustrates this point. In 1970–1 the Perth inner L.G.A.s and City accounted for 10.7 per cent and 7.8 per cent of houses, as compared with 4.1 and 0.6 in Sydney inner L.G.A.s and City, the M.S.D. with the next highest figures.

The population in the inner L.G.A.s rose slightly in absolute terms (from 145,000 to 148,000), but fell as a proportion of total metropolitan population from 26 per cent to 21 per cent. Non-residential building in the inner suburbs rose from 18 per cent of total metropolitan building to 30 per cent, mainly attributable to the office boom in the City. It is clear that the number of jobs in the inner L.G.A.s must have risen much more quickly than the number of residents, resulting in longer journeys to work.

Hobart

Building statistics in the remaining metropolitan division, Hobart, have to be placed in a State context as L.G.A.s are so large that the selected inner L.G.A.s virtually cover the whole area of the metropolitan statistical division. It should be pointed out that therefore building statistics for the inner L.G.A.s will include a considerable proportion of building on vacant land as well as redevelopment of existing sites. A good indicator is the inner L.G.A.s' share of houses, as detached dwellings are seldom erected in areas of urban renewal. The high percentage for houses in the inner L.G.A.s, 37 per cent in 1965–6 and 40.0 per cent in 1970–1, confirms that a considerable amount of new development is included.

The percentage of the State population in the inner L.G.A.s was 36 in 1966, the same as in 1971. Non-residential building in these areas increased from 21 per cent in 1965–6 to 25 per cent in 1970–1, indicating little relative change in the distribution of jobs and people. Total building in these inner L.G.A.s as well as in the City has increased in absolute and in relative terms. All types of building have contributed to this increase with the most important rises occurring in flats and in the health category. There is an interesting difference between the relative importance of office building in Hobart and in Sydney. Offices account for less than 20 per cent of total building in the City of Hobart in 1970–1 but for more than 50 per cent in the City of Sydney. The boom in high rise offices, which has been active for some time in Sydney and also in Melbourne, has not been marked in Hobart.

New financial resources

It was mentioned earlier in this chapter that urban redevelopment in recent years has been influenced by the emergence of new financial structures in the development industry. Since the early 1960s various new financial arrangements have emerged and traditional lenders have assumed new roles. As for urban redevelopment, the most important aspect of these changes has been the increasing equity investment in property by the big institutional lenders, the finance companies, the life offices and super-annuation firms. The traditional form of finance through long-term fixed rate mortgages has virtually disappeared and has been replaced by a multiplicity of new contracts. In *Development Activities in Four Sydney Suburban Areas*[8] Vandermark and Harrison discuss in more detail the magnitude of these changes and the forces behind the new forms of investment, culminating in the increasing participation by financiers in the role of developers in their own right.

There are no figures available to indicate the total amount of capital invested in property by traditional institutional lenders. The size of the new equity investment and the speed of the process can be judged, however, by the figures for one of the main groups of firms in this category, the life insurance companies. In the eight years from 1962 to 1970 life offices almost doubled the proportion of their total assets invested in property and ordinary shares and in 1970 alone increased investment in these two categories by $245m. Although the Commonwealth government uses tax incentives to make sure that a considerable portion of the funds of life offices are invested in public loans, there is still scope for much more investment in property before tax restraints become operative.

These changes in investment policy are relevant to urban renewal as they affect the volume of finance available and the type of project that will be supported. Life offices, like other large investors or developers, prefer big projects, mainly because the administrative overhead on large projects is not much greater than on small projects. Also these companies are not geared to handle a multitude of small projects. There is little doubt that the major share of property investment by the traditional institutional 'lenders' has gone into city office buildings. Although there are no official figures for the size of this investment, it is well known in the business that behind the names of many of the new development companies displayed on development projects, there stands a life office with a significant if not a 100 per cent interest. In Sydney alone, it is estimated that 2.6 million sq. ft. of office space will become available in 1972 and 1973, involving an investment of at least $1,500m (excluding land costs) and of this probably well over half can be traced back to the life offices' 'coffers'.[9] The boom in office construction in Australia, which began in the late fifties and rose in value from about $50m in 1960 to almost $250m in 1971, was not sparked off by the financiers. But its mushrooming growth during the sixties and its continuation in the coming years would hardly be possible without the financial resources that these companies channelled in that direction.

The magnitude of these investments raises the question of allocation of resources. Private redevelopment on this scale will require enormous public investment, especially in roads and other transport services. This question will be discussed later. But the question of profitability in private economic terms also needs consideration. Australia is now reaching a situation in which those who control the flow of capital are also acquiring the capability of producing real estate goods. This may lead to a general oversupply of income-producing property if decisions for future projects are largely guided by confidence gained with previous projects supported by forecasts of continuing growth in and around existing urban centres. The upshot will be severe overbuilding and overinvestment. In Sydney the drop in office rentals and 'To Let' notices, mainly in older buildings, shows that this has already occurred. An expert estimate by a spokesman for one of Australia's largest developers put the amount of uncommitted office space in Sydney at 800,000 to 900,000 sq. ft. in October 1972.[10] Another estimate set the amount of office space becoming available throughout the Sydney metropolitan area in 1972 at 1.82 million sq. ft., of which 920,000 sq. ft. still had to be let.[11] It is estimated that by 1975–6 there could be 5 million sq. ft. of vacant office space in the City of Sydney and another 2.5 million sq. ft. in North Sydney. However, developers are optimistic that the surplus will be absorbed in later years as the city continues to grow. In the meantime, considerable resources will have been put to uneconomic use, but the financial facts will be well hidden from the public eye, buried in the consolidated balance sheets of the new generation of developers, the institutional lenders.

Government participation in urban renewal

Housing Commissions

As mentioned before, direct government involvement in urban renewal in Australia is mainly restricted to the activities of two State Housing Commissions. The role of the Federal government is even more limited and consists of the provision of loan money. Since 1945, when the first Commonwealth State Housing Agreement was signed, the Commonwealth has provided State Housing Commissions with cheap loan money (prior to the latest agreement the interest rate has been 1 per cent below the long-term bond rate). The total amount of these advances has steadily increased from about $75m in 1960 to some $150m in 1971. Although the States have regularly asked for a special allocation towards slum clearance this has been refused. It seems likely that the Federal government will play a more active role in urban development with the announcement in October 1972 that the Federal government had decided to form a National Urban and Regional Development Authority (N.U.R.D.A.). This initiative has to be seen in the context of the Federal elections. The role and scope of the new authority are not clear at present.

In Victoria and N.S.W. the State Housing Commissions have actively taken part in slum clearance. Until 1969 the Victorian State Housing Commissions had cleared a total of 139 acres with another 100 acres in the process of being redeveloped. The N.S.W. Housing Commission had cleared 75 acres by 1969 and seemed to have lost interest in further large-scale projects. Measured in terms of areas that have been declared 'in *need* of slum clearance' it appears that little advance has been made. In Sydney it was estimated in the 1948 Report of the Cumberland County Council that some 3,000 acres of substandard development were in need of 'immediate action'. In Melbourne the V.H.C. in its 1957 Annual Report announced that some 600 acres of decayed property existed. This estimate was raised to 1,000 acres the following year on the basis of a survey by two senior Commission officers.

It is more likely, however, that the historical estimates of 'slum areas' are no longer valid. M. A. Jones in *Housing and Poverty in Australia*[12] severely criticizes 'block slum clearance'. The main culprit is the V.H.C. which, if Dr Jones is right, has hit on the ultimate in mismanagement, dispossessing and displacing owners or tenants in areas declared 'slums' on the basis of a most superficial inspection. In recent years a considerable amount of spontaneous renovation has taken place in the inner suburbs, often carried out by migrants who have moved in and bought properties. The replacement of medium-density low-cost terrace housing with high-density, high-cost blocks of flats of up to thirty storeys is also questioned. Whereas the V.H.C. can build a brick-veneer, free-standing house for $10,000 it is estimated that a three bedroom flat in a thirty-storey block will cost $19,000. The V.H.C. has also resold some of the reclaimed land to private developers for flats for middle- to high-income families at considerable loss. Reclamation and clearance costs for a block in north Melbourne amounted to an estimated $605,000. The sales price to a private developer was $209,000.

It appears that the V.H.C. has modelled a part of its operations on the American example, justifying its activities in terms of new objectives such as diversifying population and supporting ailing municipalities. There seems to be good reason to re-examine these objectives in the light of the findings by Rothenberg and Muth in the United States and Jones in Australia.

Planning schemes

Government involvement in urban renewal through statutory planning has been minimal. Metropolitan plans prepared for the capital cities did not attempt to establish a set of objectives or policies for redevelopment in the inner suburbs. Each of the metropolitan plans, except for Brisbane, left the detailed planning to the city councils or municipalities in the areas.

In Sydney's first post-war metropolitan planning scheme, the Cumberland County Planning Scheme, adopted in 1951, the greater part of the City of Sydney area (about 1,000 acres) was marked 'County Centre'. The preparation of a 'local' scheme was left to the City. Several areas were designated for 'Comprehensive Redevelopment'. The State Planning Authority, the successor to the Cumberland County Council, published its Sydney Region Outline Plan in 1968. The document had very little to say about the redevelopment of the inner suburbs, apart from a few comments suggesting that higher densities in these areas were unlikely in the light of current redevelopment trends.[13]

The Sydney City Council was the first of the central cities to prepare a plan for the C.B.D.[14] A draft scheme was exhibited in 1954 but was not finalized till 1971, when the City of Sydney Planning Scheme was promulgated. The most contentious issue during that period was the attempt to restrain building through the imposition of floor space ratios (F.S.R. is the ratio of floor area to site area). The City Planning Scheme did not fix a ratio but a code of floor space controls has been adopted since.

Very recently a few large-scale comprehensively planned redevelopment projects have commenced or are being planned. The two most important are the schemes for The Rocks and for Woolloomooloo. Plans for Bondi Junction and for Church lands in Edgecliff and Glebe are also of considerable size. The Rocks' redevelopment is part of the Sydney Cove Redevelopment Scheme presented in 1970 by the Sydney Cove Redevelopment Authority, a body specifically created to direct activities in an area of about 50 acres of mostly State-owned land, and of considerable historical significance to Australia. The S.C.R.A. Scheme provides for the construction of about 4.5 million sq. ft. of office space as well as retail and residential accommodation, expected to increase the population (residents and commuters) by some 35,000.

Proposals for the redevelopment of Woolloomooloo, one of the oldest residential areas just outside the C.B.D. boundaries, are at present in a state of confusion as several plans have been put forward in the last three years. A plan prepared by the State Planning Authority in 1969 and accepted by the Council provides for extensive commercial redevelopment on a basic floor space ratio of 5:1, but with provision for various bonuses. The suggested employment level was set at 35,000. On the basis of this plan developers began assembling land and prices rose from $12 per square foot, the price paid at first by the biggest land owner in the area, to almost $100 at present.

The City Council, however, also hired a firm of consultants to prepare the Sydney Strategic Plan, which recommended that the whole of Woolloomooloo be residential. To complicate matters further, the City of Sydney Planning Scheme of 1971 includes the whole of the city centre, i.e. as commercial.

The New South Wales Housing Commission also renewed its interest in redeveloping land in the inner suburbs. In 1972 it proclaimed an area of 26 acres in Waterloo (South Sydney) as a Rehousing Area. This move was possibly a result of the Commission's inability to acquire cheap land on the outskirts of the metropolitan area.

In Melbourne, the 1964 *Report on a Planning Scheme for the Central Business Area* recommended floor space ratios ranging from 8:1 in retail areas to 12:1 in commercial blocks. The proposals have not been adopted in their entirety but floor space controls are now being administered on an even more liberal basis.[15] The passing of the Urban Renewal Act by the Victorian parliament in December 1970 constituted a landmark in government participation in urban redevelopment. The Act provides for Urban Renewal Authorities and nominates the Housing Commission of Victoria as one. Other Authorities can also be recognized, either specifically constituted for the purpose or an existing municipal council. Before renewal activities are commenced, the Authority is required to consult with local municipalities and any other government authorities involved.

The Victorian Housing Commission, in line with its new responsibilities, has added an Urban Renewal Branch. A significant development reflecting some compassion for persons in areas subject to renewal was the concern that the areas concerned 'be not destroyed by factors beyond the control of individual home owners'.[16]

Developments in the Adelaide metropolitan area were based on a Metropolitan Development Plan endorsed by the South Australian parliament in 1963 and again in 1967. Development in the city centre has been actively promoted by the City Council, but the decision to prepare a plan and policies for the City was taken only recently.

The South Australian State government has taken the initiative in planning for the redevelopment of an area of about 14 acres in Hackney, just outside the Adelaide central business district. The State Planning Authority released its report in March 1972, in which it is described as a 'blight area'. The proposal speaks of a 'face lift' with a mixture of high-rise and terrace housing to be carried out by the South Australian Housing Trust and private enterprise. Government expenditure on land acquisition was estimated at $500,000, most of which was to be recouped. The proposals raised a storm of protest, mainly from property owners faced with compulsory acquisition. One result has been the establishment of a new form of communication between the State Planning Authority and local Ratepayers' Associations. At the time of writing, the plan was being re-examined in the light of the objections received.

Conclusions

At the end of June, 1966 the inner L.G.A.s as defined in this study contained 13.8 per cent of Australia's population, yet during that year 21.3 per cent of all building was carried out in these small areas. In 1971 the figures were 12.5 and 20.6 per cent respectively.

Looking at non-residential building alone, our figures show that the inner suburbs of all capitals, except Adelaide and Hobart, experienced considerable increase in construction of business premises, whereas their populations decreased. Non-residential building increased from about $240m in 1965–6 to $435m in 1970–1, an increase of 75 per cent. There are no figures available to indicate what type of buildings were demolished but there is no doubt that the redevelopment of non-residential property was at a higher density and that a larger number of jobs was provided in the new buildings. One of the implications of these building statistics and population figures is therefore that the problems associated with the commuting of workers have increased considerably over the period.

Figures in Table 13.1 show that some $320m was invested in building of all types in the inner L.G.A.s in 1965–6, rising to about $550m in 1970–1. This large amount of urban renewal took place virtually without any active and direct government participation. Only in the last few years have attempts been made to regulate development in the inner areas of the capital cities through statutory planning schemes. Direct government participation in comprehensive renewal has been limited to the operations of State Housing Commissions in Victoria and New South Wales, which have taken part in block slum clearance. The effectiveness of planning controls in controlling the forces behind urban renewal may be doubted, as illustrated in the controversies which arose during the preparation of some of the plans and the various compromises that have been developed.

Lack of a public policy towards urban renewal does not mean that the government will not be involved in it. Sooner or later the private investment in the inner areas will have to be matched by complementary public investment. The obvious forms of public investment are roads and transport, but it may be expected that several utility services will also require augmentation. The alternatives for public involvement in urban renewal are therefore either to follow in the paths of private investment or to try to direct and control both the size and location of private investment. Considering the peculiar characteristics of the property market and the need to take account of non-economic aspects of urban renewal, there is a convincing case for government initiative and direct participation in the process.

The consequences of private investment in the inner cities in recent years are now becoming manifest in serious traffic, transport and air pollution problems, notably in Sydney. Future policy towards urban redevelopment in Australia's large cities should be based on acceptance of the proposition that the inner suburbs of our metropolises have reached an economic and environmental saturation point, beyond which continued development in orthodox terms produces at least as much social damage as it does individual benefit. Without determined *Federal* and *State* government action, it is most unlikely that private investment will provide a solution.

NOTES

1 Harry W. Richardson, *Urban Economics*, Penguin Books, 1971.
2 Jerome Rothenberg, *Economic Evaluation of Urban Renewal*, The Brookings Institution, Washington, 1967.
3 Ibid. p. 205.
4 Richard F. Muth, *Cities and Housing*, University of Chicago Press, 1969.
5 Ibid. p. 14.
6 Ibid. p. 325.
7 G. J. R. Linge, 'Building activity in Australian metropolitan areas: a statistical background', in P. N. Troy (ed.), *Urban Development in Australia*, Urban Research Unit, Australian National University, Canberra, 1967.
8 Elzo Vandermark and Peter Harrison, *Development Activities in Four Sydney Suburban Areas*, Urban Research Unit, Australian National University, Canberra, 1972.
9 *Rydge's*, April 1971.
10 Sales manager of L. J. Hooker Corporation during television interview, October 1972.
11 *Sydney Morning Herald*, 10 August 1972.
12 M. A. Jones, *Housing and Poverty in Australia*, Melbourne University Press, 1972.
13 For a detailed study of Sydney's townplanning see P. F. Harrison, 'Planning the metropolis – a case study', in R. S. Parker and P. N. Troy (eds.), *The Politics of Urban Growth*, A.N.U. Press, Canberra, 1972.
14 Most of the information on C.B.D.s is from an unpublished seminar paper by Peter Harrison, 'Questions about the central business district', Urban Research Unit, Australian National University, Canberra, October 1972.
15 *Planning Policies for the Melbourne Metropolitan Region*, Melbourne and Metropolitan Board of Works, Melbourne, November 1971.
16 *Housing is People*, Housing Commission of Victoria, Melbourne, May 1972.

in Australia (as in the earlier stages of the industrial revolution and urbanization on the North American continent) that rural–urban migration was a major factor in growth. In post-war Australia, inter-city migration has almost certainly been more voluminous, although this is not to suggest no internal migration to the primate cities – there simply have been compensating outflows.

At this point, significant growth changes of the large urban nodes became evident after the war. First, there was the rapid growth of Brisbane, Perth and Adelaide, their growth in part being boosted by migration from Sydney and Melbourne as well as immigration and some rural–urban migration; second, the very fast growth of the secondary centres, Canberra, Wollongong and Geelong, each specialized centre gaining through internal migration from Sydney and Melbourne mainly – hence the latter two cities' negligible gain through internal migration.

Finally, some comments on the urbanization process *within* the large cities. Broadly, a concentric zone pattern of population change, invasion and succession took place in the central areas, but multiple nuclei or sectoral patterns distorted the model with the presence of industrial areas in some outer fringe suburbs. Although densities over 10,000 per square mile occurred in inner Sydney and Melbourne, and higher occupancy per room rates with southern European migrants, significant overcrowding did not take place except perhaps with recent migrants. While urban renewal has taken place in inner city run-down residential areas, the role of government has been limited to Commission housing apartment blocks, which increased densities from 20 families per acre in terrace housing in Redfern (Sydney) to 60 families in high-rise apartment blocks. Basically residential renewal has been of the spontaneous (or spot renewal) variety with the dispersed erection of walk-up home unit or rented apartments by private developers (and as mentioned some over-large estates). The other spontaneous form of renewal has been refurbishing of run-down properties and neighbourhoods by incoming migrants. The result has been a pleasing differentiation of residential areas, which should not allow us to turn a blind eye to the potentially serious segregation patterns concealed behind the bright facades.

NOTES

1 Ernest W. Burgess, 'The growth of the city: an introduction to a research project', in R. E. Park, E. W. Burgess and R. D. McKenzie (eds.), *The City*, University of Chicago Press, 1925, p. 47.
2 Ibid.
3 Norton Ginsburg, 'The great city in South East Asia', *American Journal of Sociology*, 60, no. 5, 1955.
4 I. H. Burnley, 'The rural population of Australia in 1990', Proceedings of the Symposium *People and Production in Australia*, Academy of Science, Canberra, 5 October 1972.

Author index

Subject index